THE GLOBAL HISTORY SERIES

Under the general editorship of Leften Stavrianos

This series aims to present history in global perspective, going beyond national or regional limitations, and dealing with overriding trends and forces. The various collections of original materials span the globe, range from prehistoric times to the present, and include anthropology, economics, political science, and religion, as well as history.

The editor of this volume, George Alexander Lensen, is Professor of History and Director of Asian Studies at the Florida State University. He holds three degrees from Columbia University. He has traveled widely and knows Russia and Asia at first hand. During World War II he served as a United States Military Intelligence Officer in India, China, and Japan. He returned to Japan in 1953-54 as a Fulbright professor. In 1961 he pursued postdoctoral research at the Leningrad State University under the official U.S.-U.S.S.R. educational exchange program. Dr. Lensen is the author of numerous books, including *Report from Hokkaido: The Remains of Russian Culture in Northern Japan; Russia's Japan Expedition of 1852 to 1855; The Russian Push Toward Japan: Russo-Japanese Relations, 1697-1875;* and *The World Beyond Europe.*

The Three Valiant Knights: Ancient and Modern

RUSSIA'S EASTWARD EXPANSION

EDITED BY GEORGE ALEXANDER LENSEN

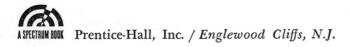 Prentice-Hall, Inc. / *Englewood Cliffs, N.J.*

To Kristin / *a born traveler*

PREFACE

The frontispiece illustrates the changing character of Russian leadership and expansion. The famous painting by V. M. Vasnetsov shows three armored knights on horseback. The warrior on the left uses one arm to hold a round shield and with the other unsheathes his sword. The hero in the center, holding a lance across his steed, shields his eyes with the right hand, and overlooks the field. As he does so, a mace dangles from his right forearm. The third knight is armed with bow and arrows. The Soviet cartoon by V. Kiunnap portrays the new heroes, still mounted and in the same position, but in proletarian garb and with bureaucratic weapons. Instead of a helmet, mailed suit of armor, shield, and sword, the rider on the left displays a visored cap, a polka dot sports shirt, abacus, and fountain-pen. The lance of the central figure has turned into a nibbed pen, the mace into an office blotter, and the mailed armor into an undershirt, while the third valiant knight, a pencil stuck behind his ear, carries a ruler and a record book as his weapons. And—crowning touch—as the three comrade heroes overlook the field, the women of the collective farm, on truck and tractor, do all the work.

The Soviet cartoon, a large poster designed to prod Soviet bureaucrats into rolling up their sleeves and getting down to work, is reprinted through the courtesy of *Boevoi Karandash*. Thanks are due also to the M. E. Saltykov-Shchedrin State Public Library and the Library of the Academy of Sciences of the U.S.S.R. in Leningrad, from whose collections some of the Russian readings have been drawn; to the American Council of Learned Societies which supported their microfilming; and to the Inter-University Committee on Travel Grants, which provided the editor with first-hand knowledge of European Russia and Siberia—the people, places, and trends described. The reliance on sources in the English language for the bulk of the selections has been deliberate: to

v

acquaint the general reader with works readily available to him for further study.

The romanization of Russian and Oriental names has undergone many changes. Differences existing even now are multiplied by writers of different generations. Nevertheless, in this collection of readings it was deemed best to remain true to the style of each author rather than to impose the preferences of the editor. Nor was it thought appropriate to weigh down the text with footnotes. In fact, footnotes have been deleted from the selections quoted. It is hoped that the excerpts will draw the reader to the originals for greater detail and documentation.

G.A.L.

CONTENTS

INTRODUCTION

The clash of American and Russian interests in the Far East antedates the Communist revolution. In 1855 Commodore Matthew C. Perry predicted that sooner or later it would involve the two countries in a mighty battle on the outcome of which would depend "the freedom or the slavery of the world." Since the second half of the nineteenth century Russia's eastward expansion has been viewed with alarm if not with hostility in the United States. Preoccupied with the adverse effect of Russian policies on the spread of both American trade and influence in such regions as Manchuria, Americans have regarded Russia's eastward expansion in the American, rather than the Russian or over-all historical context as a "menace," rather than an "accomplishment" or a "contribution." Yet contemporaries in the seventeenth and eighteenth centuries, even some hostile English critics in the nineteenth, marveled at the dynamic drive with which the Russians had burst their old frontiers— across the continent and the seas beyond.

Russia's eastward expansion was part of the European tide that inundated Asia and America in the Age of Exploration. Russian pathfinders, traders, missionaries, and soldiers of fortune had their counterparts elsewhere. The benefits and shortcomings of European civilization were disseminated here and there with equal abandon, the general effect on the "natives" depending more on the cultural level of the local inhabitants than on the relative proselytizing skill of Russians, Spaniards, or Americans. The impact of the various Western pioneers on tribesmen in Asia and America differed in degree more than in kind. The Age of Imperialism saw changes in Russian interests and policy, similar to developments elsewhere. The story of Russia's eastward expansion thus is.

of interest not only in its own right but as a facet of European expansion in general.

The polarization of the United States and the Soviet Union as standard-bearers of conflicting ideologies obscures the fact that the two countries have much in common. Their size and diversity of population are the result of similar (though not identical) historical development and the cause of similar outlook. Beneath the crust of their political institutions Americans and Russians, with their wide-open spaces and gigantic distances (as well as their remoteness from the homeland of Western civilization) share a bigness of vision and heart, a sentimental attachment to frontier-type social equality and a romantic idealism, typical of the frontiersman ever in search of the Utopia just beyond the horizon. Diametrically opposed as the principles of laissez-faire democracy may be to both the mercantilism of Tsarist Russia and the communism of the Soviet Union, there is an affinity in the cocksure and somewhat naïve Messianic zeal with which Americans and Russians confront each other.

Throughout their history Americans and Russians have striven to create a "new" society, cut loose from the umbilical cord of Europe. Present attempts to "conquer the cosmos" are but a natural extension of the explorations and the great treks which drove restless Americans and Russians across the continents and oceans. Ironically, histories of explorations, engrossed in the voyages of Portuguese, Spanish, Dutch, English, and French navigators, have tended to gloss over the remarkable achievements of American and Russian pathfinders, whereas studies of imperialism generally overlook that the lands separating the eastern and western extremities both of America and Russia were at one time as forbidding as the waters between the European states and their possessions, and that the territories of the American West Coast and of Siberia and the Maritime Province were originally colonial acquisitions.

The magnetic force of the West in American history, as embodied in Horace Greeley's immortal words, "Go West, Young Man!" has its counterpart in Russia history, though, of course, in the opposite direction. As much nonsense has been written about Siberia in the United States as about the American West in Europe. What was the nature of the land that the Russians traversed? What manner of men extended the Russian frontier? What were the motives and methods of Russia's eastward expansion in the days of the dogsled, the railroad, and the intercontinental missile? Such are the questions that form the backdrop of this collection of readings.

I / ACROSS THE CONTINENT

INTRODUCTION

The place of origin of the Russian people is not certain, but there is general agreement that the early Russians entered Russia from the west. They pushed northward and eastward into European Russia and continued pushing eastward, past the Ural Mountains, until the tremendous plain that stretches from the Baltic and Black seas to the Pacific Ocean was in their hands.

The movement of Russians into Siberia dates back to the Middle Ages. Adventure, trade, oppressive living conditions in Europe, and frequently the desire to put as many miles as possible between themselves and the law lured people east. As they pushed on and on the lust for fur, the "golden fleece," became the mainspring and a common denominator of Russian and American expansion. The Russian thrust was given direction by the natural barrier of mountains, deserts, and inland seas which frame the Eurasian plain on the south and by the great rivers whose tributaries run parallel to this barrier.

Led by individuals, Russia's eastward expansion swept along the central government, for the government was the chief fur trader. Fur was exacted from the natives as tribute and from the traders and trappers as tax. But neither the central government nor its local representatives can be said to have initiated or planned the push east. Plunder and loot sufficed to draw adventurers and freebooters of every sort to the regions beyond the restraining arm of the government. Only eventually did the government seek to secure the new frontiers with specially organized Cossack settlements.

Spearheaded by such men as Yermak (Ermak Timofeevich), colorful conqueror of the Tartar City of Sibir and of the Tobolsk region in the early 1580's, Russian adventurers penetrated ever farther east. In 1587

3

they founded Tobolsk; in 1596, Narym; in 1619, Eniseisk; in 1632, Yakutsk. By 1649 they reached the Pacific Coast at the shores of the Sea of Okhotsk. At times the rigors of the Siberian climate tempted some to seek a more southerly route, but fierce opposition on the part of local Asian tribes gave added meaning to the cry of "Eastward Ho!"

The transcontinental trek of Russia proceeded at a faster pace than its American counterpart. Yermak crossed the Urals about the same time as Sir Walter Raleigh reached Roanoke; yet by 1649, when the Russians got to the Pacific, the Americans were still at the Appalachians. The difference in tempo was due to many factors. For example, fierce as the opposition of Asian tribes was in Siberia, it did not measure up to that of the American Indians, and European and Russian Asia formed a topographical unit, whose network of rivers and tributaries formed a natural highway east.

1 / RUSSIAN EXPANSION IN THE MIDDLE AGES

Medieval Russian contacts with Asia were primarily the work of the city of Novgorod. They were led not by an absolute monarch and his obedient underlings, but by a "fickle, half-theocratic democracy," whose chief activity was commerce. "The Empire of Novgorod is above all a commercial dominion; the discoveries and conquests of her pioneers are primarily victories of a remarkable trade-expansion," C. Raymond Beazley, an English geographer and historian, writes. He then asks rhetorically: "But has anything been more efficient in aiding human progress than trade-activity? What form of men's energy has done more to link together the most distant and diverse countries, to bring about the discovery of the earth, to promote truly useful knowledge, to 'clear the mind of cant,' to break down the obstacles of ignorance, fear and prejudice which once hemmed in mankind and separated its lands and races from one another?"

On any general view of European history, there are few more interesting and suggestive chapters than that which records the expansion of the Russian people—the geographical vanguard of European Christendom and civilization—towards the Arctic Ocean on one side, towards and across Northern Asia on another. Whatever criticisms may be passed upon the Russian race, it is certainly the pioneer of our Western world in these vast regions of the North and East. And nowhere in the Old World has the primitive Roman area of Christian civilization been so widened as in the lands, from the Dnyestr to the White Sea and from the

C. Raymond Beazley, "The Russian Expansion Towards Asia and the Arctic in the Middle Ages (to 1500)," *The American Historical Review,* XIII (October 1907 to July 1908), 731-41. Reprinted with permission of *The American Historical Review.*

Baltic to the Sea of Japan, which have been gradually penetrated, conquered and colonized by the Slavonic-Scandinavian *Russ*.

. . . The primitive home-land of the Russian people did not include more than a fraction, lying almost wholly in the West-Central zone, of the present Russia-in-Europe. It was the political, mercantile and adventuring ambition of Russian states, traders and freebooters, which gave in time so noteworthy an extension to the Russian name—here representative, as one faces away from Europe, of European Christianity, society and organization. . . .

The first discovery and conquest of the North and East, to the Polar Ocean and the modern province of Tobolsk, seems to have been primarily the work of the leading Russian city of the North-West, that Old Novgorod on the Volkhov, which in position and importance, as the chief town of the Neva or Gulf of Finland basin, roughly answers in medieval history to St. Petersburg in modern. Probably about the time of the First Crusade (1096) and certainly before the second (1147) the men of Novgorod had already come into touch with the country of the Lower Ob, just beyond the Ural Mountains. Long ere this, perhaps as early as the closing years of the tenth century (950-1000), the Novgorodian pioneers seem to have penetrated into Lapland and the upper valley of the Northern Dvina. The latter formed a waterway conducting either towards the White Sea or towards the Ural; and following the latter direction, probably along the course of the Vychegda, the Russians in the course of the eleventh century reached the Pechora, most distant of European rivers. By the head-streams of the Pechora one naturally ascended into the heart of the Northern Ural highland, and it seems reasonable to fix in one of the North Ural passes those Iron Gates which the Novgorod pioneers vainly attempted to force in 1032, suffering a disastrous repulse at the hands of the native Finnish tribes.

The beginning of the next century shows us Novgorod in communication with the Asiatic lands immediately beyond the dividing range. Speaking of a year which apparently answers to A.D. 1112, the *Fundamental Chronicle,* usually known as Nestor's, tells how one Guryata Rogovishch of Novgorod had sent his servant to the Pechora, how the Pechora folk then paid tribute to *Novgrad,* and how from the Pechora the messenger went on to *Yugra.* . . .

Now this Siberian connection . . . is not a passing incident, like the early Russian dominion on the Azov or in the Crimea, or the early Russian raids towards and even beyond the Caucasus. On the contrary, it appears fairly persistent throughout the central and later Middle Ages;

and when in the fifteenth century the Novgorod sphere-of-influence in the North is finally torn away by Moscow, the Moscovite power, without loss of time, begins to interfere in Yugra, subjugating it far more thoroughly than before to its new Russian overlord.

For the greater part of the twelfth century, it is true, Novgorod history tells only of matters nearer home, though the tribute-gathering expedition of 1169 in the *Trans-Volok* (or regions beyond Byeloe Ozero) may have been concerned with payments as far as Asia, and the foundation of Vyatka in 1174 carries Novgorod settlement far nearer to Siberia than before, along a more southerly track. But in 1187 we hear again of Yugra to some purpose; both here and in lands west of Ural the natives now rose and massacred their Russian masters or customers. The punitive expedition of 1193 failed to restore Novgorodian power; though one Yugrian town was taken, and another besieged, the whole Russian force was ultimately destroyed, save eighty men, who in 1194 made their way home to the Volkhov.

How and when intercourse with Siberia was restored we are not told; but this restoration had evidently taken place by the middle of the thirteenth century, for in a celebrated agreement made in 1264 between the Novgorodians and their Prince Yaroslav, the Yugrian country, like the Pechora, appears reckoned among the domains (or at least in the sphere-of-interest) of Novgorod. Sixty years later, in 1323 and 1329, the Novgorod Annals complain of outrages—robbery and murder—upon the citizens of the Republic on their way to Yugra. These outrages were the work of Russian enemies from Ustyug in the Upper Dvina basin, planted conveniently upon the flank of the trade-route from Novgorod to the North-East, and thus a constant danger to the commerce in furs and precious metals which the great Hanseatic market carried on with the forests and mountains of its sub-Arctic sphere in both the European and the Asiatic Siberia. Again, the demand of Moscow, in 1332-1333, for tribute in silver for the lands beyond the Kama—the first sign of the coming Moscovite overlordship, advanced by the founder of the earliest Moscovite power, the bursar-prince Ivan Kalita—clearly refers to the mining wealth which Novgorod had long exploited in the Northern Ural.

Lastly, in 1445, within a generation of the ruin both of the Novgorod empire and of the independence of the Republic, we hear of a last vigorous effort to assert Novgorodian rule in Siberia. Again the *Chronicle* tells of initial successes; two generals, we read, gathered a force in the Trans-Volok, attacked the Yugrians, and made many prisoners. Then, as before, victory ends in ruinous defeat. The natives, pretending to submit, drew together in force, fell suddenly upon the Russians, and stormed their chief fastness; only a part of the Novgorod army had the good fortune to get out of the country which they had so nearly mastered.

In 1471-1478 Moscow crushed Novgorod and took over the Novgorodian empire. But even before this Moscovite forces had begun the conquest of that Yugrian Siberia with which Novgorod had dealt so long. A new Grand Prince had begun his reign in the White Stone City—the "Re-uniter of Russian lands," the future conquerer of Novgorod and of the Tartars, the founder of the Moscow tsardom, Ivan III, the Great (1462-1505). The ubiquitous energy of this eastern Louis XI made itself felt in the Urals and Asia, when, in 1465, at the very opening of his reign, Ustyug adventurers, his faithful vassals, raided Yugra and brought two Yugrian princes, with many other prisoners, to Moscow. Ivan received oaths of fidelity and promises of tribute from these "people of the Ob"; as the first Moscovite to assert dominion in Siberia, he shortly after took the style of Lord of Yugra.

In 1483, now master of Novgorod and victorious over the Golden Horde, he resumed his Asian conquests. His troops, crossing the Urals, descended by the Tavda river to its junction with the Tobol, the Tobol to its junction with the Irtysh, in that Siberian Khanate, far south of Yugra, which was not permanently subdued for another century; from where Tobolsk now stands they followed the Irtysh northward into Yugra, where it joined the Ob. The Yugrians submitted afresh; their southern neighbors the Voguls also became tributaries of Moscow; terms of peace were arranged by Philothei, bishop of Perm; and the Vogul prince Yumshan accompanied Philothei to the court of Ivan.

Yet a third expedition was undertaken by the same tsar, sixteen years later, to complete and extend the Moscovite empire in the North-East. In November and December of 1499 three of his generals, with 5000 men, after building a fortress on the Pechora, crossed the Ural on snow-shoes, in the face of a Siberian winter, and broke with fire and sword upon the Yugrians of the Lower Ob. The native princes, drawn in reindeer sledges, hurried to the invaders' camp to make their submission; the Russian leaders scoured the country in similar equipages, their soldiers following in dogsledges. Forty townships or forts were captured; fifty princes and over 1000 other prisoners were taken; and Ivan's forces, returning to Moscow by the Easter of 1500, reported the entire and final conquest of Yugrians and Voguls.

2 / RUSSIA'S ORIENTAL HERITAGE

It is generally recognized that the Russians are adept in dealing with Asians. By some this is ascribed to a common racial origin. "Scratch a Russian, and you will find a Tartar." But racially the Slavs, blond and fair in complexion, are no more Asian than the Anglo-Saxons. Their Asian "touch" stems from centuries of close contact and often bitter experience with Asian peoples, as well as from an Oriental strain in their cultural heritage—Byzantine no less than Mongol.

This Oriental heritage provided the Russians with a frame of mind that smoothed the path of their eastward expansion; it was bolstered in turn by increased contact (and some intermarriage) with the Asian peoples of Siberia and beyond. This Oriental heritage (merely one of many strains in Russian culture) had its political implications. Not only was there Byzantine and Mongol precedent for the absolutism of Russian rulers, but the latter could and did lay claim to a share of the territorial legacy of the Byzantine and Mongol empires.

Professor Vernadsky, in the concluding pages of his monumental study The Mongols and Russia, *examines the aftermath of two centuries of Mongol rule and the nature of Russia's Oriental heritage.*

I

When East Russia emancipated herself from the authority of the khan she emerged much stronger than before the Mongol invasion. All of "Great Russia" was now politically united under the guidance of the grand duke of Moscow and, to emphasize his independence of foreign rule as well as his authority in the internal affairs of the country, he assumed the titles of autocrat (*samoderzhets*) and tsar. The Jesuit Antonio Possevino, one of the shrewdest diplomats of the second half of the 16th century and well acquainted with East European affairs, was apparently right when he commented that the "haughtiness" of the Moscow rulers was the result of their emancipation from Tatar domination. The two titles "tsar" and "autocrat" were used occasionally in the latter part of the reign of Ivan III and more frequently in the reign of Vasili III. Ivan IV was officially crowned tsar with the sanction of the church (1547). In his subsequent polemics against Prince Kurbsky Ivan IV used "autocrat" in the sense of a ruler absolutely supreme in the internal affairs of the country.

It will be recalled that the title "tsar" was first applied by the Russians to the Byzantine emperor and then to the Mongol khan also. It so hap-

George Vernadsky, *The Mongols and Russia* (New Haven, Conn.: Yale University Press, 1953), pp. 385-90. Reprinted with permission of The Yale University Press.

pened that at the time Russia was shedding the already half-broken fetters of the khan's control the Byzantine Empire was destroyed by the Ottoman Turks. Ivan III's marriage to Sophia Paleologus, a niece of the last Byzantine emperor and the pope's ward, could be understood as his becoming heir to the Byzantine tsars. The pope and the Venetians who wanted to solicit Russian help against the Osmanlis lost no time in pointing out the significance of the marriage from this point of view. The Russians themselves were aware of its implications but did not attribute too much value to the event. However, they used the Byzantine traditions in many other ways. Russian political thought had been influenced by Byzantine doctrines from the time of Russia's conversion to Christianity. Yet no elaborate theory of monarchy was built up by the Russians during the Kievan period, since the Russian political background was at that time quite different from the Byzantine. Then conditions changed, a strong centralized state came into being in Muscovy, and the Russian literati could turn for inspiration to those currents in Byzantine thought which they had neglected earlier. There is no doubt that the Muscovite monarchic theories of the 16th century reflected the Byzantine doctrine in many respects.

More than that, the Muscovites now attempted to find historical evidence for claiming a direct connection between the Byzantine and the Russian monarchies. Among various semihistorical and pseudohistorical arguments which were brought forward was the assertion that Vladimir the Saint at the time of his conversion was crowned tsar by the emperor and the patriarch of Constantinople. Another popular story had it that Prince Vladimir Monomach received the insignia of tsardom from the Byzantine emperor. On the basis of that legend the jeweled and fur-trimmed crown of the Moscow rulers became known, in the 16th century, as Monomach's Crown. . . .

It is hard to tell whether the Muscovites themselves seriously believed in the stories of the crownings of Vladimir the Saint and Vladimir Monomach. In any case they did not put all their eggs in the Byzantine basket, being well aware of the historical connection between the Tsardom of Moscow and the Golden Horde. And indeed it was but natural for the Muscovite ruler to take the title of his former suzerain. Moreover, when the Russian counterattack started and the Russians conquered the khanates of Kazan and Astrakhan (in 1552 and 1556 respectively), the Russian tsar could claim to have become heir to at least two of the Golden Horde succession states. . . .

An important aspect of the continuity of Mongol traditions in the Muscovite monarchy was the Mongol influence on the etiquette of diplomatic negotiations. Many a Western envoy to Muscovy complained of the stiff and ridiculous formalities of the diplomatic ritual. As a matter of fact, when we look back now on those mutual offenses and claims and counterclaims about etiquette by the Russian and Western diplomats of the 16th and 17th centuries, some of the notions of the Western envoys seem to us as absurd as the Muscovite. At the root of the misunderstandings lay the fact that Westerners and Russians followed different bodies of rules, and that the Russian ceremonial reflected the Mongol pattern in many respects.

The basic Muscovite concept of the duties of a government toward foreign ambassadors and of the rights of ambassadors with respect to the government in the country of their destination differed markedly from the Western concept. From the Mongol point of view—shared by the Muscovites—an ambassador was a guest of the ruler to whom he was accredited. That ruler had to provide him, and his suite, with free transportation, lodgings, food and drink, and to guard his safety. While the Westerners did not object to free lodgings and food, they protested on many occasions that Moscow's care for their safety amounted to keeping them constantly under guard. On the other hand, the Russian ambassadors who had to travel in the West were indignant when they had to pay—and sometimes exorbitantly—for their transportation and maintenance. In both Mongol and Muscovite diplomatic ceremonial much attention was paid to mutual gifts. Not only did the rulers exchange presents but ambassadors were expected to offer appropriate gifts to the ruler they visited. A Muscovite rule, patterned on Mongol etiquette, forbade any foreign envoy to be armed when received in audience by the tsar. Many a Western ambassador resented being required to part with his sword before entering the audience hall, but all had to comply with the rule. When the foreign envoy entered Russia he was met at the frontier by a special official (*pristav*). Muscovite (as well as Tatar) etiquette required that envoy and pristav dismount simultaneously to greet each other in the name of their respective sovereigns. Then the pristav rode at the right of the ambassador. For reasons hard to understand, the Westerners objected violently to these two rules and tried every possible device to circumvent them. Most however had to accept the inevitable.*

The familiarity of the Muscovites with Mongol ways of diplomacy helped them greatly in their dealings with Oriental powers, especially

---

* It would not be amiss to mention that the Muscovite etiquette in foreign relations was abolished by Peter the Great and the Western body of rules introduced instead. In the 18th and 19th centuries Russian diplomatic ceremonial was identical with the Western.

with the succession states of the Golden Horde. In a sense Russia herself was such a succession state, and after the breakup of the Golden Horde the ruler of Russia seemed to be entitled to present his claims for leadership in the Mongol-Tatar sphere. Since as we have seen the so-called Golden Horde was actually known as the White Horde, the tsar of Moscow, as successor of the khans of this horde, was now called the "white tsar." As late as the 18th and 19th centuries the Russian emperor was still the white khan (*tsagan khan*) to the Kalmyks and the Buriats. The feeling among many Turkish and Mongol tribes that the Russian tsar was the successor of the Mongol khans created a favorable situation psychologically for the extension of the tsar's rule over those tribes. Moscow diplomats consciously or subconsciously took advantage of the situation. In this sense it may be said, as Prince Nicholas Trubetskoy did, that the Russians inherited their empire from Chingis-Khan.

II

The emancipation of East Russia from Mongol rule was the result of a combined effort of the Moscow grand dukes, the church, the boyars, the gentry, and the commoners—in fact of the whole nation. The new monarchy which was created in the tortuous process of emancipation was based on principles alien to the Russians of the Kievan period. All classes of East Russian society were now subordinated to the state. It might have been expected that once the goal of emancipation was achieved the Muscovite regime would relax and at least some of the old liberties would be restored. Actually, as we know, the opposite happened. Regimentation of the social classes progressed unchecked and reached its peak about 1650, two centuries after the end of the Mongol rule.

Why this seeming historical paradox? The answer is obvious: the precarious position of the Moscow monarchy on the international scene and the constant danger of war. In the southeast and south Muscovy was still threatened by the Tatars; in the west the struggle for power between Moscow and Lithuania (after 1569, between Moscow and Poland) continued to flare up at almost regular intervals; in the northwest, after having annexed Novgorod, the Moscow government had to take over the task previously performed by the Novgorodians, that of containing the pressure of the Livonian Knights and of Sweden in the area of the Gulf of Finland and Karelia. When Moscow defied the authority of the khan of the Golden Horde, there still remained several Tatar succession states, and the Tatars continued to raid the southern and eastern provinces of Muscovy almost yearly, looting and seizing thousands of captives. Thus the drain on Russian resources increased rather than decreased after the emancipation of the grand duke of Moscow from Mongol rule. There were no natural boundaries in the steppes between Muscovy and the Tatars, and the Moscow government had to keep the whole frontier constantly guarded. Both the Kasimov Tatars and the frontiersmen and Cossacks proved useful, but regular army troops had to be mobilized every year as well. An elaborate system of fortified defense lines was built up, but on many occasions the Tatars would pierce them and pour into the country between and behind them. Under the circumstances, the only way to solve the problem seemed to be to establish firm Russian control of the steppes, by either conquest or diplomacy. From the geopolitical point of view, Ivan IV's dash down the Volga to Astrakhan was an important move since it cut the steppe zone into two sectors, each of which could now be taken care of separately. But that was only the beginning of Russia's bid for sovereignty over the peoples of the steppes. The process continued throughout the 17th and the 18th centuries, ending, in the south, with the annexation of the Crimea in 1783.

The struggle in the west, while not continual and not as exasperating as the process of containing the Tatars, was on the whole no less costly since it required, in the periods of acute crises, stronger and better-equipped armies and more expenditure for armament plants. The situation was certainly not propitious for any relaxation of governmental controls. On the contrary, new taxes were required and the taxation system was to be tightened rather than liberalized. The creation of the new army based on the pomestie system raised the problem of supplying agricultural labor to the pomestia [tenant estates granted by the tsar], and this, as we have seen, led to serfdom. As a result of all this, the regimentation of the social classes which started during the Mongol period and was originally based on the Mongol principles of administration, was carried further and completed by the Muscovite government. Autocracy and serfdom were the price the Russian people had to pay for national survival.

3 / TO THE URALS

There was no natural barrier between European Russia and Asia. A weak Russia, therefore, lay exposed to foreign invasion, a fact of life as responsible for the development of absolutism in Russia as her Oriental heritage.

The absence of a natural frontier worked, of course, in either direction. If there was no barrier to shelter a weak Russia, neither was there one to hem in a strong Russia. Forced to gird her loins in a struggle for survival,

Prince A. Lobanov-Rostovsky, *Russia and Asia* (New York: The Macmillan Company, 1933), pp. 33-38. Reprinted with permission of A. Lobanov-Rostovsky.

Russia tended to distend ever more, her defensive and offensive measures flowing together in a torrent of expansion that eventually inundated a major part of the Eurasian continent.

Prince Lobanov-Rostovsky, in his pioneer work on Russia in Asia, shows how Russian expansion traditionally proceeded hand-in-hand with Russian "quest for peace" and irresistibly led the Russians to the Ural Mountains and beyond.

The overthrow of the Mongol domination coincided with and was the result of the emergence of the Czardom of Muscovy as a powerful empire which had reunited the Russian nation and was taking its rightful place in the world. As it coincided also with the fall of the Byzantine Empire, Russia now took the position so long held by the Eastern Roman Empire, that of a balancing force between East and West. . . .

This great rhythmic movement in history, the Roman influence first expanding into Asia, then counterbalanced by the subsequent Asiatic invasions into Europe, was now once more marked by the recurrent wave of white expansion eastward. On the other hand, just as Russia was holding out against the Mongols on one flank of Europe while Spain was doing the same against the Moors on the other flank, so now at the time when Spain and Portugal were discovering a vast new world to the west, Russia was doing the same in the East. The balance of power between Russia and Asia having turned definitely in favour of Russia, her advance into Asia was to be remarkably rapid and in a century she was to sweep across to the Pacific.

After the overthrow of the Golden Horde, there remained three moribund Mongol states, the Khanates of Crimea, Kazan and Astrakhan. The first of these, becoming a vassal of the Turkish Empire, escaped Russian domination until the 18th century, but the other two were immediately attacked by John [Ivan] the Terrible shortly after his accession. In 1552 he led an expedition against Kazan. To this war he gave the character of a religious crusade, and though the Crimean Tartars showed their solidarity with their co-religionists on the Volga by invading Muscovy, John was not deterred from his task. After besieging Kazan and making a passage through its mighty defences by the explosion of a mine, he stormed the city and captured it. Astrakhan followed in 1556, and by these two victories Russia at one stroke reached the Ural Mountains and the Caspian Sea. The way into the heart of Asia was now open.

The Crimean Tartars continued to give trouble. In their peninsula, separated from the mainland by a narrow neck of land, the Perekop, they not only had a hiding-place but also a convenient base for the Turks to land. According to Kluchevsky, more than 120,000 Tartars participated in the attacks upon Moscow in 1571 and 1572. Minor raids on the border occurred once or twice yearly, for the purpose of capturing slaves. The usual tactics were to creep up to the Russian border secretly, avoiding roads and taking care not to light fires which might be discovered by the Russian watches. Then profiting by the population being scattered in the fields during harvest time, they threw out detachments in all directions to capture as many boys and girls as possible. These were taken to Kaffa, the great slave exporting port in Crimea, and from there were dispatched on Turkish ships to the Levant, to Africa, and also to Europe. Western Europeans were not particularly reluctant to purchase Christian slaves. . . .

Notwithstanding the conquest of the Tartar states along the Volga, it became obvious that the Moscow government was still faced with the all-important task of making its frontiers safe from the disastrous incursions of nomads. This was particularly urgent along the southern frontier facing Crimea, but it was also necessary along the eastern border beyond the Volga. Only continuous expansion and the establishment of chains of fortified posts would establish security, by placing the central provinces of the empire further from the borders.

Thus expansion and colonization ran hand-in-hand in this quest for peace, and the Government soon discovered what use could be made of the Cossack communities which were springing up in the frontier regions. The great steppe was not solely the abode of the hostile nomads but also, lured by a promise of freedom and adventure, a motley crowd of Russian freebooters. These were either peasants escaping taxes and military service, or criminals escaping justice, or even young men of rich families in search of excitement. At the time of John's expeditions against the Volga Khanates, bands of these adventurers, profiting by the weakening of the Tartar rule on the steppe, pushed far ahead of the Russian settlement and were to be found along the course of the Upper Don in the very heart of no-man's land. A little later, on the Dnieper, a peculiar free military republic of Cossacks sprang up and prospered by participating in the wars fought between Russia, Poland and the Tartars. Being very restless, the Cossacks formed a doubtful asset to the side they were supporting; however, they carried out looting raids against the infidel, i.e. the Turks and the Tartars, sometimes even menacing Constantinople in their light crafts. A vague feeling of Russian nationalism and communion in the Orthodox faith made them less of a menace to the Russian Government than to the Poles whom they hated, and hence the attempt to enlist them for frontier service was more successful on the part of the Moscow Czars than on the part of the King of Poland. Gradually as the power of the government grew, so the hold on the Cossacks tightened. Finally they were organized into special "hosts"—both a military and administrative term—and they systematically settled along the border to form military settlements of colonists, agriculturalists who at a moment's notice might be turned into a cavalry force.

As Russia expanded in the East, new hosts were established along the shifting border. This policy was carried out right up to the 20th century. The names of the various hosts tell the tale of the Russian expansion: Don, Kuban, Terek, Astrakhan, Ural, Orenburg, Siberian, Semiriechensk (Turkestan), Transbaikal, Amur, Ussuri. . . .

Thus we see that once Russia was started on her expansion towards Asia, the forces driving her made this movement irresistible. These were, first, the quest for security against the Tartars; then, the growing consciousness of an imperial destiny as a result of her adoption of the Byzantine political ideals, and finally, the adventurous quest of the Cossacks. To these must also be added the enterprise and vision of certain merchant families who carried on the great Novgorodian tradition of commercial exploration. Under the pressure of these forces the Russians crossed the Urals only thirty years after the fall of Kazan.

4 / DOMAIN OF DOOM

The name "Siberia" sends shivers down the spine of the average American, who conjures up exile, salt mines, and everlasting cold. But Siberia is a many-splendored land, full of natural beauty and freedom as well as suffering. The splendor of Lake Baikal on a calm summer day or the simple warmheartedness of the inhabitants of Siberia are not readily duplicated in European Russia today.

Senator Beveridge, who visited Siberia at the beginning of the twentieth century, pointed to the prejudiced view that Westerners had of that region in his day. Years fraught with momentous change have passed since the Senator penned his lines, but the stereotype blinders are still on our faces. The observations of Senator Beveridge sound remarkably up-to-date.

Two influences operate to deflect the judgment of the American, the English, and the German traveller through Siberia. The first is that all of us have had it fixed upon our minds that Siberia is the land of terror, the region of exile, the domain of doom. We have been told that it was a snowy desert where wander the men and women whom Russian oppressors drove from their homes. It has been pictured to us as a country of prisons, a waste peopled by destroying wolves and sentinelled by grim

Albert J. Beveridge, *The Russian Advance* (New York: Harper & Row, Publishers, 1903), pp. 209-10, 219-220.

and savage Cossacks, the agents of a secret, ruthless, and terrible power. For years popular plays have pictured the infamy of this barren world of outcasts; and at the present moment more than one melodrama, played at theatres patronized by the masses of the people, portrays the awful tyranny of the Czar and the bitter lot of his unfortunate subjects who people that dreadful land called Siberia.

Even the best-informed traveller enters Siberia with the above impression constituting his subconscious viewpoint. Fortify ourselves as we will with the tolerance of the scientist and the impartiality of the judicial mind, we find the feelings formed in our childhood days by shuddering tales of this Slav inferno asserting themselves. We have crossed the Urals, and Siberia proper is before us. Now, therefore, for the chain-gang, now for the knout, now for the stench, degradation, and death of those pens of incarceration where Russia herds her rejected till they go mad or expire.

On the other hand, the American, German, or Englishman comes suddenly into this territory from his own land. And his land is thickly settled, highly developed, and organized up to the ideals of modern civilization. He comes from countries of quick despatch, of frequent towns, of mammoth cities, of a perfected commerce, whose complexity has eliminated non-essentials, and is still eliminating them. He comes from a land of comforts, a place where the luxuries of a century ago are the common necessities of to-day.

On the one hand, therefore, Siberia is, in contrast to the first of these influences, a surprise and delight; on the other hand, and in contrast to the conditions surrounding him in his own home, he will declare Siberia to be undeveloped. . . .

Against both of these influences the fair-minded man who visits Siberia must contend. He must take into account that Siberian development has only just begun. He must remember the racial characteristics of the Slav. He must bear in mind the serious conditions of climate and distance with which the government has had to contend. Above all, he must remember the Russian ideal of preserving for the Russian people themselves every foot of territory which Russian blood, Russian diplomacy, and Russian enterprise have won for the empire of the Czar.

Over and over again the analogy of these Slav frontiersmen with their American counterparts in the period of the early settlement of our own country suggested itself. Here were the same fearlessness, the same daring of the unknown, the same severance from the place of their birth, the same intention to plant in the wilderness the institutions which they had left. With the American pioneer it was Anglo-Saxon individualism and the institutions of a representative government; with the Russian emigrant it is Slav communism and the institutions of autocracy. . . .

5 / YERMAK

If there be one man who above all others personifies Russia's eastward expansion, it is Yermak, tracker, Cossack, river pirate, and "Conqueror of Siberia." His thrust into the trans-Ural region had been financed by the Stroganovs, a family of wealthy merchant-capitalists, who sought to enlarge their already vast landholdings, where they plied most profitably in the fur trade as well as in iron and silver mining and salt making. The private enterprise of such families rather than the initiative of the state or the ambition of roving adventurers was the actual mainspring of the conquest of Siberia. Yet it is not the quiet daring and organizing ability of the capitalist, but the bravado and physical courage and fight to the death of the swashbuckling marauder that captures the heart of the nation.

There are many colorful versions of the exploits of Yermak. In his lifetime he was rumored to have been invulnerable to bullet or sword, and after his death he was worshiped as a saint both by Russian wanderers in Siberia and by native tribesmen. The story of Yermak, set down by John F. Baddeley, an English scholar who had the good fortune of doing research in Russia before the Revolution, when the Far Eastern regions and Foreign Office Archives were still open to foreigners, is one of the more restrained and accurate.

From the days of the Vikings, at least, except, perhaps, when the Mongol power was at its height, the Volga had been not only a channel of commerce but the chosen haunt of piratical outlaws. When the power of the Horde declined, that part of the river between the mouth of the Kama and the Samara bend or loop had, in especial, acquired an evil notoriety. Here passed all the merchandise coming to the heart of Russia from north, east, and south; from the Ural Mountains and the Orenburg steppes; from Khiva and Bukhara; from the Caucasus and from Persia. Here, too, passed the caravans of ambassadors and envoys coming or going between the rulers of many States and the Court of Moscow, and it was the despoiling of one such embassy that filled to overflowing the cup of Ivan's wrath ever bubbling near the brim. He sent orders to his lieutenants to take drastic measures against the culprits, whereupon they dispersed in various directions, some to the Don, to the Caspian some, and the river Terek while others, to the number of 540 men, under the

John F. Baddeley, *Russia, Mongolia, China: Being some Record of the Relations between them from the beginning of the XVIIth Century to the Death of the Tsar Alexei Mikhailovich* A.D. *1602-1676* (London: Macmillan & Co., Ltd., 1919), vol. I, lxix-lxxiii. Reprinted with permission of Macmillan & Co., Ltd., and St. Martin's Press.

leadership of Yermak, went up the Kama to the Chusovaya. The date of their arrival on that river is 1579 and, apparently, they took service at once with the Stroganoffs, who probably saw no other way out of a dangerous situation. They had been commanded, moreover, by the Tsar seven years previously, on an occasion when 87 Russian traders were massacred by natives, to hire "free" cossacks and others and arm them against the Cheremiss, Votiaks, Ostiaks, and Nogais "who have played traitor to Us." It was not unnatural, therefore, that the Stroganoffs should think of employing the new-comers in this way. They did so, in any case, providing them with what arms and munitions they needed, and with food; and the marauders, thus furnished, seem, during two years and two months, to have followed their old calling with renewed zest and greater security. For, in a menacing letter dated 16th November 1582 addressed to the Stroganoffs, who had doubtless arranged with Yermak that they should not suffer in person and property even if they did not actually share the plunder, the Tsar complains that they had betrayed his interests. . . . The Tsar's wrath was justified. The enemy had wasted all this flourishing region with fire and sword, and nearly taken Cherdin. But the letter came late. Yermak and his marauding band, now grown to a total of 840 men by the addition of 300 of the Stroganoffs' militiamen, Lithuanians, Germans, Russians, and Tartars, "daredevils all," had already crossed the Urals by way of the Chusovaya, the Serebrianka, and the Tura to where Tumen still stands. The force was well armed, but, as a Russian writer points out, the idea that their fire-arms struck panic terror into the hearts of Kuchum's Tartars, as something new and super-human, is untenable. Possibly, some of the Voguls and Ostiaks were unacquainted with fire-arms, but the Mongols and Tartars had doubtless known them little later than the Russians. Still, a band such as this was likely, so long as its strength was kept up, to hold its own against anything that Kuchum could bring against it.

The winter of 1582 was spent on the Tura and not without loss, from attacks made by the natives; from disease, too, and from accident. In spring with the breaking of the ice Yermak moved down the Tura, but where it enters the Tobol met with armed opposition, and from here to the mouth of the Tavda could fight his way but slowly. When, after a week's rest at this spot, the expedition started again, the opposition grew even stronger; the natives of many tribes lined both banks of the river and harassed the adventurers night and day, occasionally giving battle on a larger scale, and only at the end of September did the Russians reach the Irtish and succeed in occupying some high ground on the left bank of that river. Here they waited three weeks in great uncertainty what next to do. However, on the opposite bank there was a native stronghold, Podchuvashi, and this, at last, on the 23rd October, Yermak stormed. Three days later the enemy, who were commanded by Prince Mametkul, his uncle, Kuchum, being, it is said, blind, abandoned neighbouring Iskir or Sibir (not far from where Tobolsk was afterwards built) and fled up the Irtish. The Russians wintered here, perforce, but the situation was rendered somewhat easier by the fact that the local tribesmen—Ostiaks and Voguls—recognising in the new-comers the stronger side, gave in and acknowledged their supremacy, presenting *yasak* [tribute]. The Chronicles tell us that Yermak now sent a deputation to the Tsar in Moscow, with rich tribute in fur, announcing the capture of Sibir, and that Ivan IV, rejoicing greatly at the news, sent back a gracious letter with full forgiveness of past offences, at the same time making grants of land to the Stroganoffs for their services. . . .

Yermak and his men spent the whole winter of 1583-84 in huts at the mouth of the Tobol. The enemy were on the watch not far off and, soon, a party of twenty cossacks was caught napping and killed to a man, at a neighbouring village, Abalatskoe. On the other hand, in February, the Russians fell suddenly upon the enemy fifty versts up the Irtish, below the mouth of the river Vagai, killed many and took Mametkul alive. Meantime, a strong party of cossacks went north on snow-shoes, as far as the Ob, using force or cajolery to procure the submission of the natives and obtain help and food from them. They returned at the end of May, by boat, with plentiful supplies, such as they were.

The hostile relations between the families of the Sheibanids and Tai-bughids, to which, mainly, no doubt, the Russians owed what success they achieved, now came into play once more. Seidak, Edigher's heir, attacked the usurper Kuchum and drove him beyond the river Vagai. This somewhat relieved Yermak's position, and he now started up the Tobol and the Tavda to meet the reinforcements under Prince Bolkhovsky which were said to be on their way from Russia, leaving his atamans Koltso (or Koltsoff) and Mikhailoff in Sibir. But when summer had come and gone, when winter was at hand, yet nothing could be seen or heard of Bolkhovsky, Yermak, heavy at heart, turned back to rejoin his companions. The journey was begun by water, but the boats, caught half-way by the ice, had to be abandoned and the journey finished on foot.

At Sibir, during his absence, all had changed for the worse. Koltso, his ablest lieutenant, with forty companions, had fallen a victim to native "treachery"—what was laudable ruse in a Russian was, of course, the vilest treachery in a native. Mikhailoff, hurrying to help him, had likewise been killed, with many of his men. Kuchum's forces—he had apparently got the better of Seidak for the moment—took courage and pressed hard upon the enfeebled garrison of Sibir.

Yermak, on arrival, did what he could to improve the position and prepared to pass another winter. Then, in November, most unexpectedly, the longed-for reinforcements arrived, to the unspeakable relief of the forlorn adventurers. But their joy was short-lived. Bolkhovsky's men had suffered great privations on the way and far from strengthening the garrison actually weakened it; for with added numbers food ran short, scurvy made its dread appearance, many died, and one chronicler (Remezoff) declares that the bodies of the dead were devoured by their starving comrades. Bolkhovsky himself fell a victim to privation and hardship, and from March 1585 the enemy grew more and more threatening. In May or June, however, a bold sally relieved the situation. The besiegers retired once more beyond the Vagai.

Meantime, Mametkul had been sent prisoner to Moscow soon after Bolkhovsky's arrival, with the latter's written confirmation of what had already been accomplished, and what more might be expected. Moscow, therefore, thoroughly roused, despatched a further reinforcement under the command of the *voevoda* [governor of a province] Mansuroff. But Yermak found his position intolerable, and to improve it, whether by negotiation or fighting, had to make all possible use of the open water. Sailing, therefore, and rowing up the Irtish, he is said to have reached a point not far from the present town of Tara, with what precise object does not appear; he then turned back, and, when nearing the mouth of the Vagai, received information that a caravan from Bukhara . . . with goods for Sibir had been stopped on the Ishim steppes by Kuchum. It was a simple trick enough, but it answered its purpose. Yermak turned up the Vagai and made his way to the point where the caravan track crossed that river—at Atbash, some say, others at Aghib. Having waited some days in vain, the Russian leader started back, and at the river-mouth bivouacked on shore, apparently without any precaution. The night was dark and rainy—it was the 6th August 1585—and the cossacks were asleep, when the enemy fell upon them in overwhelming numbers. Yermak alone reached the river's brink, and leaped for a boat—but missed his footing, fell into the water, and, encumbered by his armour, sank.

When this terrible news reached Sibir, the remaining Russian forces beat a hasty retreat; and Kuchum with his son Alei re-entered their capital in triumph, to be promptly beaten, however, and turned out again by Seidak. While still on the river Tura the refugees met the voevoda Mansuroff with the new forces from Moscow. Together they came down-stream and wintered at the mouth of the Irtish. Then, Ivan IV being dead and the reins of government, under his feeble son Theodor, in the capable hands of Boris Godunoff, to whom more than to any one the consolidation of Russian power in Siberia is due, still further reinforcements arrived from the capital under the voevoda Chulkoff, and in 1586 the town of Tumen was founded, on the site of a native *gorodok* [small town], the first permanent Russian settlement beyond the Urals. The founding of Tobolsk followed in 1587. Russia had come to stay.

Seidak, who still gave trouble, was now taken prisoner by a really treacherous deed, being seized, and his companions slaughtered, at a banquet to which he had been invited by the Russians in all apparent friendliness. The chroniclers have not a word of reprobation or excuse for this atrocious crime, nor would one expect it from them. *"No son cristianos"* was the grumbling answer of a South American *arriero,* when remonstrated with for cruelty to animals. In Yermak's day—and after—to be pagan, "poganny," put men, similarly, without the pale of humanity.

Yermak's name can never die. For many generations of Russians he has been not merely the conqueror of petty Sibir, but of all Siberia. The cut-throat of the Volga has been metamorphosed into a knight-at-arms, *sans peur et sans reproche,* a happy mixture of Hernan Cortes and King Arthur, with, in one version at least, more than a touch of Sir Galahad —for all which there is scant foundation in history. On the other hand it is very evident that he was not merely a vulgar brigand or bandit, but a leader of men, of a personality quite beyond the common. His lawless followers, a motley crew, stood by him to the last, through those long years of hardship and privation. There is not a hint of insubordination or revolt in circumstances that would strain the constancy and loyalty of most men to breaking-point, and by that alone we might judge him a man amongst men. But, after all, it is less, even, the devotion of friends and companions than the respect of enemies that sets the crown on a hero's fame. Yermak alive kept a Khanate at bay; Yermak dead became to Tartars and Mongols a miracle-worker and saint; to the ruder tribes of Siberia, Ostiaks and others, even as the bear they first kill and then worship, a God. When his body was dragged from the Irtish river the hero was known by the armour he wore, a hauberk or coat of chain-mail, brass-hemmed and emblazoned with the two-headed eagle, the fatal gift of the Tsar. When rough hands removed it, blood gushed from mouth and nose. The news went flying to Kuchum and his sons; they arrived to find, after many days, a body untouched by corruption. With the points of their arrows they pierced the flesh—it bled like that of a living man. Then, filled with awe, they buried Yermak by the river brink at the foot of a pine; and made all present swear that never in any circumstances would they reveal the spot to the Russians. After this, for a while, by night, columns of fire stood over the place, to dwindle, in course of years, to corpse-lights, visible to none but natives. With earth from the grave sick men were made whole, rich booty secured on raiding ventures; and, after two generations, Prince Ablai, the Kalmuk chief, intimate friend of "living Buddhas," zealous builder of lama monasteries, begged and obtained Yermak's mail-coat from Tzar Alexei's representative, assured that in it he could fight and conquer the Kazak horde, no matter what the odds.

From Russian outlaw to hero of Delhi is a far cry; yet both were of that rare stamp men follow living and worship dead.

6 / YERMAK'S SUCCESSORS

Yermak had his successors. Slowly the Russians made their way across the continent. In the following selection George Frederick Wright gives a chronological account of their progression to the Pacific Coast.

Interest in the occupation of Siberia was maintained and stimulated by the opportunities for trade which were soon opened. In Mexico and Peru it was gold and silver which stimulated the Spanish explorers. It was the valuable fur-bearing animals scattered over the vast wastes which excited the cupidity of the Russian adventurers in Siberia. Of these the most highly valued was the sable, now almost exterminated by the hunters, but which in 1640 yielded no less than six thousand eight hundred skins, being in fact so common that the Siberian Cossacks used its fur for their coat linings; while already in European Russia they had become so scarce as to bring an exorbitant price. Not only sable, but foxes, snow foxes, ermines, squirrels, bears, reindeer, and hares provided a great store of furs which it was profitable to transport to the mother country. To obtain these treasures, independent hunting and trading parties of Cossacks set out in all directions, oftentimes interfering and quarreling with each other when they chanced to meet in the same locality. A large tribute of furs was also exacted from the Ostiaks and Samoyedes. As early as 1593, or a year before the founding of Tara, the Cossacks had descended the Obi River to the sixty-fourth degree of latitude, N., seven hundred miles below Tiumen, and founded the trading-post of Berezof, which is still an important Siberian town.

Following the lines of water communication offered by the wide-spreading branches of the Obi, the Russian adventurers reached the Yenisei River in 1620, though probably sporadic expeditions had visited the river

George Frederick Wright, *Asiatic Russia* (New York: McClure, Phillips and Co., 1902), I, 135-50.

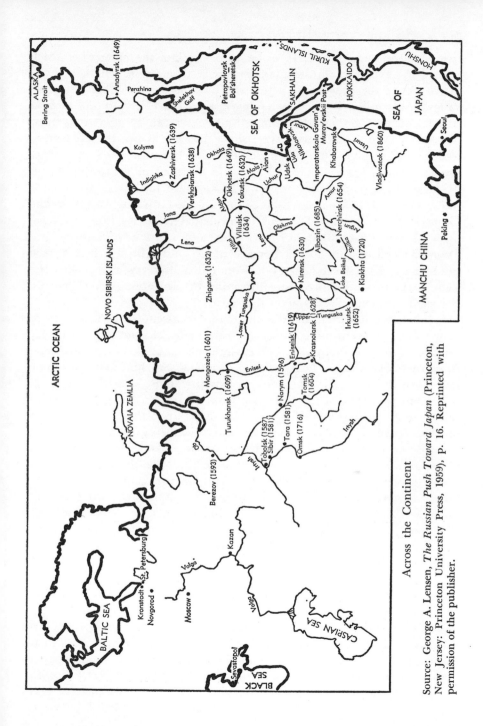

Across the Continent

Source: George A. Lensen, *The Russian Push Toward Japan* (Princeton, New Jersey: Princeton University Press, 1959), p. 16. Reprinted with permission of the publisher.

two or three years earlier. In order to appreciate the enterprise which carried the explorers thus far, it is necessary to note the length and the difficulties of the journey by which the passage is made from one river valley to the other. First, after having crossed the Ural Mountains by a journey of not less than four hundred miles to reach Tiumen, they must descend the Tura and Irtysh rivers for a distance of five hundred miles to the Obi, at about the sixty-first degree of latitude, when they must ascend the Obi for a distance of fully six hundred miles, to the mouth of the River Ket, which in turn must be ascended for a distance of three hundred and sixty-five miles, where the explorers, turning aside into the Lomovataya, must ascend it and its principal tributary, the Yazevaya, until, after fifty-five miles, they reach Lake Bolshoe, four miles in length. From the end of this lake, a portage of five miles brings them to the head of the Kas, which, after one hundred and thirty miles, joins the Yenisei about one hundred and fifty miles below Yeniseisk, the first important settlement effected upon that river.

It is possible, however, that the first explorers ascended the main stream of the Ket to a point more nearly opposite Yeniseisk, and made a longer portage of forty or fifty miles. The entire distance by the only practicable route of travel was not far from two thousand two hundred miles, one half of which in either journey, going or coming, must be made up stream. The boats used were of the most primitive kind, often being nothing but rafts, while their one-masted vessels with decks upon them were less than one hundred feet long, put together without the use of iron, their anchors, even, being made of wood loaded with stone sinkers. Their ropes and their sails were made of the skins of animals. Nevertheless, with these rude conveyances communication was kept up between a line of settlements scattered along this whole distance of more than two thousand miles, and with others established at feasible points upon either side. The junctions of nearly all the streams, as well as the portages between the headwaters of the different drainage areas, were naturally the favorite places of settlement.

But years of experience and the occurrence of repeated catastrophes of floods were needed to teach the settlers to build upon the bluffs rather than upon the low banks of the stream, whose floods, owing to the obstructions of ice in the higher latitudes of the river course, were phenomenal and terrific in their extent. The distance was so great from their starting-point that these settlements were compelled to be somewhat permanent in their character and to serve as winter quarters to which the hunting parties could retire upon the close of the season. Here in a commodious but rude log hut, with an earthen stove to furnish heat and the most primitive arrangements for admitting light, the hunters would cluster together to await the opening of spring. Oftentimes these huts would be completely enveloped in the snow, their presence being betrayed solely by the column of smoke which continuously arose from the chimney. But wherever the Cossacks went, a rude cross of wood was erected to distinguish their houses from those of the natives.

As time went on and success attended the exploring parties, settlers of a more permanent order followed in the wake of the early adventurers. To some extent the first explorers intermarried with the natives, but the number of such marriages is surprisingly small; much less, for example, than those which took place between the French trappers and the Indians of America. Then, as at all times in Siberia, Russian women were ready to follow their husbands and lovers wherever they went. In 1630, one hundred and fifty women and girls emigrated to Tobolsk at one time. Still the men were always somewhat in excess and in advance of the women, and the efforts of the home government, both to protect the natives, and to preserve the morality of the explorers and adventurers, were not altogether successful. The exercise of justice and humanity was always freely enjoined upon them; but, in the absence of oversight, many irregularities occurred, and the traders often degenerated to the level of freebooters, robbing the natives of what they should have obtained only by fair purchase. As late as 1662, the patriarch of Moscow complained to the archbishop of Tobolsk that his subjects were grossly neglecting their religious duties, and violating the plainest rules of morality in their associations with native women, even going so far, it was alleged, as to sell them and exchange them in a most scandalous manner.

On the Yenisei River, the Cossacks met the Tunguses, a branch of Mongols, related to the Manchus, who extend from the Yenisei to the Pacific Ocean. These stoutly resisted the collection of tribute, and were brought into subjection only by several years of war; while the Buriats, another Mongol race, occupying the upper portions of the river, succeeded in maintaining their independence for twenty or thirty years longer, and temporarily turned the tide of Russian emigration from the upper part of the Yenisei Valley into that of the Lena. It was not until 1648 that the Russians succeeded in following up the Angara River to Lake Baikal, and in establishing a fort on the east side at the point which is now known as Verkhni Udinsk.

Meanwhile, in 1628, the enterprising adventurers had crossed from the Yenisei to the Lena, and established a fort at Yakutsk in 1637. This they accomplished only by a long and most tedious route up the Angara and its tributary the Ilim to a difficult portage near the fifty-sixth degree of latitude. The distance from Yeniseisk to this portage is not less than seven hundred miles, which had to be made against numerous rapids where the water was often insufficient, so that the Cossacks were compelled to resort to the old device of Yermak of securing a sufficient depth by damming the streams with their sails. The portage also was long and difficult. For thirty or forty miles, the sledges had to be hauled overland, and each sledge could convey only about one hundred and fifty pounds of provisions.

An even longer route was established by going down the Yenisei six hundred miles from Yeniseisk to Turukhansk, at the mouth of the Lower Tunguska River, and thence, following up that stream for a thousand miles, to where it approaches near Kirensk, still closer to the Lena than the Ilim does, the portage here being but ten miles. After reaching the Lena River, however, by either of these portages, it was still nearly one thousand miles down the river to Yakutsk. To increase the difficulty, the Russians were bitterly opposed at these portages by the Buriats, and were compelled to carry on a long and expensive warfare before they were freed from molestation. In 1641, and soon after, two expeditions were sent against them,—one under Vassil Vlasieff, and a later one under Vassil Bugor,—which succeeded in accomplishing their objects only by the total annihilation of the existing force of Buriats. Vassil Bugor, in reporting upon the success of the one hundred and thirty Cossacks under his leadership, says, "By the grace of God and the good luck of the Emperor, the imperial soldiers stood firm, and the Bretski (they were five hundred) were all destroyed to a man." Such was the vigor of this resistance that, as already remarked, it was not until 1648 that a fort was established on the east side of Lake Baikal at Verkhni Udinsk; while Irkutsk was not founded until 1651, fourteen years after the establishment of Yakutsk.

With their headquarters now in the valley of the Lena, about four thousand miles away from their starting-point in the valley of the Kama, the restless Cossacks continued their explorations in almost every direction beyond. In 1630, two years after reaching the Lena, we find them following up the channel of the Aldan River to its sources in the Stanovoi Mountains, from which they could almost look over into the waters of the Pacific. Here the difficulties of farther progress were greatly increased by the rapidity of the descent upon the eastern side; for, as we have seen in describing the country, the entire descent was made in a distance of twenty or thirty miles in the narrowest place, and even where the distance is greater by streams that were utterly unnavigable. Nevertheless, in 1639, they succeeded in crossing the mountains and in descending the Ulia

River to the Sea of Okhotsk, about fifty miles south of the present town of that name. . . .

In 1647 Ivan Athanasieff, with a company of fifty-four Cossacks, crossed the valley of the Aldan River, a distance of five hundred miles in a straight line eastward from Yakutsk, and, having descended the short eastern slope of the Stanovoi Mountains, permanently intrenched himself on the bay of Okhotsk. Here he was vigorously resisted by the Tungusian warriors, who outnumbered him twenty to one, but the superiority of his arms and of his discipline gave him the advantage, and they were speedily brought into subjection, and compelled to pay exorbitant tribute. Infuriated by the exactions of their conquerors, the Tunguses made repeated efforts to free themselves from the yoke, and maddened the Cossacks by mutilating the bodies of those whom they had slain in battle. It is to be deplored, yet not to be wondered at, that the Cossacks retaliated by the practice of similar barbarity.

The result is the same whether in the wilds of Siberia or of America: the pioneers who are far beyond the reach of the central government become a law unto themselves, and in dealing with the aborigines descend to their methods and manners. The story of the Cossacks in their dealing with the native races of Siberia can be easily enough equaled in that of the frontiersmen of the United States, who have by similar means gradually wrested the continent of America from the improvident hands of the Red Indian.

7 / PLEAS FOR GOVERNMENT SUPPORT

Siberia was conquered on a shoestring. The remarkably small number of men involved and the meager resources at their disposal, as well as the slow, limited, almost casual, if not reluctant, role of the central government in the exploration and annexation of the eastern regions are clearly brought out in seventeenth-century documents. Two such documents follow. The first is the request of military commanders in Fort Yakutsk for

"Otpiska iakutskikh voevod V. N. Pushkina i K. O. Suponeva v Sibirskii prikaz o kolichestve sluzhilykh liudei v Iakutskom ostroge i v zimov'iakh, o rasprosnykh rechakh Ivana Erastova ob otkrytii im r. Anadyr' (Pogychi), o naselenii po ee beregam" (Report of the Yakutsk Voevods V. N. Pushkin and K. O. Suponev to the Siberia Office about the number of serving people in Fort Yakutsk and in the wintering places, about the testimony of Ivan Erastov concerning his discovery of Anadyr [Pogychi] River, about the population along its shores), in N. S. Orlova (comp.), *Otkrytiia russkikh zemleprokhodtsev i poliarnykh morekhodov XVII veka na severo-vostoke Azii* (The discoveries of Russian pathfinders and polar navigators of the 17th century in the northeast of Asia), A Collection of Documents (Moscow: Gosudarstvennoe Izdatel'stvo Geograficheskoi Literatury, 1951), pp. 212-16. Translated by G. A. Lensen.

more men and the second is the pathetic plea for back pay by the most celebrated of early explorers, debt-ridden Senka (Semen) Dezhnev, who on one of his combined river and sea journeys in 1648 discovered the Bering Strait, eighty years before the man after whom it was named.

Report from Yakutsk, 1646

To your Majesty, Tsar and Grand Duke Mikhail Feodorovich of all Russia, your humble servants Vaska Pushkin, Kirilko Suponev and Petrushka Stenchin knock their heads [against the ground in humble request]. On the first of June of this year, 1646, on your Majesty's orders, we, your humble servants, arrived in your Majesty's service at Fort Yakutsk on the great Lena River, and with us, your humble servants, your Majesty, there came from Tobolsk 50 serving people as escort and military replacement. In Fort Yakutsk, your Majesty, according to your Majesty's Tobolsk payroll of serving people, there are 5 boyars and 395 serving people, 2 gunsmiths and salaried men, 1 monk, 1 priest, a deacon, a Yakut and a Tungus interpreter, and 2 blacksmiths. Some of these had been sent out with your Majesty's sable treasury and some in your Majesty's service to collect tribute. . . .

After counting all those who have been sent away, there will remain in Yakutsk by winter only fifty people. And with these fifty serving people, your Majesty, it will be most difficult for us, your humble servants, to winter in Fort Yakutsk, because, your Majesty, the Yakutsk land near Fort Yakutsk is populous, and in winter at the time of tribute collecting there come to Fort Yakutsk to pay your Majesty's tribute fifty or more Yakuts at a time, and it will be frightening in view of our small number. According to your serving people, who are now being sent in your Majesty's service to collect your Majesty's tribute, they sent on your missions small numbers of people and they have great hardship in collecting your Majesty's tribute.

And the Yakuts and Tunguses, seeing their smallness in number, pay your Majesty's tribute and gifts as they please; whatever they give, the others will take. . . .

And there are no firearm muskets and carbines of your Majesty at Fort Yakutsk on the Lena, of which we, your humble servants, wrote you earlier to Moscow from the Ilimskii Lena portage. And in your Majesty's distant land on the great Lena River one cannot get along without additional serving men of your Majesty, because in Fort Verkholenskii and Fort Bratskii the serving men for lack of strength can barely protect themselves against their fellow soldiers. . . .

Petition of Senka Dezhnev

To [you] the Tsar, Sovereign and Grand Duke Aleksei Mikhailovich
. . . your humble servant, the [military] serving man Senka Dezhnev of
the Great Lena River and Fort Yakutsk, knocks his head [against the
ground in humble request].

I, your humble servant, have served His Majesty the Tsar and Grand
Duke Mikhail Feodorovich of all Russia—blessed be the memory of His
Majesty your father—on the Yana, Indigirka, Alazeika and Kolyma Rivers with the [military] serving and clerical men Dmitrii Mikhailov and
Mikhail Stadukhin, and we have brought great profit to your Majesty's
treasury through the collection of tribute. And from the Kolyma River
I, your humble servant, went up by sea to explore new rivers and discovered in addition to those former rivers the new river Anandyr. And
on that new Anandyr River, while in your Majesty's service, I established
a wintering place and a fort, captured some hostages, and collected, on
that new river, as tribute for your Majesty and as tithe 234 sables, 280
sable backs [?] and 4 sable umbilical cords [?] and about 573 pounds of
walrus tusk fish bone. I too, your humble servant, with my comrades on
the Anandyr River humbly gave your Majesty 2 walrus tusks weighing
32 pounds. And tribute from that new Anandyr River is continuing to
come to your Majesty to this day. And I, your humble servant, set out
on your Majesty's service to those new rivers on my own money and my
own traveling expenses, and received no salary whatsoever from you,
great Sovereign, either in cash or grain or salt from 1642 to 1661. And
last year, in 1661, your Majesty, the Stol'nik and Voevoda of Fort Yakutsk,
Ivan Bol'shoi Golenishchev-Kutuzov, gave me, your humble servant, the
salt payment for the period of 1642 to 1661 from your Majesty's treasury,
but I, Senka, did not receive your Majesty's cash and bread salary for
the past years to cover my poverty in cash and grain. . . . And Fort
Yakutsk wrote your Majesty about that service of mine. And being in
your Majesty's service, giving myself and serving your Majesty a long time
without salary from your Majesty, having natives as hostages, I have risked
my life, suffered great wounds and shed my blood, suffered cold and great
hunger, and starved. And being in that service, I was impoverished by

"Chelobitnaia Semena Dezhneva o zhalovanii za sluzhby na rr. Iane, Indigirke, Alazee
i Kolyme" (Petition of Semen Dezhnev about salary for service on the rivers Iana,
Indigirka, Alazeia and Kolyma), in N. S. Orlova (comp.), *Otkrytiia russkikh zemleprokhodtsev i poliarnykh morekhodov XVII veka na severo-vostoke Azii* (The discoveries of Russian pathfinders and polar navigators of the 17th century in the northeast of
Asia) (Moscow: Gosudarstvennoe Izdatel'stvo Geograficheskoi Literatury, 1951), pp 279-
81. Translated by G. A. Lensen.

piracy and incurred heavy debts beyond my ability to repay, and am now perishing in these debts.

Merciful Majesty, Tsar and Grand Duke Aleksei Mikhailovich, . . . grant me, your humble servant, for my service to your Majesty and for my fervor and for my hostages, and for my wounds and for the blood and the piracy, and for all I had to suffer the full amount of the salary due me in grain and money for the past years from 1642 to 1661, lest I, your humble servant, be tortured to death in shackling debts and be unable to continue serving your Majesty, and finally perish.

Tsar, Sovereign, be merciful, grant it to me.

8 / THE KAMCHATKA REBELLION

*The Kamchatka Peninsula was an appendage to the continent, and, there-
fore, was explored and subjugated only after the Pacific Ocean had been
reached. "Out of the way" even from a Siberian point of view, it remained
for a longer time outside the pale of civilization. Barbarism feeds upon
barbarism, and in Kamchatka Cossacks and natives seemed to pull each
other down to the lowest possible level rather than to lift each other up.
The celebrated* History of Kamchatka *by the Russian explorer Stepan
Petrovich Krasheninnikov describes a native rebellion against the Russians
in about 1730.*

The natives had resolved for a great while to destroy all the *Russians* who were in *Kamtschatka;* but since the discovery of the passage over the *Penschinska* sea, and the arrival of vessels with new people, it appeared to them too dangerous: but when Captain *Bering* with his fleet sailed on the expedition of *Kamtschatka,* and most of the Cossacks who were settled in *Kamtschatka* were ordered to join Captain *Paulutskoy* at *Anadir,* to suppress the rebellious *Tchukotskoi,* very few Cossacks were left in *Kamtschatka.* This the natives looked upon to be the wished-for opportunity; and during the whole winter the *Nishnashaltalski, Klutchefski,* and *Yalofski Kamtschadales,* under pretence of visiting one another, travelled through all *Kamtschatka,* and instigated the other inhabitants to join in their designs, under pain of being intirely destroyed. By these means all *Kamtschatka* entered into a state of open rebellion; and hearing that *Shesticof* was killed by the *Tchukotskoi,* they reported that these people were marching against *Kamtschatka,* with a view either to have a pretence for collecting themselves together, or that the *Russian* Cossacks, out of fear of these people, might desire the *Kamtschadales* to guard

Stepan Petrovich Krasheninnikov, *The History of Kamchatka, and the Kurilski
Islands, with the countries adjacent,* trans. James Grieve (Gloucester: printed by
R. Raikes for T. Jefferys, 1764), pp. 258-63.

them. Their measures were so well concerted, that it was a singular instance of Providence that any of the *Russians* were preserved; for if they had once been driven intirely out of the country, it would have been difficult for them to have re-established themselves. The counsels of the *Kamtschadales* were far from being such as one would expect from savages; they endeavoured to prevent any correspondence with *Anadirsk,* and kept a strong guard upon the sea-coasts, where they might seize upon any of the Russians that arrived. The chief authors of this rebellion were *Yalofski Toyon,* or chieftain called *Fetka Harchin,* who had frequently served the Russians as an interpreter, and a chieftain of the *Klutchefski,* called *Chugotche.*

While this conspiracy was in agitation, the commissary *Shacurdin* was on his departure from *Kamtschatka,* with a considerable party to guard the tribute. They had sailed from the mouth of the river *Kamtschatka* towards *Anadir,* but soon after contrary winds obliged them to return. The *Kamtschadales,* informed of their departure, and ready for the revolt, gathered together, and sailing up the river *Kamtschatka* killed every *Russian* Cossack they could find, burned their summer huts, and carried off their wives and children into slavery. Their chief strength was directed against the fort; where arriving in the night, they set fire to the priest's house, concluding that the fire would bring out all the inhabitants. In this they succeeded too well, murdering almost every person, without sparing either sex or age. They burned all the houses, except the fortifications and church, where the goods both of the publick and private people were kept. Those who escaped this massacre fled to the mouth of the river, and carried the news to their countrymen, who had not yet left the coast. When the *Klutchefski* chief, *Chugotche,* heard of the taking the lower *Kamtschatka* fort he marched thither, killing or taking prisoners all the Russians he met with; and joining *Harchin,* he informed him that the Russian vessels were yet upon the coast, for which reason he judged it proper to strengthen themselves in the fort; and sending accounts of their success to all their countrymen, ordered them to join him. The next day they divided all the plunder, and dressed themselves in the *Russian* habits, and some of them, putting on the priest's robes, celebrated their own religious ceremonies and conjurations. *Harchin* ordered a new-baptised *Kamtschadale,* who had learned to read *Russ,* to say mass in the *Russian* manner, and dressed in the priest's robes; for which he made him a present of 30 red fox-skins.

The 3d day after taking of the fort arrived a *Russian* skipper, *Yacob Hens,* with 60 Cossacks, who was sent with a design to recover the fort from the rebels. He endeavoured by all methods to persuade them to return to their duty, assuring them of a general pardon; but they would not give ear to him; nay, *Harchin,* their chief, told him that he had no business there, and that he was commissary of *Kamtschatka,* and would himself gather the taxes, so that they did not want any Cossacks among them. Upon which *Hens* sent to his vessels for some cannon, and began on the 26th of July to fire upon the fort, where he made a very large breach, which caused great confusion amongst the besieged, and gave an opportunity for the women that were prisoners to escape. *Harchin,* finding it impossible to defend the fort, made his escape disguised in women's cloaths; and although he was pursued by several, yet he made such expedition that they could not overtake him. After this 30 of the besieged who remained surrendered themselves; but a *Klutchefski* chieftain, *Chugotche,* with a few people that joined him, held out to the last man. During their defence the powder magazine was set on fire, which reduced the fort and all the riches in it to ashes. In this siege the Cossacks had four men killed, and a great many wounded. How many of the *Kamtschadales* were killed was not known, their bodies being consumed in the fire; not one escaped alive, for those who surrendered were killed by the Cossacks, in revenge for the loss of their wives and children.

The sudden return of the *Russian* party was the occasion that this revolt was so easily quelled; for it prevented their assembling in such numbers, as they otherwise would have done. However, it was not intirely over, for *Harchin,* with some other chieftains, collected a good number of people together, and resolved to march to the sea side, and attack the *Russian* vessels which were there. But, in the very beginning of his march, he was met by a party of *Russians,* which obliged him to fortify himself upon the left side of the river *Kluchefka;* the Cossacks encamping upon the right, several skirmishes ensued between them. When *Harchin* saw that he could not accomplish his design, he proposed to treat with the Cossacks, and offered to come to their camp, if they would send one Cossack as an hostage for him; which they granted. He demanded, That they should not intirely ruin the *Kamtschadales,* and promised that for the future they would all live peaceably, only desiring that they would allow him to go and prevail upon his friends and relations to consent to this agreement; which being granted, he sent word, that he could not prevail with them to make peace; and that even his own brother, and a chieftain, *Javatche,* who had accompanied them, had refused to return.

The next day *Harchin* came to the bank of the river with some other chiefs, and desired, that the Cossacks would send a boat to bring him over, and give him two Cossacks in hostage; which they agreed to: but no sooner was he come over than they made him prisoner, and ordered the hostages to throw themselves into the river, and swim over, while they fired upon the *Kamtschadales* on the opposite bank, who, when their chief was made prisoner, presently separated; but, being pursued by different parties, most of them were destroyed. The chieftain *Teghil,* having defended himself for a great while, at last murdered his wife and children, and killed himself; the chieftain *Chugotche,* in vain solliciting the inhabitants upon the river *Koseretska Shapina* to join him, was in the end murdered by them. After this rebellion, which appeared at first very dangerous, and threatened the intire destruction of the Cossacks, was quieted by the arrival of succours, things continued in pretty good order at *Kamtschatka* until the year 1740, when the *Russians* had seven people killed by the natives.

When this rebellion was over, orders were sent as soon as possible to Major *Merlin,* with another officer and some regulars, together with *Major Paulutskoy,* to inquire into the cause of this rebellion, and the murder of the *Japanese,* and to send the report thereof to *Jakutski;* he was at the same time to build a new fort, which he did a little lower than the mouth of the river *Ratuga:* this was called the lower fort of *Kamtschatka.* Having examined into the cause of the rebellion, three of the *Russians* were found guilty of death and executed; and two of the chief rebels, with some others, both Cossacks and *Kamtschadales,* were punished. All the natives, whom they had either taken prisoners, or had made slaves of, were restored to their liberty. Those *Kamtschadales* who were put to death, seemed to go to execution without the least concern, and under the torture they were scarcely heard to moan; nor could they force them to confess any thing more than what they had done voluntarily before.

Since this time all things are intirely quiet there; and it is hoped they will continue so, affairs being brought into such order, that the natives themselves could not wish for more, being only obliged to pay their taxes, without the least oppression, which consist only in one skin for every man of such creatures as he is used to hunt, such as sables, foxes, or sea beavers. Justice, except in criminal cases, is administered by their own chieftains. The Cossacks are forbidden to demand former debts, which they pretend were due from the natives. Their principal happiness consists in the conversion of several of them to Christianity; to which end her Majesty has been graciously pleased to appoint missionaries and schoolmasters, who keep schools in the principal villages for the instruction of the youth, both natives and Cossacks; and they begin now to be so much improved, that they even laugh at their former barbarity.

9 / FRONTIERSMEN

Men like Yermak made possible the conquest of Siberia. Frontiersmen and settlers carried it out. So highly prized had been the furs brought back by Yermak's Cossacks that following the defeat of Kuchum a veritable stream of fortune hunters crossed the Urals in pursuit of the Golden Fleece, driven by a fur-fever akin to the gold-fever that was to grip the Forty-niners in America.

There were various types of frontiersmen. Some acted like their American counterparts, others not. For many there is no equivalent in the English language. Raymond Fisher describes the different groups of immigrants that participated in the conquest of Siberia, and explains some of the terms commonly encountered in readings on Russian expansion and colonization.

Two groups of immigrants first appeared in Siberia, drawn there by the fur trade. They were the private enterprisers and the state employees. It was by means of their activities that Siberia was conquered and brought under Russian rule. In the first group, the private enterprisers, two types are distinguishable, traders and *promýshlenniks.* The former included merchants or their agents and small traders, who sought to avail themselves of the new sources of furs. These traders (*torgovye liudi*), more particularly those who became resident in Siberia, sometimes joined the expeditions which went out to conquer new territory. However, their participation in the conquest was perhaps not as extensive as that of the second type, since their business was to acquire furs for sale in the Russian and foreign markets mainly by exchanging or purchasing them from the promyshlenniks. It was the latter who obtained the furs at the source, and for that reason participated actively and extensively in the conquest. The term promyshlenniks ordinarily referred to men who worked for themselves, exploiting natural resources. It may also be understood here to include the so-called *pokrúchenniks,* men who worked for an employer, but who in all other respects conducted themselves as promyshlenniks. The role of the promyshlenniks is akin to that of the *coureurs de bois* in Canada. They hunted and trapped fur-bearing animals, or got them from the natives by trade, extortion, or as tribute. So active were they in the fur trade in Siberia that in that country the term "promyshlennik" became synonymous with fur hunter or trapper. By the very nature of their occupation they became explorers and conquerors.

Raymond H. Fisher, *The Russian Fur Trade 1550-1700* (Berkeley, Calif.: University of California Press, 1943), pp. 29-33. Reprinted with permission of the University of California Press.

The second group drawn to Siberia by the fur trade, the state employees, was sent there to further and protect the interests of the state. Because the exploitation of the fur wealth of the country was the principal interest of the state, the fur trade became the chief activity of the state employees; and because conquest was a means of establishing regular sources of furs, the state employees participated actively in the conquest. In fact, the tribute exacted from the natives—*iasak* (pronounced yahsáhk)—always attended conquest and constituted the objective of Moscow's conquest of Siberia.

Of the state employees the highest in rank and authority were the *voevodas* (pronounced vaw-yeh-vóe-das). They were the military and administrative heads of the towns and forts and the adjacent territories, and were appointed for a short term, usually from two to four years. Upon them rested the responsibility of seeing that Moscow's orders were carried out and of preserving the interests of the state.

The rank and file of state employees were the "serving men" (*sluzhilye liudi*). The ranks of the serving men who performed military service included cossacks, *streltsý*, boiar-sons (*deti boiarskie*), and foreigners— Poles, Lithuanians, and Swedes sent to Siberia as prisoners of war for military service. The cossacks were the most numerous and active of the serving men. A social caste, not a national or racial group, they were a kind of irregular troops stationed on the frontier, whose duties were to maintain order and to guard the frontier, to impose and collect iasak. They were selected from freemen in Russia and Siberia, and in return for their military service, which was compulsory, they received a salary and were granted the use of a plot of land for cultivation. They were organized into detachments (*sotni,* originally "hundreds"), each of which elected its own leaders, or atamans. When their services were not in demand by the local authorities, they were free to explore and conquer on their own account. During the earlier stages of the conquest streltsy were sent to Siberia to supplement the cossacks. They were fewer than the latter and by the middle of the seventeenth century there were enough Russians in Siberia from which to fill the ranks of the cossacks. The streltsy were ordinarily infantrymen, commanded by regularly appointed officers. The boiar-sons belonged to a rank higher than that of the cossacks and streltsy, a rank sometimes granted to individual serving men in return for a special service. Their numbers were much smaller and they served usually as military leaders, both of cossacks and streltsy. The foreigners composed a small element among the serving men and, quickly adapting themselves to their new environment, they soon became barely distinguishable from their Russian companions. Ultimately all of these military serving men came to be known by the one name, cossacks. They and the promyshlenniks were the conquerors of Siberia.

At first glance the state employees and promyshlenniks seem to constitute two different types of invaders: the one an official representative or servant of the state, the other a private profiteer who entered Siberia at his own expense and risk. Actually, they differed but little; their psychology and interests, their duties, and their organization and mode of life were the same.

As individuals they displayed like qualities of character—boldness, courage, great persistence and endurance. They both possessed a passion for adventure and a greed for booty—to such an extent that they often disregarded the means they employed. The fur trade occupied them both, and the serving man was almost as much a fur trader as the promyshlennik; in fact, many serving men were erstwhile promyshlenniks, for the new serving men were recruited principally from the ranks of the latter. The official duties of the serving men brought them into a direct contact with the natives which offered them excellent opportunities for acquiring furs. Up to 1625 they participated freely in the fur trade, and though the reforms of Suleshev in that year forbade further participation by them, they commonly disregarded the prohibition. In turn, the promyshlenniks were almost as much state employees as private enterprisers. Frequently the numbers of the serving men were inadequate, and promyshlenniks had to be utilized for state service. They assisted as volunteers (okhotniki) in the collection of iasak and in the conquering expeditions. Or sometimes the promyshlenniks were commissioned by the voevodas themselves to collect iasak and to conquer new lands in the name of the tsar.

Likewise in their organization and mode of life the serving men and promyshlenniks resembled each other. Under an acknowledged leader (peredovshchik), the promyshlenniks joined together in armed bands, or vatágas, which were no different from the cossack bands organized by the serving men, since the military service of the serving men was not the disciplined routine associated with a settled society. Considerable freedom existed for the play of initiative and enterprise; their instructions "to collect iasak and seek new lands" amounted to a roving commission. In a country where they were the force of the law, the bands of serving men acted as independently of authority and of each other as did the vatagas of the promyshlenniks. Like the promyshlenniks, too, the serving men shared the booty among the members of the band.

Thus promyshlennik bands and cossack bands alike, or frequently parties composed of both promyshlenniks and serving men, roamed the wilds of Siberia, hunting wild animals and seeking new lands and natives from whom iasak could be taken. Differing originally in function, the one a fur trader, the other the agent of the state, promyshlennik and serving man became hardly distinguishable from one another. The merging of the interests of one and the duties of the other fashioned the conquerors of Siberia, adventurous undisciplined freebooters in pursuit of valuable furs.

10 / SETTLERS

Neither the marauding Cossack nor the roving trapper or trader could secure Siberia. It remained for a different breed of man, the peasant, to settle and truly conquer Siberia.

The popular American image of the Russian peasant as a downtrodden serf without substance or thought of freedom requires modification. Emancipation of the serfs in "reactionary" Russia was proclaimed two years before emancipation of the slaves in the "progressive" United States, and without a civil war. To be sure, in Russia, as in the United States, there was a gap between legal and actual emancipation, but, if legal emancipation did not of itself bring freedom and equality, it removed the shackles which restrained their attainment. Given a taste of freedom, the Russian peasant developed an appetite for more, and migrated to Siberia, away from the restrictions and inhibitions of the old society.

Donald Treadgold reviews the causes of the great migration following emancipation and discusses the meaning of democracy *in the Russian context.*

What attracted the migrants to Siberia? The quest for land and freedom. What did they find there? More of both than they had ever known before. Often the settler gave his reason for departure as "lack of land," but if that is the only thing he sought he could often have had it at home by renting. Of course hard work and money were needed to make a land rental successful, but not only toil and cash were required of a prospective migrant, but also a break with his whole past and that of his ancestors. . . .

To break away from a life in which the peasant felt secure and safe, whatever his wants, required more than simply the desire for a few more desiatinas of land. For millions of peasants, freedom was *not* to be found in their native village, and the opportunity to seek it even thousands of miles away compelled them to uproot themselves and risk everything for its sake. To separate "economic" freedom from "political" freedom is not

Donald W. Treadgold, *The Great Siberian Migration: Government and Peasant in Resettlement from Emancipation to the First World War* (Princeton, N.J.: Princeton University Press, 1957), pp. 239-45. Reprinted with permission of the Princeton University Press.

warranted either in trying to analyze man's aspirations or in attempting to build a good state and society. Oppression and misery had never managed to extinguish in the peasant the desire for both "land and liberty" —the chance to care for his family decently and to call his soul his own.

The peasant's desire to seek afield for land in part reflected the crisis in communal land tenure and the three-course system of land use in south-central Russia. The growing density of population had rendered these institutions obsolete and inadequate to feed either the Russian village or the city. The Siberian migration showed the individual peasant family the way to realize its goals. For the Russian peasantry as a whole, migration had a double significance. It furnished the homeland a useful, and for the overcrowded central provinces perhaps an indispensable, catalyst for the successful execution of land settlement. It also created in Siberia a dramatic example of how rapid agricultural improvement could occur and what social and economic benefits it might produce.

The peasant's search for freedom was in part a consequence of his having already been relieved of the bondage of serfdom. He learned what a degree of independence could be like, and was eager for more. The breakdown of the legally stratified class system inaugurated by Alexander II's Great Reforms gave the peasant a chance to develop a sense of citizenship which he had hitherto experienced in only a very limited fashion within the village commune, where the power of the landlord—not to mention the state—was ever present. In European Russia, the destruction of class barriers—as in western Europe since the French Revolution— had deprived the upper classes of certain privileges and had given the lower classes more. Migration had a rather different effect. At first the prerogative of the lower and "protected" class of peasants, by its success migration attracted members of the "upper" classes, who sought to obtain the benefits of being a peasant (though by the last years of Tsarism, "farmer" may be a better word for the Siberian settler). In Siberia, the peasant learned that he could bend the law and officialdom to recognize and provide for his own needs; he even found it possible, as our evidence has repeatedly suggested, to evade the hand of the government entirely. There could be nothing servile about a man who managed to complete Siberian migration successfully.

The effects of Siberian migration . . . were in certain ways comparable to those of the American frontier movement. Turner believed that they included the development of a "composite nationality" of differing ethnic stocks, stimulation of a "nationalizing tendency" simultaneous with the creation of what he called "sections," and the encouragement of democracy and individualism.

The mixing of ethnic groups which occurred in Siberia was of less dramatic dimensions than in America's melting pot, but it is still noteworthy. First of all, a considerable amount of intermarriage between Russians and the Siberian natives took place. . . .

More important numerically than mingling with natives was the amount of intermingling of Russians from different regions. . . . In all parts of Siberia there were villages with settlers who came from ten or fifteen different provinces.

These phenomena had a linguistic side. . . . Siberian speech came to exhibit both a synthesis of European Russian features and an admixture of native influences; that is, it was at the same time more national and more regional than European Russian speech.

Siberia likewise developed both strong national and strong regional feeling. . . . As in America, nationalism and sectionalism both developed powerfully. . . . The opportunities which arose for Siberian autonomism and the successes and mishaps of attempts to exploit them during the Civil War . . . make a climax to the whole story of the Great Migration. Despite the fact that the Soviets did not feel the need for even nominal recognition of Siberian regionalism—since the Siberians did not make up a minority "nationality"—it is possible that such aspirations may one day be heard again.

Finally, what may one say of the development of democracy and individualism in Siberia? Democracy in the sense of popular participation in government had not been fully attained. On the village level there had long been self-government, as in European Russia. Although the Siberian commune was nearly defunct as a manager of agriculture, the village assembly was a functioning organ of democracy, subject to far less outside interference in Siberia, where there was no gentry, than in the homeland. . . .

The equality of the Siberian frontier did not exclude feelings of self-sufficiency and the spirit of initiative. The Siberian peasant, according to *Aziatskaia Rossiia,* accepted complex machines of whose very existence he had been unaware in the homeland, and came to accept and act on the aid and advice of the local agronomist in trying new methods. The settler showed "an exceptional capacity for self-help, by means of cooperatives, credit unions, and other types of unions and societies." The growth of the Siberian cooperatives was impressive enough to deserve a full-length study of its own. The most dramatic development of all—the emergence of the individual family homestead in Siberia at the expense of the commune and in the face of the legal universality of state ownership— has already been traced. Economic and social individualism were far advanced, and some of the political interest and experience necessary to a functioning democratic government were at hand. There could be no democracy in the full and true sense while the autocratic state remained, but that the Siberian population was in many respects prepared for democracy seems a reasonable supposition.

11 / THE STRATEGY OF SIBERIA'S CONQUEST

The fur trade, as we have seen, was the dynamo that generated Russian expansion. As hunting grounds were exhausted, adventurous trappers and traders pushed eastward. Conquest followed, and at times preceded, the exploitation of new hunting grounds, as the government and local officials sought to share in the furry wealth of Siberia by exacting tribute from the natives. The tremendous demand for peltry was responsible for the rapid exhaustion of hunting ground after hunting ground and consequently the speedy subjugation of Siberia. Dr. Fisher examines the basic strategy by which this conquest was effected.

The process by which Siberia was conquered is not peculiar to it. It repeats for the most part that by which a large part of the United States and most of Canada were explored and were subjected to European rule. The major difference lies in the practice by the Russian state of exacting formal tribute in furs from the Siberian natives. This had the effect of bringing about the political subjugation of a given area more quickly in Siberia than in North America. But otherwise both regions owe their opening and first exploitation to the fur trade.

The search of the Russian invader for valuable furs and his passion to learn what lay beyond the frontier knew no limits. No land was too distant, no risk too great for him if it promised the chance for gain and adventure. Siberia was a vast land, almost every part of which yielded the precious sable and other prized fur-bearing animals. Beckoning promyshlenniks and serving men alike, they drew these restless conquerors always eastward, until nearly all of Siberia was brought under the sovereignty of the Russian tsar.

Although the nature of the Russian advance changed in its progress across Siberia, its strategy remained essentially the same. This strategy was based on the river, the portage, and the *ostróg*, or fort. Four large river systems and several smaller ones spread themselves over Siberia and form natural lines of communication. Along these rivers the Russians advanced. With the boats then in use most of the rivers in Siberia were

Raymond H. Fisher, *The Russian Fur Trade*, pp. 33-36. Reprinted with permission of the University of California Press.

navigable for long distances, and in flat-bottomed boats the Russian invaders moved up and down these waterways, pulling their boats when wind or current was against them. Separating three of the four great river systems of Siberia are only low rolling mountains, and the Russians were enabled, thereby, to establish short portages between them. Joined by these portages, the rivers formed an extensive system of natural highways and afforded the basis for effective control of the country. Although the Russians used overland routes as well, traveling in sledges in the winter when the rivers froze over and in horse-drawn carts in the summer, the rivers were their main lines of communication, and their strategy of conquest was essentially a river strategy.

As the means of controlling the rivers the Russians set up forts, the ostrogs. The ostrog was constructed in the form of a rectangular wooden stockade, ten to twenty feet high, along which a parapet was built. Bastions housing artillery stood in each corner, over the gateway, and sometimes along the sides; within the stockade were contained various buildings, the voevoda's office, . . . the customhouse, living quarters, granary, church, and other buildings. Around the main stockade was a second stockade, and a moat. The Russians located their ostrogs so as to command strategic points, such as the confluence of rivers, the ends of portages, or tenable points along the rivers. With these ostrogs they secured their conquests and provided themselves with bases for advancing into unconquered areas. The ostrogs served also as centers of the state's fur trade. A supplementary agency of control was the *zimovie,* or blockhouse (literally, "winter quarters"). Blockhouses were built in the forests, on the tundras, along the rivers, on the shores of lakes and the ocean, at portages—in general, in places where there were no other habitations. Built for defending the Russians against the natives, these blockhouses, quartering as many as fifty men, served equally as winter quarters, outposts for the collection of iasak, and headquarters for the serving men and promyshlenniks who roamed the outlying and distant regions of Siberia. It was not unusual for a blockhouse to be enlarged into an ostrog, for the steady influx of Russians into Siberia made additional administrative centers necessary.

Within eighty years after the fall of Sibir the Russians overran almost all of Siberia. Only the Amur Valley, the peninsula of Kamchatka, the Kirghiz steppes, and the uppermost part of the Enisei did not come under Russian rule during that period. The conquest, by virtue of its river strategy, assumed the geographical pattern of a series of advances in which the river systems were successively explored and brought under Russian control.

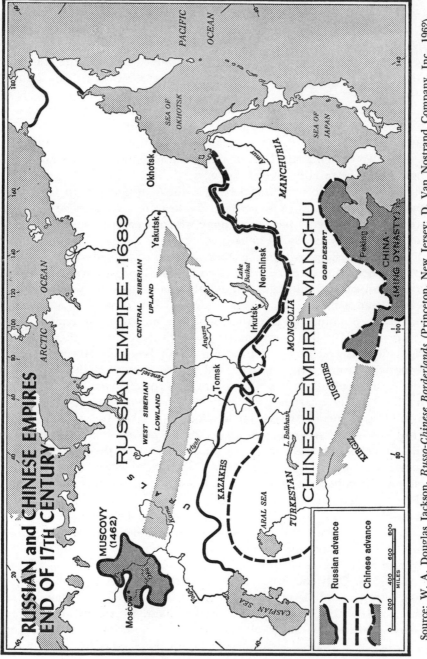

Source: W. A. Douglas Jackson, *Russo-Chinese Borderlands* (Princeton, New Jersey: D. Van Nostrand Company, Inc., 1962), p. 29. Reprinted with permission of the publisher.

12 / KHABAROV

In their expansion across the continent the Russians collided with the Chinese and the Manchus, who ruled China after 1644. The first contacts were indirect, through native tribes who paid tribute to China. Eventually the Russians were to run head-on into the Manchus to whom the natives appealed for protection, for unlike the indigenous tribesmen who gave in to Russian pressure, the mighty rulers of the Celestial Empire went out to meet the Russians with overwhelming force and blocked their advance in this direction for better than a century and a half.

The experiences of Erofei Pavlovich Khabarov, after whom the city of Khabarovsk is named, are a case in point. With a band of about 150 men, recruited at his own expense, Khabarov set out in 1649 to impose tribute on the inhabitants of the Amur region, expecting to recoup his outlays by plunder. As he pushed along the Olekma river across the mountains, however, he found the region deserted. Such had been the cruelty of earlier Russian explorer-conquerors that the population had fled upon hearing that "the Cossacks are coming." After withdrawing to Yakutsk to replenish his resources and equip himself with cannon, Khabarov resumed his advance in the summer of 1650. He surprised the Dauri and, defeating them, made Albazin his headquarters.

. .Frank A. Golder, an American historian of Russian birth, describes Khabarov's exploits. Khabarov has just taken Albazin and decimated the fleeing Dauri.

In knowing how to make use of the opportunities of the moment, Khabarof showed himself an able leader. He hurriedly fortified Albasin, leaving it in charge of a small garrison, and with the bulk of his men, drawing cannon and supplies on sleds, he started, on November 24, in pursuit of the demoralized natives. On the tenth day out he came in touch with a force of Dauri horsemen and fought them all day and, as the woewod [voevoda] in his report to Moscow puts it, "against their [Russian] fighting and their cannon, they [Dauri] could not stand." These successive defeats broke temporarily the resistance and spirit of the native chiefs, nearly all of whom offered tribute; and with these sable skins, prisoners, and spoils of war the Siberians returned to Albasin for the winter. In his report for the year 1650, Khabarof is enthusiastic about the resources of the country and states that at Albasin alone there was

F. A. Golder, *Russian Expansion on the Pacific, 1641-1850: An Account of the Earliest and Later Expeditions Made by the Russians along the Pacific Coast of Asia and North America; Including Some Related Expeditions to the Arctic Regions* (Glendale, Calif.: Arthur H. Clark Company, 1914), pp. 38-51. Reprinted by permission of the Arthur H. Clark Company.

enough grain on hand to last five years, and that the natives of the Amur could be made to supply a quantity large enough to feed twenty thousand men or even a larger number.

On June 2, 1651, Khabarof took the field once more, having under him at the time over two hundred well armed men, and, at least, three cannon. His plan of campaign was to move quickly and take the enemy unawares. For this purpose he had built light boats to seek, surprise, and engage the foe until the heavier boats containing the main force, the cannon, and the horses should come up. Four days he sailed down the river without meeting a human being. As far as he could see the settlements had been destroyed and the inhabitants had fled, repeating the tactics of 1649. From an old woman who had been left behind and whom he tortured, he obtained a clew which led him to several huts; but at the sight of the Russians the inmates set fire to their homes and ran away. Towards sunset of the fourth day, Khabarof surprised Guigudar, a settlement sheltering about one thousand human beings, including women, children, and several Chinese. All during that summer night the cannon of the Russians bombarded the walls, tearing large holes in them and striking terror into the hearts of the women and children who had probably never before seen the flash of a gun. Daybreak found the two outer walls in ruins and the panic stricken natives huddled together behind the third and last one which was being rapidly knocked to pieces. When that frail defense was no more the natives attempted to escape, but it was too late, the enemy was upon them. The shouts of the Cossacks whose bloodthirsty appetites had been whetted by a night of excitement and fighting were drowned by the cries of children and women as they were being butchered or dragged into the arms of the Cossacks whose hands were dripping with the bloods of fathers, husbands, and brothers. . . .

Six or seven weeks the victors rested at this place enjoying their captives and the good things which they had conquered. They were not altogether idle, for they sent messengers in different directions calling upon the natives to pay tribute or suffer the fate of Guigudar. These threats had no effect, there was still another alternative—flight, and as far as the Dseya the country was deserted. Here and there a straggler was caught and tortured to reveal where the inhabitants had gone. By these tactics Khabarof learned of several inhabited villages near the mouth of the Dseya, and with the light boats he hurried to the spot and surprised them so completely that they could neither fight nor run away. Captives there were many: and these pleaded that they had just paid tribute to China and had very little left, but they would give up that little to regain their liberty. . . . He went on board his boats on September 7, to go down the river, passing on the way the mouth of the Sungari and out of the country of the pastoral Ducheri, killing many of them and taking their families and property with him.

When Khabarof had come among the fish eating Achani, he decided to go no farther, and on September 29, he pitched and fortified a camp probably near the site of the present town of Khabarofsk. The Achani showed themselves friendly and the Russians thinking they had nothing to fear from them, sent one hundred of their men on the river to fish for a few days. In their absence the Achani and the Ducheri, numbering, according to Khabarof, eight hundred to a thousand men, attacked the camp on October 8. The cannon and guns proved themselves once more superior to the bows and arrows, and the natives were driven off. During the winter parties of Cossacks sought out their encampments and helped themselves to whatever they found.

Being well provided with the necessaries of life, the Russians believed themselves safe, being quite ignorant that a Chinese army was moving against them. Khabarof's campaigns of 1650 and 1651 had caused so much suffering among the Dauri and the Ducheri that they, in the early fall or late summer of 1651, sent their leading men to the Chinese officers in charge of the Amur to lay before them the true state of affairs and to petition that China either protect them or allow them to come under Russian jurisdiction. Their petition was forwarded to Peking and from there orders came to send an army to drive out the invaders, and it was this army which was now looking for Khabarof. In their first fight against the Russians the Chinese blundered, failing to understand the quality of the antagonist and the meaning of the invasion. At the beginning of the fight the Chinese had the best of it and for a time it looked as if they would carry the ostrog. It may have been that the Chinese commander was over confident or it may have been in obedience to instructions that, just about the time when the Russians were most hotly pressed, he ordered his soldiers not to kill or injure the Cossacks but to take them alive. This was the turning point in the battle. When the Russians understood the situation they determined not to be taken alive and, calling upon the holy saints, they charged the Chinese and gradually drove them back. No other result could have been expected under the circumstances. An army cannot be shot at and not be allowed to return the deadly fire and yet retain the field. The Chinese soldiers became demoralized and retreated, leaving behind seventeen muskets, two cannon, eight flags, eight hundred thirty horses, and stores of provisions. On the Russian side ten men were killed and seventy-eight were wounded. On inquiry among the natives, an unreliable source, Khabarof was told that six hundred seventy-six Chinese lost their lives.

Although the Chinese had been forced to withdraw from the field, their fight was not without important consequences. It checked the boldness of the Russians and filled them with fear. . . .

Khabarof's victory over the Chinese was his last great achievement on the Amur. From now on he plays an insignificant rôle, due in part to his loss of control over his men. . . .

Khabarof was undoubtedly the ablest of the Cossacks on the Amur. For the period during which he was in command he made the power of Russia felt and feared along the whole of the great river. He did, however, very little more than this. His policy, on the whole, did much harm to the cause of his country. It involved her in undertakings which she could not at that time carry out successfully. His lust for wealth led him to antagonize all the people with whom he came in contact and to make friends with none. He destroyed the source from which the riches were to come, for even in his day the Amur region was in great part deserted. His weapons were always force and cruelty and never diplomacy and kindness. It was during his administration, and originating in his own command, that lawless bands began terrorizing the Amur and plundering not only natives and Chinese but their own countrymen as well.

13 / NEGOTIATING WITH MANCHU CHINA

Russian inroads in the Amur region were a thorn in the flesh of the Celestial Empire. To pacify the borderlands the Manchu rulers were willing to resort to diplomatic negotiation as well as to force. The resultant treaties of Nerchinsk (1689) and Kiakhta (1727) delineated the Russo-Chinese frontier (the longest frontier in the world), provided for limited commercial relations in the form of Russian overland caravans, and authorized the establishment of an Orthodox mission in the Chinese capital. As intercourse between China and the other Western powers was confined to Macao and Canton, the Russians, with their commercial and intellectual foothold in Peking, were at an advantage in understanding and confronting Manchu China. Russo-Chinese relations remained peaceful until the second half of the nineteenth century, Manchu might deflecting the Russian thrust eastward again.

Negotiating from a position of strength China had made the Treaty of Nerchinsk an "equal" one. Yet she too had made concessions in demands and attitude, conferring, as she did, on foreign soil. The dignified bearing of the Russian Ambassador Feodor Alexeevich Golovin at Nerchinsk, described by the Portuguese Jesuit Thomas Pereira, who assisted the Man-

chu negotiators, could not be maintained by his fellow countryman, Ambassador Ivan Lorents de Lange, in Peking (1721-22), where, as the Scottish traveler John Bell, another eyewitness, relates, conformity with Chinese etiquette was demanded.

At Nerchinsk

The Moscovite had sent to inquire of our ambassadors if they wanted him to prepare a common meeting place, or if each party should prepare its own. They answered without my advice in a way which for them showed great knowledge of the world: they had their tent and His Excellency should prepare his. The Moscovite then erected in a north-south direction a large and well-ordered oblong tent with pictures and a floor covered with beautiful carpets. At its head, which was the southern side and towards us, he had a large desk, occupying almost the whole area, on top of which was a beautiful gilded writing table in European style. Besides this there was a clock, which kept the time of the proposals and answers, and also two fine, large, silver vessels decorated with reliefs. From them the ambassador was served either with a sour drink of vinegar and cold water or honeyed water, which he took frequently. Above the table, hanging from the tent, there was a beautiful cross decorated with precious stones which the Moscovites held in great reverence and respect. To the west there was another smaller, well-painted tent which I think served the purpose of which I shall speak in due course. There was an excellent chair of yellow damask for the ambassador with nails either of gold or gilded. One in ordinary bright red and smaller, on which the Governor of those parts was sitting, and a bench covered with carpets on which another man, whom we thought to be an official of rites, sat. There was no other seat; the rest of the company consisting of many honorable officials of war, captains and colonels, remained on their feet and no one dared to sit in the presence of the ambassador. From this fact we gathered that he was a man of great authority, respect and rank. He signed his name as follows: Odolnicius Locitenens Brancensis Theodorus Alexius Oviez Golovin.

Our ambassadors sent their own Tartar-styled black tents, well but more modestly made, to be put up next to the Russian ambassador's in such a way that the desk served both parties but was dominated by its owner. To the east of this tent they put a smaller one for the same purpose as the Moscovites had put one to the west. Our ambassadors departed from the Court in Peking as if they were alone in the world (which I

Joseph Sebes, J.J. *The Jesuits and the Sino-Russian Treaty of Nerchinsk (1689): The Diary of Thomas Pereira, S.J.* (Rome: Institutum Historicum Societatis Iesu, 1961), pp. 227-33. Reprinted with permission of Institutum Historicum Societatis Iesu.

cannot fail to repeat in order to be truthful and sincere in my report and not to omit their conceit) with an army as described above. They gloried justly in their great number, for I sincerely believe that for no other monarch would it have been possible to send such a mounted army on a forty day trip through the desert (although it took us forty-nine days, taking all necessary things and supplies with us on camels and ox-carts), with ninety boats all to transport artillery, with one thousand soldiers and with two thousand servants who, when they appeared at Nipchu, caused the Moscovites no end of concern. The style of their tents, however, was common and unelaborate; they had some coarse grass mats instead of carpets with which they covered the floor of their modest tents. Knowing that the Moscovite had beautiful chairs and that they had nothing on which they sat on the floor according to their custom, they ordered the carpenters to work all night in order to fabricate such rough benches as time permitted and on which there was hardly enough room to place their cushions. They had sixteen lances for the guards, but knowing that the Moscovites had many more as well as arquebuses and other arms in the ancient Roman style, they thought it better to leave their sixteen lances behind.

We crossed the river in the manner mentioned before. All the Mandarins, who were in great number, dressed in their best attire decorated with dragons and other animals, the insignia of their respective offices, which on the golden background made a great impression on the eyes but were not of any great value. The rest of the soldiers were dressed in damask or other similar material. After crossing the river we all rode on horses which had swum across the river before us. There were four beautiful saddles: mine, which the Empeor had given to me and which, decorated with gold, was of great value; my companion's; and those of the two ambassadors, T'ung Kuo-Kang, uncle of the Emperor, and Songgatu, uncle of the heir apparent. The others were very ordinary in Chinese style but good enough. Before the Moscovite left his lodging, there came out two companies of soldiers with great pomp and with their captains and officers in order marching slowly as if in a procession, preceded by some bands of well-harmonized flutes and four trumpets which from time to time united their tunes with those of flutes with much applause. They were followed by some drums mounted on horses, after which came in order those arms and insignia in Roman style of which I spoke before. Then came the ambassador on horseback with a suite which though not excessive was quite adequate. He was flanked by two persons on horseback. His saddle was very small, similar to those used in racing and not large enough to be decorated. The blanket which covered the whole upper part of the back of the horse was the color of Milano silver and in European style.

As they approached the tents both parties stopped; their flutes and trumpets continued to play, but we were in silence. It had been decided that both parties would descend simultaneously from their horses and this was readily done. Both parties entered the tents. All the Moscovites, except the three which we mentioned before, remained standing. Our ambassadors wanted to imitate this impression of grandeur and consequently obliged all the Mandarins, more than one hundred and some of them in high office, to stand during the whole time; only the four most important ones received a bench. In order to honor their ambassadors they all consented to this. My companion and myself were seated between the two delegations. The Moscovite was dressed in an array of magnificent furs covered with damask which he changed everyday to another equally impressive one. He also changed caps (as they do not use hats), the price of one of which, together with its precious stones, I think was more than one thousand cruzados. At his right, close to him, there was a young man holding a baton of great value which was of gilded silver at least, ornamented with many precious stones. Seated, he filled the chair materialiter with his bulk and filled it formaliter with the air of experience and directness with which he spoke. He was an intelligent man, acute and experienced in negotiations, and though he knew Latin he always used the interpreter who had been his teacher of this language. Master of himself without ostentatious show, he was all in all worthy of this function. Among our group there were some intelligent and prudent men, but all were lacking in experience of the world outside China. The Moscovite, however, would never have had this advantageous position had he come to China, because there they would have obliged him, as they did those who came in the past, either to submit to the Chinese customs or return home without peace. Since he did not want to go to the Court of China, he achieved equality in honor through obliging them to leave their own country and to negotiate peace at the pretended borders.

At Peking

On the 28th, the day appointed for the ambassador's publick audience of the Emperor, horses were brought to our lodgings for the ambassador and his retinue; the Emperor being then at a country house, called TZAN-SHU-YANG, about six miles westward from PEKIN. We mounted at eight in the morning, and about ten arrived at court; where we alighted, at the

John Bell, *Travels from St. Petersburg in Russia, to Diverse Parts of Asia* (Dublin: Robert Bell, 1764), II, 5-8.

gate, which was guarded by a strong party of soldiers. The commanding officers conducted us into a large room, where we drank tea, and staid about a half an hour till the Emperor was ready to receive us. We then entered a spacious court, enclosed with high brick-walls, and regularly planted with several rows of forest-trees, about eight inches diameter, which I took to be limes. The walks are spread with small gravel, and the great walk is terminated by the hall of audience, behind which are the Emperor's private apartments. On each side of the great walk are fine flower-pots and canals. As we advanced, we found all the ministers of state, and officers belonging to the court, seated upon fur-cushions, cross-legged, before the hall, in the open air; among these, places were appointed for the ambassador and his retinue, and in this situation we remained, in a cold frosty morning, till the Emperor came into the hall. During this interval, there were only two or three servants in the hall, and not the least noise was heard from any quarter. The entry to the hall is by seven marble steps, the whole length of the building. The floor is finely paved with a neat checker-work of white and black marble. The edifice is quite open to the south; and the roof supported by a row of handsome wooden pillars, octangular, and finely polished; before which is hung a large canvass, as a shelter from the heat of the sun, or inclemencies of the weather.

After we had waited about a quarter of an hour, the Emperor entered the hall at a back-door, and seated himself upon the throne; upon which all the company stood. The master of ceremonies now desired the ambassador, who was at some distance from the rest, to walk into the hall; and conducted him by one hand, while he held his credentials in the other. Having ascended the steps, the letter was laid on a table for that purpose, as had been previously agreed; but the Emperor beckoned to the ambassador, and directed him to approach; which he no sooner perceived, than he took up the credentials, and, attended by ALOY, walked up to the throne, and kneeling, laid them before the Emperor; who touched them with his hand, and inquired after his Czarish Majesty's health. He then told the ambassador, that the love and friendship he entertained for his majesty were such, that he had even dispensed with an established custom of the empire in receiving his letter.

During this part of the ceremony, which was not long, the retinue continued standing without the hall; and we imagined, the letter being delivered, all was over. But the master of the ceremonies brought back the ambassador; and then ordered all the company to kneel, and make obeisance nine times to the Emperor. At every third time we stood up, and kneeled again. Great pains were taken to avoid this piece of homage without success. The master of the ceremonies stood by, and delivered his orders in the TARTAR language, by pronouncing the words *morgu* and *boss;* the first meaning to bow and other to stand; two words which I cannot soon forget.

II / ACROSS THE PACIFIC OCEAN

INTRODUCTION

Russia's eastward expansion extended beyond the Pacific coastline. Free-booters and explorers, trappers, traders, and settlers ranged anywhere from the Kuril Islands and Sakhalin to the Aleutians, and to the Marshall and Sandwich (Hawaiian) Islands. The Russian-American Company staked out a colonial empire in America and sought to establish commercial relations with Japan.

The mainspring of Russia's eastward expansion remained fur, the most important single item in Russian commerce with Europe and China. But in time Russian penetration to the American continent assumed also strategic and political meaning, since here, unlike Siberia, her interests touched upon those of other Western powers. The reopening of Japan, a more convenient source of supplies for settlements in the Russian Far East and America than was the European homeland, likewise entailed international implications, for Japan was as convenient a steppingstone for Americans moving West as for Russians moving East.

14 / TO AMERICA

On Christmas Day, 1962, American newspapers carried an AP dispatch which announced theatrically:

> In fourteen hundred and ninety-two,
> Columbus sailed the ocean blue.
> In nineteen hundred and sixty-two,
> the Russians say he was No. 2.

M. B. Synge, *A Book of Discovery: The History of the World's Exploration, From the Earliest Times to the Finding of the South Pole* (New York: G. P. Putnam's Sons, 1925), pp. 312-18. Reprinted with permission of Thomas Nelson & Sons Ltd.

The story, reporting the speculation of a Soviet historian that the English navigator Nicholas Lynn had discovered Hudson Bay in 1360, was headlined in the Florida St. Petersburg Times, "Oh, No—Now The Russians Say Columbus Did NOT Discover America in 1492," and was dismissed by a noted American historian as "another propaganda scheme" of the Soviet Union. The American reaction makes no sense—for how could the U.S.S.R. benefit by the glorification of an English explorer at the expense of a Genoese seafarer in the service of Spain—until one realizes the possessiveness of patriotism, which has managed to metamorphose Columbus into an American national hero.

Russian efforts to play down the role of Columbus are not new. If his priority of discovery has not been challenged before, his discovery of America, in the sense of the whole continent, has been challenged all along. Explorers of many countries participated in this task. There is more than propaganda in the Soviet assertion that the honor of exploring a large part of the northwestern extremity of the American continent belongs to Russia. To be sure, among her navigators there were men of foreign birth or extraction, but they were Russian in loyalty and service and conscientiously furthered the Russian cause. To draw another parallel —they were as Russian as the Old World immigrants to the United States were to be American.

In the following pages M. B. Synge describes the celebrated expeditions of Bering and Chirikov to America.

In the great work of Arctic exploration during the eighteenth and nineteenth centuries, it is to England and Russia that we owe our knowledge at the present day. It is well known how Peter the Great of Russia journeyed to Amsterdam to learn shipbuilding under the Dutch, and to England to learn the same art under the English, and how the Russian fleet grew in his reign. Among the Danish shipbuilders at Petersburg was one Vitus Behring, already a bold and able commander on the high seas.

The life of the great Russian Czar was drawing to its close—he was already within a few weeks of the end—when he planned an expedition under this same Vitus Behring, for which he wrote the instructions with his own hands.

"(1) At Kamtchatka two decked boats are to be built. (2) With these you are to sail northward along the coast and, as the end of the coast is not known, this land is undoubtedly America. (3) For this reason you are to inquire where the American coast begins, and go to some European colony and, when European ships are seen, you are to ask what the coast is called, note it down, make a landing, and after having charted the coast return."

Were Asia and America joined together, or was there a strait between the two? The question was yet undecided in 1725. Indeed, the east coast of Asia was only known as far as the island of Yezo [Hokkaido], while the Pacific coast of America had been explored no farther than New Albion.

Peter the Great died on 28th January 1725. A week later Behring started for Kamtchatka. Right across snow-covered Russia to the boundary of Siberia he led his expedition. March found him at Tobolsk. With rafts and boats they then made their way by the Siberian rivers till they reached Yakutsk, where they spent their first winter. Not till the middle of June 1726 did Behring reach the capital of East Siberia. The rest of the journey was through utterly unknown land. It was some six hundred and eighty-five miles eastwards to Okhotsk through a rough and mountainous country, cut up by deep and bridgeless streams; the path lay over dangerous swamps and through dense forest.

The party now divided. Behring, with two hundred horses, travelled triumphantly, if painfully, to Okhotsk in forty-five days. The town consisted of eleven huts containing Russian families who lived by fishing. Snow lay deep on the frozen ground, and the horses died one by one for lack of food, but the undaunted explorer had soon got huts ready for the winter, which was to be spent in felling trees and pushing forward the building of his ship, the *Fortuna,* for the coming voyage of discovery. Behring himself had made a successful journey to the coast, but some of the party encountered terrible hardships, and it was midsummer 1727 before they arrived, while others were overtaken by winter in the very heart of Siberia and had to make their way for the last three hundred miles on foot through snow in places six feet deep. Their food was finished, famine became a companion to cold, and they were obliged to gnaw their shoes and straps and leathern bags. Indeed, they must have perished had they not stumbled on Behring's route, where they found his dead horses. But at last all was ready and the little ship *Fortuna* was sailing bravely across the Sea of Okhotsk some six hundred and fifty miles to the coast of Kamtchatka. This she did in sixteen days. The country of Kamtchatka had now to be crossed, and with boats and sledges this took the whole winter. It was a laborious undertaking following the course of the Kamtchatka River; the expedition had to camp in the snow, and few natives were forthcoming for the transport of heavy goods.

It was not till March 1728 that Behring reached his goal, Ostrog, a village near the sea, inhabited by a handful of Cossacks. From this point, on the bleak shores of the Arctic sea, the exploring party were ordered to start. It had taken over three years to reach this starting-point, and even now a seemingly hopeless task lay before them.

After hard months of shipbuilding, the stout little *Gabriel* was launched, her timber had been hauled to Ostrog by dogs, while the rigging, cable, and anchors had been dragged nearly two thousand miles through one of the most desolate regions of the earth. . . . On 13th July 1728 the sails of the *Gabriel* were triumphantly hoisted, and Behring, with a crew of forty-four, started on the great voyage. His course lay close along the coast northwards. The sea was alive with whales, seals, sea-lions, and dolphins as the little party made their way north, past the mouth of the Anadir River. The little *Gabriel* was now in the strait between Asia and America, though Behring knew it not. They had been at sea some three weeks, when eight men came rowing towards them in a leathern boat. They were the Chukches—a warlike race living on the north-east coast of Siberia, unsubdued and fierce. They pointed out a small island in the north, which Behring named the Isle of St. Lawrence in honour of the day. Then he turned back. He felt he had accomplished his task and obeyed his orders. Moreover, with adverse winds they might never return to Kamtchatka, and to winter among the Chukches was to court disaster. After a cruise of three months they reached their starting-point again. Had he only known that the coast of America was but thirty-nine miles off, the results of his voyage would have been greater. As it was, he ascertained that "there really does exist a north-east passage, and that from the Lena River it is possible, provided one is not prevented by Polar ice, to sail to Kamtchatka and thence to Japan, China, and the East Indies." . . .

There was dissatisfaction in Russia with the result of Behring's voyage, and though five years of untold hardship in the "extremest corner of the world" had told on the Russian explorer, he was willing and anxious to start off again. He proposed to make Kamtchatka again his headquarters, to explore the western coast of America, and to chart the long Arctic coast of Siberia—a colossal task indeed.

So the Great Northern Expedition was formed, with Behring in command, accompanied by two well-known explorers to help, Spangberg and Chirikoff, and with five hundred and seventy men under him. It would take too long to follow the various expeditions that now left Russia in five different directions to explore the unknown coasts of the Old World. "The world has never witnessed a more heroic geographical enterprise than these Arctic expeditions." Amid obstacles indescribable the north line of Siberia, hitherto charted as a straight line, was explored and surveyed. Never was greater courage and endurance displayed. If the ships got frozen in, they were hauled on shore, the men spent the long winter in miserable huts and started off again with the spring, until the northern coast assumed shape and form.

One branch of the Great Northern Expedition under Behring was composed of professors to make a scientific investigation of Kamtchatka! These thirty learned Russians were luxuriously equipped. They carried a library with several hundred books, including *Robinson Crusoe* and *Gulliver's Travels,* seventy reams of writing-paper, and artists' materials. They had nine wagonloads of instruments, carrying telescopes fifteen feet long. A surgeon, two landscape painters, one instrument maker, five surveyors accompanied them, and "the convoy grew like an avalanche as it worked its way into Siberia." Behring seems to have moved this "cumbersome machine" safely to Yakutsk, though it took the best part of two years. Having left Russia in 1733, it was 1741 when Behring himself was ready to start from the harbour of Okhotsk for the coast of America with two ships and provisions for some months. He was now nearly sixty, his health was undermined with vexation and worry, and the climate of Okhotsk had nearly killed him.

On 18th July—just six weeks after the start—Behring discovered the continent of North America. The coast was jagged, the land covered with snow, mountains extended inland, and above all rose a peak towering into the clouds—a peak higher than anything they knew in Siberia or Kamtchatka, which Behring named Mount St. Elias, after the patron saint of the day. He made his way with difficulty through the string of islands that skirt the great peninsula of Alaska. Through the months of August and September they cruised about the coast in damp and foggy weather, which now gave way to violent storms, and Behring's ship was driven along at the mercy of the wind. He himself was ill, and the greater part of his crew were disabled by scurvy. At last one day, in a high-running sea, the ship struck upon a rock and they found themselves stranded on an unknown island off the coast of Kamtchatka. Only two men were fit to land; they found a dead whale on which they fed their sick. Later on sea-otters, blue and white foxes, and sea-cows provided food, but the island was desolate and solitary—not a human being was to be seen.

Here, however, the little party was forced to winter. With difficulty they built five underground huts on the sandy shore of the island now known as Behring Island. And each day amid the raging snowstorms and piercing winds one man went forth to hunt for animal food.

Man after man died, and by December, Behring's own condition had become hopeless. Hunger and grief had added to his misery, and in his sand-hut he died. He was almost buried alive, for the sand rolled down from the pit in which he lay and covered his feet. He would not have it removed, for it kept him warm. Thirty more of the little expedition died during that bitter winter on the island; the survivors, some forty-five persons, built a ship from the timbers of the wreck, and in August 1742 they returned to Kamtchatka to tell the story of Behring's discoveries and of Behring's death.

15 / TO THE SHORES OF JAPAN

The Bering expedition, described above, encompassed a number of ventures, including an attempt to establish commercial relations with Japan. While Chirikov accompanied Bering to the shores of America, another assistant, Martin Spanberg, a Dane, was to proceed to Japan, assisted by Lieutenant William Walton, an Englishman, and Ensign Alexei Shelting, the young son of a Dutch seaman.

Europeans had reached Japan as early as the sixteenth century and had frequented its shores for close to a hundred years, but they had come from the opposite direction. The northern route, from Russia, was unknown. Russian contacts with Japan may be dated back to 1697, when a Japanese castaway was found on Kamchatka. From him and other castaways in later years the Russians gained an exaggerated impression of Japanese wealth, so that the prospect of silver and gold joined fur as the lure beckoning Russian adventurers across the Pacific. Earlier attempts to find Japan by canoe and rowboat had ended in failure. The offshoot of the Bering expedition was the first realistic effort to locate the Island Kingdom.

Spanberg's vessels were ready at Okhotsk in the autumn of 1737, three years before the completion of the somewhat larger St. Peter *and* St. Paul, *which were to head for America in 1741. They consisted of the newly constructed flagship* Arkhangel Mikhail, *a one-masted brigantine sixty feet long and eighteen feet wide, carrying sixty-seven men; the newly built* Nadezhda, *a three-masted double sloop, seventy feet in length and eighteen feet in width, carrying forty-six men; and the renovated* Sviatoi Gavriil, *also with a complement of forty-six men. In 1738 the vessels vainly searched for Japan, but the following year, accompanied by a fourth ship, the sloop* Bolsheretsk, *they finally succeeded.*

The following selection describes the approach of Spanberg and Walton, who had separated a couple of days before, ostensibly because Walton's Sviatoi Gavriil *had sustained damage in a heavy storm, but possibly because he, like other subordinate commanders of the day, wished to do some exploring of his own.*

On June 27, 1739, Spanberg and his companions sighted at long last the northeastern shores of the Japanese main island at about latitude

George Alexander Lensen, *The Russian Push Toward Japan: Russo-Japanese Relations, 1697-1875* (Princeton, N.J.: Princeton University Press, 1959), pp. 50-55. Reprinted with permission of the Princeton University Press. Copyright © 1959 by Princeton University Press.

39° N. and followed down the coast for two days, casting anchor on the 18th at latitude 38°41′ N. off the east coast of Iwate Prefecture. The Russians were dazzled by the luxurious vegetation of the countryside that stretched out before them, all the greener by comparison with the barren shores of Okhotsk and Kamchatka. They were impressed also by the numerous settlements that dotted the coastline. Two boats came within close view, and the Russians motioned them to pull up. The Japanese would not come nearer, but in turn beckoned the Russians to land. This Spanberg did not dare to do, and weighing anchor sailed farther south. On July 3 he cast anchor again at approximately latitude 38°23′ N., off Aji-shima, Ojika County, in the province of Mutsu in the domain of the lord of Sendai.

The Russian ships had been sighted here and there along the coast and reports poured into Sendai from everywhere. Even from aboard the ships the excitement on shore could be discerned. At one place Spanberg dispatched the *Bolsheretsk* to within less than a mile and a half of the coast. But he did not dare to effect a landing. The Japanese on the other hand, in spite of the strictest prohibitions, seemed anxious to deal with the foreigners. Already at sea, near the tiny island Tashirohama, fisherman Kisabei had audaciously boarded one of the Russian vessels and stared at the tall strangers. Now two junks laden with foodstuffs, tobacco, and gold coins pulled alongside and began a spirited trade. Before long officials, headed by Chiba Kanshichiro, arrived from Sendai. Without fear or hostility but with the greatest politeness they approached Spanberg, who received them with due hospitality, treating them to wine and food, showing them about the ship, and handing gifts of fur to their servants. The Kurilian interpreters whom Spanberg had brought along proved valueless. Nevertheless a great many thoughts can be conveyed by gestures. To confirm his whereabouts Spanberg produced a map and a globe. The Japanese readily pointed out Japan, saying "Nippon, Nippon," reassuring Spanberg that he had indeed found the way. And though he had instructions not to disclose the approaches to Russia, Spanberg took this opportunity to point out to Chiba the proximity of Russia to Japan.

Meanwhile the number of small boats that milled about the squadron had increased until some eight hundred or more Japanese on seventy-nine boats surrounded the Russians. As yet they showed no signs of hostility, but one could hardly foretell how long the interest of the onlookers would remain one of amicable curiosity, and Spanberg withdrew into the open sea and headed back north. As he passed Tashirohama Island, a settlement elder by the name of Zembei visited the flagship. Again Japanese and Russian eyed each other with mutual curiosity. As always,

Japanese garments called for comment: "Their dress is white and fastened with a band round the body. The sleeves are wide, like those on a European dressing gown, but without gores. None were seen with trousers and all went barefoot. Their shame they either tied up or covered with a piece of silken cloth or linen." When Zembei bowed his head, one of the Russians could not resist the temptation of stroking it. His hand became all greasy from the oily hairdo and everybody laughed heartily. Zembei did not take offense. He was too engrossed in making mental notes of everything. When he went back on shore he made a full report of what he had observed to the lord of Sendai. Sailing north Spanberg explored the southern Kuril Islands. Then on July 5 he briefly reapproached the shores of Japan at Hokkaido near latitude 41° N. before finally resuming his homeward voyage.

While Spanberg was thus carefully probing the shores of Japan, receiving Japanese visitors here and there, yet not daring to touch land, Walton actually broke the isolation of Japan and sent his men onto Japanese soil. As will be recalled, Walton had separated from the squadron on June 25. On June 27 he came upon the southeastern shore of Honshu at about latitude 37°42′ N. and turned southward. On June 30 the *Sviatoi Gavriil* cast anchor in the open sea at about latitude 35°10′ N. near Amatsu Village in Nagasa County in the province of Awa (Chiba Prefecture) and sent ashore a boat with Kazimirov, his second navigator; a navigator's mate; and six seamen to obtain fresh water.

More than a hundred Japanese boats came forth to meet the boat and surrounded it so closely that the Russians could hardly row. As the latter persisted, however, the Japanese took no measures to turn them back. On land the Russians were greeted politely and helping hands quickly filled their water barrels, possibly in the hope of expediting their departure. When Navigator Kazimirov left two soldiers to guard the boat and with Navigator's Mate Vereshchagin and the remaining four sailors proceeded to town, no effort was made to harass them. On the contrary, Kazimirov was invited into Japanese houses and regaled with wine, rice, fruit, and various delicacies. These Russians—the first of their countrymen to set foot in Japan—viewed everything with fascination; they were particularly impressed to see about them so much unaccustomed cleanliness and order. Returning to his boat, Kazimirov espied a two-sworded samurai and companion standing nearby, but though he was alarmed at their presence, they did not interfere.

As the Russians rowed back to their ship, they were followed by a multitude of boats. A Japanese official in costly robes came aboard the *Sviatoi Gavriil* with red wine and exchanged presents and drinks with

Walton while a brisk trade developed between the sailors and the Japanese, the former selling a number of trifles, mostly old shirts and stockings for a quantity of copper coin. Nevertheless the potential danger of a boarding attack by the numerically superior Japanese, who crowded about the vessel on some one hundred boats, made it seem unwise to tarry overnight; so, upon the departure of the official, Walton weighed anchor, discharging one of his cannons in salute. Unlike Spanberg he did not withdraw to the north right away, but pushed farther south, casting anchor here and there along the Japanese coast. On July 3, he stood close to shore and requested fresh water from some Japanese who had approached the vessel. The Japanese brought the water and even offered to lead the *Sviatoi Gavriil* into port. This Walton would not risk. He continued southward, and the following day (July 4) at about latitude 33°28′ N. cast anchor and sent several men ashore to gather medical herbs and some tokens of Japan. On July 5, in the general vicinity of Katsuura on the east coast of Wakayama Prefecture, Walton turned back and headed homeward.

When the Russians departed, the Japanese officials turned to their reports. The Russians had been received with politeness if not friendliness. Only once, as their southward journey brought them relatively close to the Japanese capital, had an official seemed to order his countrymen not to deal with them. Elsewhere Japanese officials themselves had sought out the Russians and had interchanged civilities. At least so the Russian records state, and we have no reason to question them on this point. The Japanese reports, though they corroborate Russian data as to the number of men who landed and as to the houses they entered, studiously avoid any reference to signs of welcome. The Russians are portrayed as having entered the Japanese houses without invitation and as having helped themselves to whatever they wanted. The Japanese records could not have stated otherwise. The officials were committed to the exclusion of foreigners. A report describing the amicable reception of the intruders on land would have been no less than a confession of neglect of duty. Thus the official who visited Walton aboard ship was described as having followed the vessel out to sea without catching up with it.

The story of the expedition, narrated above, was pieced together from both Japanese and Russian sources. At the time of the events neither the Japanese nor the Russians saw the whole picture. The Japanese did not know the foreigners were Russians until two coins and a card with a cross, which the Russians had left behind, were identified by the Dutch on Deshima as coins "from the Muscovia country" and an ace of clubs. At first their information was limited to such eyewitness descriptions of the strangers as that of the priest Ryumon who reported: "Their appearance resembled that of Dutchmen, with red wavy hair and caps of various kinds. Their noses were long and pointed. Their eyes were the color of sharks. The trunks of their bodies, however, were normal just like those of ordinary people." From the Dutch the Japanese learned more about the Spanberg expedition. The Russians knew only the latitude of the place where they had cast anchor or gone ashore. The place names have come to us from Japanese sources. Yet the Russians knew that they had been in Japan and were pleased with what they had seen. "The members of the party were loud in proclaiming their pleasure at having been able to visit the country, declaring that Japan was indeed a nation with whom friendly relations must be formed."

16 / A JAPANESE WELCOME

Russian attempts to establish commercial relations with Japan continued for the next century and culminated in a nip-and-tuck race between Vice-Admiral Evfimii Putiatin and American Commodore Matthew C. Perry. Offended by Japanese insistence on isolation, one Russian envoy, Nikolai Rezanov, of whom we shall speak later in connection with the Russian-American Company, on his own authority sought to frighten Japan into commercial relations by a number of naval raids, executed by Gavriil Davydov and Nikolai Khvostov, officers in the service of the Russian-American Company. These raids of 1807 were carried out, however, without the prior knowledge or authorization of the Russian government; thus, when the events became known, they led to the courts-martial of the officers, which triggered a series of reprisals and counter-reprisals. Among these the best known is the celebrated capture of Captain Vasilii Golovnin in 1811.

At Kunashiri, one of the Kuril Islands, Golovnin had gone ashore with great caution. Hospitably received by the Japanese, he agreed to come ashore again the next day and to call on the governor inside the fortress. The following excerpt from Golovnin's memoirs describes this visit.

Next morning, July 11 [1811], at 8 o'clock, I landed with the . . . officers [Chlebnikoff and Moor], the Kurile Alexei, and four seamen. I was so fully persuaded that we stood on a friendly footing with the Japanese, that I had not ordered the seamen to arm themselves. The officers, three in number, including myself, had each a sword, in addition to which Mr. Chlebnikoff brought with him a pocket pistol, more for the purpose of making a signal in the case of a fog, than for defence. . . . We landed

Captain Vasilii Golovnin, *Memoirs of a Captivity in Japan: During the Years 1811, 1812, and 1813, With Observations of the Country and People* (London: Henry Colburn and Co., 1824), I, 67-75 close to the fortress. The Oyagoda, and two officers whom I had seen the day before, came out to meet us, and begged that we would wait a little until every thing was prepared for our reception in the castle. Wishing by my confidence in the Japanese to extinguish any suspicion they might yet entertain, I ordered the boat to be hauled up on the shore until it was half out of the water, and left one sailor with it. The other seamen I directed to follow us, carrying seats, and the presents which I destined for the Japanese. We walked from ten to fifteen minutes on the shore, during which time I conversed with the Oyagoda. I made inquiries respecting the coast of Matsmai, of which we had a view, and the trade between their island and the peninsula of Niphon. I remarked, however, that he answered my questions with reluctance. Finally, we proceeded to the castle.

On entering the castle gate, I was astonished at the number of men I saw assembled there. Of soldiers alone, I observed from three to four hundred, armed with muskets, bows and arrows, and spears, sitting in a circle, in an open space to the right of the gate: on the left a countless multitude of Kuriles surrounded a tent of striped cotton cloth, erected about thirty paces from the gate. I never could have supposed this small insignificant place capable of containing so many men, and concluded that they must have been collected from all the neighbouring garrisons since we appeared in the harbour.

We were soon introduced into the tent, on a seat opposite to the entrance of which the governor had placed himself. He wore a rich silk dress, with a complete suit of armour, and had two sabres under his girdle. A long cord of white silk passed over his shoulder; at one end of this cord was a tassel of the same material, and at the other a steel baton, which he held in his hand, and which was doubtless the symbol of his authority. His armour-bearers, one holding a spear, another a musket, and a third his helmet, sat behind him on the floor. The helmet resembled that of the second in command, with this difference, that instead of the figure of the moon, it bore the image of the sun. This officer now sat on the left of the governor, on a seat somewhat lower than that of his superior; he too had his armour-bearers behind him. Four officers were sitting cross-legged on the floor on each side of the tent: they wore black armour, and had each two sabres. On our entrance the governor and lieutenant-governor both rose up: we saluted them in our own manner, and they returned the compliment. They invited us to sit down on a bench which was placed directly opposite to themselves, but we chose to use the seats we had brought with us. Our sailors seated themselves on the bench behind us. After the introductory civilities were concluded, they entertained us with tea without sugar, in cups which, according to the Japanese fashion, were only half filled; the cups had no saucers, but were handed to us on small trays made of varnished wood. Before they gave us the tea, they asked whether we would prefer any thing else. Pipes and tobacco were afterwards brought to us, and the conference commenced. They desired to know our names and rank, the name of our ship, whence we came, whither we were bound, why we had visited them, what had induced Russian ships to attack their villages, and further, whether we knew Resanoff, and where he now was? Our answers to these questions were conformable to the statements we had previously made, and were written down by the lieutenant-governor. We were next told that to enable them to prepare the proper quantity of provisions we wanted, it was necessary they should know the exact number of our crew. Ridiculous as this question was, they had an object in putting it. On our part we thought it advisable to make our force appear more considerable than it was, and therefore doubled it, calling it one hundred and two men. Alexei could neither understand nor express this number; and I was obliged to make an equal number of marks with a black-lead pencil on paper, which the Japanese counted off. We were further asked whether we had any other ships of the size of the *Diana* in their seas? We answered that we had many in Okotzk, Kamtschatka, and America. Among their questions were several of a very insignificant nature, relative to our dress, customs, &c. They also carefully examined the presents I had brought for the governor, among which were maps of the globe, ivory-handled knives, burning-glasses, and piastres, with which I intended to pay the Japanese for a supply of provisions, as soon as I could ascertain the number they required.

While the conference was going on, Mr. Moor observed, that naked sabres had been distributed among the soldiers who were sitting in the open space. He immediately mentioned this to me; but I supposed that a sabre or two might have been accidentally out of their sheaths; and I asked him, with a smile, whether he had not made a mistake, as the Japanese always carry swords, and could at present have no reason for drawing them. This remark appeared to satisfy him; but circumstances soon occurred which roused all our suspicion, and convinced us that some mischief was intended against us. The lieutenant-governor having withdrawn for a short time, as if to make some arrangement, returned and whispered to the governor, who immediately rose up to go away. We got up also to take our leave; and I repeated my question respecting the price of provisions, and also asked whether he intended to supply us with any? On hearing this he sat down, invited us to do the same, and, though it was early in the day, ordered dinner to be served up.

We accepted his invitation, and waited with impatience to see what would next occur, as it now appeared we were caught in a snare from which it would be difficult to escape. But the kind behaviour of the Japanese, and their assurances that we had nothing to fear, again tranquillized us, and induced us to abandon our suspicions of their treachery. They entertained us with rice, fish in a green sauce, and other savory dishes, the ingredients composing which we did not know. They also gave us sagi. After we had dined, the governor was again about to withdraw. I now declared that we could wait no longer, but must return immediately on board. On hearing this he once more sat down, and having intimated that he could not supply us with any thing without an order from the Governor of Matsmai, under whose jurisdiction he was, proposed that one of us should remain in the castle as a hostage, until a decision should be returned by that commander on the report he was about to transmit to him. The Japanese began now to throw off the mask. I desired to be informed what time would be occupied in sending the report to Matsmai and obtaining an answer; he replied a fortnight. I felt, however, that it would be dishonourable to leave an officer behind me as a hostage. There was, besides, no knowing when such an affair would be brought to a conclusion with a people like the Japanese. It was probable that when the report reached Matsmai the commander of that island would say he could do nothing without the authority of the general government: thus I perhaps should have to wait until winter for a decisive answer. I therefore stated that I could not wait so long without consulting the officers who remained on board the *Diana,* and that I would leave no officer as a hostage; upon which we rose to go away.

The governor, who had hitherto conversed in a soft and gentle voice, now altered his tone, spoke loud and with warmth; frequently mentioned Resanoto (Resanoff) and Nicola-Sandrejetsch (Nicolai Alexandroivitsch, meaning Chwostoff the captain of the company's ship) and struck several times on his sabre. In this manner he made a long speech, of which the terrified Alexei interpreted to us only the following sentence:—"The governor says that if he let a single one of us out of the castle his own bowels will be ript up." This was brief and decisive! We instantly made all the haste we could to escape. The Japanese did not venture to close upon us, but set up a loud cry, and threw oars, and large pieces of wood at us, to knock us down. On our reaching the gate they fired several times on us, but without effect, though one of their balls whistled past the head of Mr. Chlebnikoff. We now found that they had succeeded in detaining Mr. Moor, the sailor Makaroff, and our Kurile Alexei, in the castle. We ran, however, to our landing place; but on arriving there, perceived with horror that the tide had ebbed above five fathoms, and left the strand quite dry. As the Japanese saw that it was impossible for us to get the boat afloat, and had previously ascertained that it contained no arms, they became confident, advanced against us with drawn sabres, which they held in both hands, muskets and spears, and surrounded us beside the boat. I cast a look upon the boat, and said to myself;—It must be so; our last refuge is lost; our fate is unavoidable!—I surrendered. The Japanese seized me by the arms, and conducted me to the castle, into which my unfortunate companions were also conveyed.

17 / THE RUSSIAN-AMERICAN COMPANY

The discovery of America or, to be more accurate, of its proximity to Russia uncorked a flow of hunters and adventurers to the Aleutian Islands and to Alaska. Their sole concern was wealth and fortune.

The spoliation of Alaska was not in the interest of Russia, however. As the systematic exploitation of northwest America and Russian colonial entrenchment there were beyond the efforts of individual enterprisers or small groups of merchants, the government in 1798 created a Russian-American Company in the image of the highly successful Dutch, French, and British East India companies. Like the latter its activities were broader than the name implied; for example, the Russian-American Company played a major part in the attempts to reopen Japan. The Tsarist government, according to S. B. Okun, set before the Russian-American Company the goal of making the Pacific Ocean an "inland sea" of the Russian Empire.

This plan presupposed the further entrenchment of Russia along the west coast of North America, including California, the Hawaiian Islands, the southern part of Sakhalin, and the mouth of the Amur. These colonies, together with Kamchatka, Alaska and the Aleutians, which already belonged to Russia, were to make that country the all-powerful master of the whole northern Pacific.*

The Russian-American Company was an outgrowth of the company founded by the merchant Gregorii Shelikhov and developed by his son-in-law Nikolai Rezanov. Clarence A. Manning describes the company's attainment of monopoly status.

Clarence A. Manning, *Russian Influence on Early America* (New York: Library Publishers, 1953), pp. 27-38.

* S. B. Okun, *The Russian American Company*, ed. B. D. Grekov, trans. Carl Ginsburg (Cambridge, Mass.: Harvard University Press, 1951), p. 50.

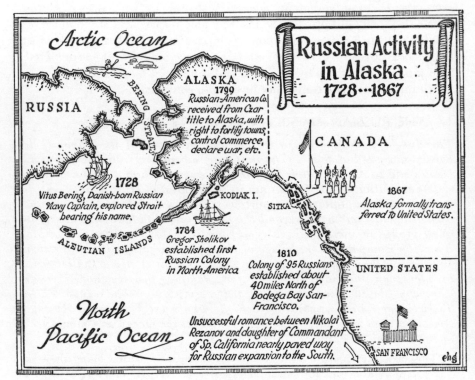

Source: AP Newsfeature, dated June 17, 1958. Reprinted with permission of the
Associated Press.

Shelikov never gave up his efforts to secure a monopoly of the Aleutian and American trade. The vision which he and his wife had formed of establishing themselves securely along the north Pacific burned brighter and brighter until the day of his death. With his strange mixture of brilliant achievement and fantastic promises, he outlined plans for establishing trading relations with the entire American and Asiatic seacoast. He drew up plans to send "trading ships to Canton, Macao, Batavia, the Philippine and Maram Islands with products and productions obtained in America and to take to America all that was necessary both for the Russians living there and for the native population."

He went further and seriously recommended the exploration of the Amur valley and the opening of a way of communication from Baikal which would give the Russians a safer harborage than they could possibly secure at Okhotsk. This was the very scheme that was to be worked out later and which led to the foundation of Vladivostok in 1858.

While Shelikov showed considerable political sense, he represented the old Cossack urge for expansion which had driven Yermak and his followers from the Volga to the Pacific Ocean. He could deluge the court with appeals which would be fatally choked in the tangled methods of the bureaucracy and after his original failure, all of the letters of his supporters among the governors of Siberia brought no positive results.

On the other hand the man was found to plan for Russian expansion and to present it in political terminology that would be acceptable to the expansionist elements at court. This man was Nicholas Petrovich Rezanov. He was a noble and was born in St. Petersburg in 1764. His father held a small post there but he had made his career at Irkutsk and had always retained his relations with the Merchant's Guild there. The boy had entered one of the Guard Regiments and in addition had become a warm friend of Gabriel Romanovich Derzhavin, the leading poet of the court of Catherine. Along with his verses, Derzhavin was a sincere, if overzealous, administrator and he held many high posts during his long life.

When Rezanov finally left the army for the Civil Service, it was at the advice of Derzhavin, and at the first opportunity the poet called him back to court. Here he became involved in the constant altercations between Derzhavin and Zubov, the favorite of the empress. He had early made the acquaintance of both Shelikov and Golikov and now, with the feud between the two courtiers at full career, he seized the opportunity of a mission from the Empress to go to Irkutsk and arrange for the carrying out of part of Shelikov's plans.

When he reached Irkutsk, he promptly fell in love with the younger daughter of Shelikov, Anna Grigoryevna. It was startling in every way. Anna was perhaps the most beautiful girl in Siberia and her father was the richest man. Still they were merchants and Rezanov a nobleman of high rank. He finally decided to ask for her hand. He was accepted and Shelikov gave him an enormous dowry with his daughter, but it was entirely in the funds of the Shelikov enterprises. The bold merchant had bound Rezanov to his cause not only by cords of affection but also of money.

The young couple returned to St. Petersburg after the marriage and Rezanov found that she was cordially received even in social circles.

Then he set to work to win Catherine's approval of the proposed company. Shelikov was working with the Governor General in Irkutsk to form a permanent company which would function steadily and not be merely a device for financing various cruises. Suddenly he died, and this left his widow, Natalya, and Rezanov as the leading champions of the Shelikov interests. Once more they had to go over the wearisome round of opposition from the rivals and just as the plans were being perfected and there was hope of success, the empress passed away.

This brought Paul to the throne and Paul made it a point to do everything contrary to his mother's wishes. As autocratic and anti-revolutionary as he was, he set free all those men whom she had imprisoned for radicalism and applied pressure on all her friends. She had favored the merchant class. He would not and he took stern action to force the American trade back into the old fetters, although he was less concerned with a possible hostile reaction of England to the new situation.

Nevertheless there penetrated through the head of the half-mad emperor a new factor that had been growing in importance with every day; that was the appearance of the citizens of the United States on the scene or, as they were dubbed, the Bostonians. Now there was not only the British fleet under such men as Captain James Vancouver on the scene, sailing with impunity through the waters that Russia claimed as her own, but there were American ships putting into Kodiak and trading with the most bitter enemies of the Russians, the Koloshi or the Tlingits, the most powerful and ferocious of the Pacific Indian tribes. These had already on more than one occasion attacked Baranov and his small forces and the Americans were now supplying them with arms and ammunition.

The Commercial College renewed its efforts to form some sort of union company and in this they had the support of Rezanov and Natalya. But they were steadily opposed by the other merchant groups as that of Lebedev-Lastochkin who were joined by Golikov, for Natalya had so arranged it that the controlling position in the Shelikov interests would always be held by one of the Shelikov family, and this ensured the freezing out of Golikov who had already withdrawn as an active participant when he had left Siberia, but who still retained large commercial interests in it.

The best that the opponents could do was to suggest that the control of the Alaskan colony should be rested in a governmental commissioner who would, so to speak, take over the entire control of the colony and run it under imperial orders. Rezanov and his friends fought this. They based their arguments on the methods of the British East and West India Companies and advanced the spectre of revolution by pointing out that the poorly Christianized and civilized natives of Alaska and the islands would be more easily the prey of revolutionary ideas if they were compelled to deal with a government instead of a company official.

The controversies raged at Irkutsk, at Okhotsk, and in St. Petersburg itself, as the various merchants struggled for powerful protectors. Rezanov, as a member of the Shelikov group and a high official of the Russian Senate had the point of advantage. . . .

The terms ostensibly worked out by the heirs of Shelikov but under the supervision of Rezanov gave the company practically all that it desired. It received as a monopoly all trade and minerals found "on the northeastern shore of America from latitude 55° to Bering Strait and beyond and also on the Aleutian, Kurile and other islands lying in the North Eastern Ocean." This phraseology may seem peculiar but it reflects the attitude of the day when it was not yet certain as to whether or not Asia and America were connected and it also stressed the Russian desire to separate the North Pacific area from the question of the rest of the Pacific.

The Company was also authorized to make "new discoveries not only north of 55° but also further to the south and to accept the lands which it discovered under Russian government on the previously prescribed rules." This clause gave the Company the right to extend its control as far south as it would, subject to the vague northern limits of Mexico. In this respect it was similar to the instructions that the Empress Anna had given to Bering. With the anti-British policy of Paul and his attitude of treating the United States as a revolting colony of Great Britain and therefore a part of the revolutionary movement which he was fighting, it was intended to exclude the Anglo-Saxons as a whole from the Pacific area. It was an unspoken but clear repudiation of the English claims to a section at least of the Pacific coast on the basis of the discovery of New Albion by Sir Francis Drake in 1579.

The Company was also given full permission to carry on trade with "the countries in the neighborhood" without specifying what these were. This in fact corresponded to the ideas of Shelikov for pushing Russian possessions down both shores of the Pacific Ocean. The inclusion of the Kurile Islands made it obvious that Japan, if it could be opened, and then China would be regarded as neighboring lands exactly as were Mexico and any other settlements on the American shore. Shelikov and with him Rezanov had dreamed of ultimately extending Russian trade and control throughout the entire Pacific even as far as the East Indies. The purpose and range of the Russian American Company was left purposely vague.

In still other clauses the governmental support of the organization was made clear. It was entitled to cut lumber in the government forests and still more important it was to have the power of drawing powder and shot from the government arsenals. In view of the Russian restrictions these clauses made it clear that for all intents and purposes the Russian American Company was to be the official arm of St. Petersburg in the Pacific area.

Finally, the company received an iron-clad monopoly which not only provided that they could exclude foreign traders from the area but also any Russians who declined to enter it and trade on its terms.

18 / BARANOV

The rôle of the individual in history is often debated. Do men make events or do events make men? The answer, of course, is somewhere inbetween. Man is the product of his environment, even as he shapes it. In the days before the telegraph and the wireless, when communication was slow and decisions frequently had to be made on the spot, individuals had greater scope for action and their characters and personalities came more prominently into play.

Shelikhov, an undaunted merchant, and Rezanov, a proud, eloquent, and able chief procurator of the Senate, had founded and developed the Russian-American Company. Alexander Baranov, who headed its operation on the American continent, was a very different type of person. A. C. Laut gives a vivid sketch of this "Viking of the Pacific" and his activities.

No wilder lord of the wild northland ever existed than that old madcap Viking of the Pacific, Alexander Baranof, governor of the Russian fur traders. For thirty years he ruled over the west coast of America from Alaska to southern California despotic as a czar. And he played the game

A. C. Laut, *Vikings of the Pacific: The Adventures of the Explorers Who Came from the West, Eastward* (New York: The Macmillan Company, 1905), pp. 316-38.

single-handed, no retinue but convicts from Siberia, no subjects but hostile Indians.

Whether leading the hunting brigades of a thousand men over the sea in skin canoes light as cork, or rallying his followers ambushed by hostiles repelling invasion of their hunting-ground, or drowning hardships with seas of fiery Russian brandy in midnight carousals, Baranof was supreme autocrat. Drunk or sober, he was master of whatever came, mutineers or foreign traders planning to oust Russians from the coast of America. Baranof stood for all that was best and all that was worst in that heroic period of Pacific coast history when adventurers from all corners of the earth roamed the otter-hunting grounds in quest of fortune. Each man was a law unto himself. There was fear of neither man nor devil. The whole era might have been a page from the hero epic of prehistoric days when earth was young, and men ranged the seas unhampered by conscience or custom, magnificent beasts of prey, glorying in freedom and bloodshed and the warring elements.

Yet in person Baranof was far from a hero. He was wizened, sallow, small, a margin of red hair round a head bald as a bowl, grotesque under a black wig tied on with a handkerchief. And he had gone up in life much the way a monkey climbs, by shifts and scrambles and prehensile hoists with frequent falls. It was an ill turn of fortune that sent him to America in the first place. He had been managing a glass factory at Irkutsk, Siberia, where the endless caravans of fur traders passed. Born at Kargopol, East Russia, in 1747, he had drifted to Moscow, set up in a shop for himself at twenty-four, failed in business, and emigrated to Siberia at thirty-five. Tales of profit in the fur trade were current at Irkutsk. Tired of stagnating in what was an absolutely safe but unutterably monotonous life, Baranof left the factory and invested all his savings in the fur trade to the Indians of northern Siberia and Kamchatka. For some years all went well. Baranof invested deeper, borrowing for his ventures. Then the Chukchee Indians swooped down on his caravans, stampeded the pack horses, scuttled the goods, and Baranof was a bankrupt. The rival fur companies on the west coast of America were now engaged in the merry game of cutting each other's throats—literally and without restraint. A strong hand was needed—a hand that could weld the warring elements into one, and push Russian trade far down from Alaska to New Spain, driving off the field those foreigners whose relentless methods—liquor, bludgeon, musket—were demoralizing the Indian sea-otter hunters.

Destitute and bankrupt, Baranof was offered one-sixth of the profits to become governor of the chief Russian company. On August 10, 1790, about the same time that John Jacob Astor also embarked in the fur trade that was to bring him in contact with the Russians, Baranof sailed to America.

Fifty-two men the ragamuffin crew numbered, exiles, convicts, branded criminals, raggedly clad and ill-fed, sleeping wherever they could on the littered and vermin-infested decks; for what did the lives of a convict crew matter? Below decks was crammed to the water-line with goods for trade. All thought for furs, small care for men; and a few days out from port, the water-casks were found to be leaking so badly that allowance of drinking water was reduced; and before the equinoctial gales, scurvy had already disabled the crew. Baranof did not turn back, nor allow the strong hand of authority to relax over his men as poor Bering had. He ordered all press of sail, and with the winds whistling through the rigging and the little ship straining to the smashing seas, did his best to outspeed disease, sighting the long line of surf-washed Aleutian Islands in September, coasting from headland to headland, keeping well offshore for fear of reefs till the end of the month, when compelled to turn in to the mid-bay of Oonalaska for water. There was no ignoring the danger of the landing. A shore like the walls of a giant rampart with reefs in the teeth of a saw, lashed to a fury by beach combers, offered poor escape from death by scurvy. Nevertheless, Baranof effected anchorage at Koshigin Bay, sent the small boats ashore for water, watched his chance of a seaward breeze, and ran out to sea again in one desperate effort to reach Kadiak, the headquarters of the fur traders, before winter. Outside the shelter of the harbor, wind and seas met the ship. She was driven helpless as a chip in a whirlpool straight for the granite rocks of the shore, where she smashed to pieces like the broken staves of a dry water-barrel. Led by the indomitable Baranof, who seemed to meet the challenge of the very elements, the half-drowned crew crawled ashore only to be ordered to save the cargo now rolling up in the wave wash.

When darkness settled over the sea on the last night of September, Baranof was in the same predicament as Bering—a castaway for the winter on a barren island. Instead of sinking under the redoubled blows of an adverse fate, the little Russian rebounded like a rubber ball. A messenger and some Indians were at once despatched in a skin boat to coast from island to island in an effort to get help from Kadiak. Meanwhile Baranof did not sit lamenting with folded hands; and well that he did not; for his messengers never reached Kadiak.

Holes were at once scooped out of the sand, and the caves roofed over with the remnants of the wreck. These underground huts on an island destitute of wood were warmer than surface cabins, and better withstood the terrible north winds that swept down from the Arctic with such force that for two months at a time the men could go outside only by crawling under shelter of the boulders. Ammunition was distributed to the fifty castaways; salmon bought from the Indians, whom Baranof's fair treatment won from the first; once a week, rye meal was given out for soup; and for the rest, the men had to depend on the eggs of sea-birds, that flocked over the precipitous shores in myriads, or on the sea-lions roaring till the surf shook on the rocky islets along the shore.

If there is one characteristic more than another that proves a man master of destiny, it is ability not only to meet misfortune but to turn it to advantage when it comes. While waiting for the rescue that never came, Baranof studied the language of the Aleuts, sent his men among them to learn to hunt, rode out to sea in their frail skin boats lashed abreast to keep from swamping during storm, slept at night on the beach with no covering but the overturned canoes, and, sharing every hardship, set traps with his own hands. When the weather was too boisterous for hunting, he set his people boiling salt from sea-water to dry supplies of fish for the summer, or replenishing their ragged clothes by making coats of birds' skin. The last week before Easter, provisions were so low the whole crew were compelled to indulge in a Lenten fast; but on Easter Monday, behold a putrid whale thrown ashore by the storm! The fast was followed by a feast. The winds subsided, and hunters brought in sea-lions.

It was quite apparent now no help was coming from Kadiak. Baranof had three large boats made of skin and wreckage. One he left with the men, who were to guard the remnants of the cargo. A second he despatched with twenty-six men. In the third he himself embarked, now in a raging fever from the exposure of the winter. A year all but a month from the time he had left Asia, Baranof reached Three Saints, Kadiak, on June 27, 1791.

Things were black enough when Baranof landed at Kadiak. The settlement of Three Saints had been depending on the supplies of his wrecked ship; and when he arrived, himself in need, discontent flared to open mutiny. Five different rival companies had demoralized the Indians by supplying them with liquor, and egging them on to raid other traders. Southward, toward Nootka, were hosts of foreign ships—Gray and Kendrick and Ingraham from Boston, Vancouver from England, Meares from

East India, Quadra from New Spain, private ventures outfitted by Astor from New York. If Russia were to preserve her hunting-grounds, no time should be lost.

Baranof met the difficulties like a commander of guerilla warfare. Brigades were sent eastward to the fishing-ground of Cook's Inlet for supplies. Incipient mutiny was quelled by sending more hunters off with Ismyloff to explore new sea-otter fields in Prince William Sound. As for the foreign fur traders, he conceived the brilliant plan of buying food from them in exchange for Russian furs and of supplying them with brigades of Aleut Island hunters to scour the Pacific for sea-otter from Nootka and the Columbia to southern California. This would not only add to stores of Russian furs, but push Russian dominion southward, and keep other nations off the field. . . .

All fear of rivalry among the Russians had been removed by the union of the different companies in 1799. Baranof pulled his forces together for the master stroke that was to establish Russian dominion on the Pacific. This was the removal of the capital of Russian America farther south.

On the second week of April, 1799, with two vessels, twenty-two Russians, and three hundred and fifty canoes of Aleut fur hunters, Baranof sailed from Prince William Sound for the southeast. Pause was made early in May opposite Kyak—Bering's old landfall—to hunt sea-otter. The sloops hung on the offing, the hunting brigades, led by Baranof in one of the big skin canoes, paddling for the surf wash and kelp fields of the boisterous, rocky coast, which sea-otter frequent in rough weather. Dangers of the hunt never deterred Baranof. The wilder the turmoil of spray and billows, the more sea-otter would be driven to refuge on the kelp fields. Cross tides like a whirlpool ran on this coast when whipped by the winds. Not a sound from the sea-otter hunters! Silently, like sea-birds glorying in the tempest, the canoes bounded from crest to crest of the rolling seas, always taking care not to be caught broadsides by the smashing combers, or swamped between waves in the churning seas. How it happened is not known, but somehow between wind and tide-rip, thirty of the canoes that rode over a billow and swept down to the trough never came up. A flaw of wind had caught the mountain billows; the sixty hunters went under. From where he was, Baranof saw the disaster, saw the terror of the other two hundred men, saw the rising storm, and at a glance measured that it was farther back to the sloops than on towards the dangerous shore. The sea-otter hunt was forgotten in the impending catastrophe to the entire brigade. Signal and shout confused in the thunder of the surf ordered the men to paddle for their lives inshore. Night was coming on. The distance was longer than Baranof had thought, and it was dark before the brigades landed, and the men flung themselves down, totally exhausted, to sleep on the drenched sands.

Barely were the hunters asleep when the shout of Kolosh Indians from the forests behind told of ambush. The mainland hostiles resenting this invasion of their hunting-fields, had watched the storm drive the canoes to land. On one side was the tempest, on the other the forest thronged with warriors. The Aleuts lost their heads and dashed for hiding in the woods, only to find certain death. Baranof and the Russians with him fired off their muskets till all powder was used. Then they shouted in the Aleut dialect for the hunters to embark. The sea was the lesser danger. By morning the brigades had joined the sloops on the offing. Thirteen more canoes had been lost in the ambush.

Such was the inauspicious introduction for Baranof to the founding of the new Russian fort [Archangel] at Sitka or Norfolk Sound. . . .

All went well as long as Baranof was on the ground. Sea-otter were obtained for worthless trinkets. Sentries paraded the gateway; so Baranof sailed back to Kadiak. The Kolosh or Sitkan tribes had only bided their time. That sleepy summer day of June, 1802, when the slouchy Siberian convicts were off guard and Baranof two thousand miles away, the Indians fell on the fort and at one fell swoop wiped it out. Up at Kadiak honors were showering on the little governor. Two decorations of nobility he had been given by 1804; but his grief over the loss of Sitka was inconsolable. "I will either die or restore the fort!" he vowed, and with the help of a Russian man-of-war sent round the world, he sailed that summer into Sitka Sound. The Indians scuttled their barricade erected on the site of the present Sitka. Here the fort was rebuilt and renamed New Archangel—a fort worthy in its palmy days of Baranof's most daring ambitions. Sixty Russian officers and eight hundred white families lived within the walls, with a retinue of two or three thousand Indian otter hunters cabined along the beach. There was a shipyard. There was a foundry for the manufacture of the great brass bells sold for chapels in New Spain. There were archbishops, priests, deacons, schools. At the hot springs twenty miles away, hospitals and baths were built. A library and gallery of famous paintings were added to the fort, though Baranof complained it would have been wiser to have physicians for his men. For the rest of Baranof's rule, Sitka became the great rendezvous of vessels trading on the Pacific. Here Baranof held sway like a potentate, serving regal feasts to all visitors with the pomp of a little court, and the barbarity of a wassailing mediæval lord.

But all this was not so much fireworks for display. Baranof had his motive. To the sea-captains who feasted with him and drank themselves torpid under his table, he proposed a plan—he would supply the Aleut hunters for them to hunt on shares as far south as southern California. Always, too, he was an eager buyer of their goods, giving them in exchange sealskins from the Seal Islands. Boston vessels were the first to enter partnership with Baranof. Later came Astor's captains from New York, taking sealskins in trade for goods supplied to the Russians.

How did Baranof, surrounded by hostile Indians, with no servants but Siberian convicts, hold his own single-handed in American wilds? Simply by the power of his fitness, by vigilance that never relaxed, by despotism that was by turns savage and gentle, but always paternal, by the fact that his brain and his brawn were always more than a match for the brain and brawn of all the men under him. . . .

To pass judgment on Baranof's life would be a piece of futility. His life, like the lives of all those Pacific coast adventurers, stands or falls by what it was, not what it meant to be; by what it did, not what it left undone; and what Baranof left was an empire half the size of Russia. That his country afterward lost that empire was no fault of his. Like all those Vikings of the North Pacific, he was essentially a man *who did things,* not a theorizer on how things ought to be done, not a slug battening on the things other men have done.

19 / SEWARD'S FOLLY

Russian expansion in those days was less menacing than it appeared, for it lacked the backbone of government initiative and support. As the American press recalled in 1958, on the day after the United States Senate voted to admit Alaska to statehood:

> Russia's pioneers were in Alaska more than thirty years before the thirteen American colonies rebelled against the rule of England's King George III. They were hunting sea otters off the California coast when no white man had ventured west of the Missouri River. They were in the Hawaiian Islands while the United States was still licking the wounds of the War of 1812.

Yet the Russians "merely marked time" in Alaska and California, while Americans "pushed relentlessly westward" until Russia could do little more than withdraw gracefully and recognize "the manifest destiny of America." Recalling the dreams and schemes of Rezanov and his associates, the American press commented:

> These men were empire builders denied their tools, architects of expansion whose plans died on the drawing board. Had their visions and energies been

Alexandre Tarsaïdzé, *Czars and Presidents: The Story of a Forgotten Friendship* (New York: Ivan Obolensky, Inc., 1958), pp. 235-41. Reprinted with permission of Alexandre Tarsaïdzé.

shared in the courts of the tsars in St. Petersburg, Alaska might yet belong to Russia; Northern California, Oregon, and Washington might today be under the hammer and sickle.*

A number of factors had brought the Russian government to the decision to sell its American possessions: the commercial failure of the Russian-American Company; the government's inability to defend the colonies from foreign attack; fear that the British, Russia's major rivals, might take Alaska, and Russian preference to see Alaska, if it could not be kept, in what then seemed friendly American hands; the adverse effect that Russian entrenchment on the American continent was having on diplomatic and commercial relations with the United States; the desire to strengthen the latter to the disadvantage of Great Britain while feeding Anglo-American rivalry with the sale of Alaska; and a shift of interest back to the Asian continent.

The sale was negotiated on American initiative. During the Crimean War Senator William McKendry Gwin of California and Secretary of State William L. Marcy had inquired whether Russia might sell her colonies in America. Though the Russian Minister had replied at the time that his country "never had such intentions," the Crimean War, which laid bare Russian weakness, and the zealous activity of Secretary of State William H. Seward, "a man of keen but sometimes wayward imagination," paved the way for the transaction. Alexandre Tarsaïdzé, an American author born in Imperial Russia, traces the peculiar steps Eduard de Stoekl, the Russian Minister to the United States, had to take in Washington to persuade the Senate to ratify "Seward's Folly" and to acquire for a relative pittance the territory that in our day was to form the fiftieth state of the Union.

Stoekl arrived in New York on February 1, 1867, where he was stricken ill and in bed for six weeks. The time was not wasted, however, as he used it to drop hints and spread rumors that Russia was considering the sale of Alaska. He was aided by several other events. For nearly a year pressure had been exerted on the Johnson Administration by the Pacific Coast settlements to secure trading rights in Alaska, or, failing in that, to purchase the territory. Also, a group of Californians, aware that the Russian-American Company lease would expire in June, 1867, had conceived the idea of forming a company to take over the charter on a twenty-five year lease. Moreover, the citizens of the Washington Territory had requested the United States government to attempt to obtain Alaskan fishing rights and privileges for them.

Secretary Seward took up the various proposals with Stoekl. Stoekl

* *The Tallahassee Democrat,* July 1, 1958, p. 7.

replied that the Russian Government must refuse them. "Very well," said Seward. "Will Russia sell the whole territory?"

"Such a solution might offer advantages to both Russia and the United States," replied Stoekl.

Seward announced that he would take the matter up with President Johnson.

The President, who was not enthusiastic, agreed to leave the matter to his Cabinet. On their urgent advice, he authorized Seward to negotiate. A few days later Seward and Stoekl met and proceeded directly to the matter of price. Seward offered five million, which Stoekl refused. "Five and a half million," said Seward. "That's our final offer!"

"I'm afraid I couldn't consider less than seven million," replied Stoekl, who later that same day made out a report to his government that negotiations had begun and that he had high hopes of obtaining $6,000,-000, a million more than he had been instructed to obtain.

But as Seward continued to reveal eagerness in subsequent interviews, Stoekl decided he could risk holding to his $7,000,000 declaration. Seward came up to it, a little at a time, complaining bitterly that he was exceeding his instructions and would probably never be able to get it approved by Congress. Stoekl was aware that there was truth in this, because Seward was regarded as a crack-pot by many Senators and Representatives. He cautioned Seward, therefore, that if they did reach an agreement, it would be better to have a member of the Senate claim the initiative for having made the purchase. Congress would then be more kindly disposed. Seward, however, refused to consider such a thing. It was his duty as United States Secretary of State to carry out the negotiations, and he had no intention of being stripped of the honor of presenting the Nation with a new important territory.

The next day, Stoekl cabled the joyful news to St. Petersburg that the United States had agreed to pay seven million dollars. Chancellor Gorchakov, seeing that the United States was anxious to acquire Alaska, or at least that Seward was, decided to try to tempt the United States Government into taking over the debts of the Russian-American Company, to have the money deposited in London, and to pay the incidental gold-exchange fees.

But this time Seward balked. Seven million had been the price, and the United States had met it. "I consider the price too high as it is," said Seward. "I have gone far beyond the wishes of my Government in order to prevent unnecessary bickering. But I will not for one moment entertain any suggestion of taking over the obligations incurred by the chartered company. And my Government will not clear the transaction in London. We had our bellyfull of London in the late war."

Stoekl, who personally felt that his task of trying to wheedle a few more concessions was unpleasant and unfair, agreed to drop these. Seward then admitted that there might be some justice in the Russian Government's objection to paying exchange fees, and said that his government would add a couple of hundred thousand dollars to cover it. Thus the final figure of $7,200,000 was reached, the price for Alaska "free and unencumbered by any reservations, franchises, etc."

It is small wonder that the world, to this day, believes that when the United States deals with European diplomats it is like a sheep going to the shearing. It may seem strange in the light of Alaska's present value that there could have been so much discussion over the purchase of a vast land at two cents an acre—though no one then knew the actual acreage of Alaska. But it was really much more strange that Congress ratified the purchase, and in four hurried days. The ratification of "Seward's Icebox" took place in a kind of hands-thrown-in-the-air manner, with Congress playing the role of a resigned father paying the gambling bills of an irresponsible son. . . .

Most Americans feel that the Russians were "out-foxed," that they did not have accurate knowledge of the wealth of Alaska. The fact is that both the Russian Government and the directors of the Russian-American Company were aware of the extreme richness of Alaskan mineral deposits.

As early as 1848 a mining engineer by the name of Doroshin had discovered deposits there of limestone, marble, graphite, coal, and gold. In 1855, a vein of gold was opened and a small shipment sent to San Francisco. But the Russians had no way of exploiting these resources. Having at their disposal insufficient ships, money, and trained engineers, both the Russian Government and the Russian-American Company had no choice but to remain silent about their Alaskan treasure trove, any hint of which would "bring not only an army of foreigners with shovels, but an army of enemy soldiers." Had Alaska still been a possession of Russia at the time of the Klondike gold-rush, the horde of Americans who swept north would have either driven the Russians out or caused such friction as to make a war inevitable between the two countries.

A Soviet Marxist historian analyzes the situation fairly accurately: "The Czar of Russia knew perfectly well what he was selling, and the U.S. knew just as well what they were buying." This should perhaps be amended by adding that at least those Americans who wanted to buy Alaska knew what they were buying.

Seward and Stoekl reached an agreement just as Congress was on the verge of its annual spring recess. Seward, who knew that on such occasions Congress was prone to passing bills and treaties which they did not like in order to get away from frenetic Washington, was so anxious to have the sale ratified by the Emperor and ready for Congress at this propitious moment, that he told Stoekl to cable the draft of the treaty to St. Petersburg at America's expense, a mere $9000. On Friday evening, March 29th, Stoekl went to Mr. Seward's residence where he found him playing whist with his family.

"I have a dispatch from my government," he said. "The Emperor gives his consent. Tomorrow, if you like, I will come to the Department."

"Tomorrow?" said Seward. "Why wait until tomorrow?"

"But the Department is closed. You have no clerks, and my secretaries are scattered about town."

Seward called for his hat and coat. "You muster your Legation," he said. "You'll find me waiting at the Department at midnight!"

At four o'clock on the morning of March 30, 1867, the treaty lay on Mr. Seward's desk—signed, sealed, and ready for delivery to the Senate.

The Senate at first refused to have anything to do with a measure sponsored by the Johnson Administration. It required all the power and prestige that Senator Sumner possessed to keep the debate open until there was some chance of success. Sumner personally did not care about Alaska, but as Chairman of the Senate Foreign Relations Committee, he supported the purchase partly for Seward's sake, and partly to cement Russian-American relations. Then, as the pressure mounted, Sumner finally urged Stoekl to withdraw the treaty. He feared that it would not be approved and that it might cause political damage to his own career. Stoekl refused. "The honor of the United States is involved, for it was not Russia who took the initiative," said Stoekl. "Refusal of the Senate to ratify a treaty which my Government made in good faith can only be regarded as an insult."

Sumner returned in despair to the floor of the Senate. Then, without warning, the Senate opposition vanished, and the treaty was ratified on April 4th by the comfortable majority of 37 to 2. This feat of magic has always been graciously attributed to Sumner's oratorical powers. But in 1912 Professor William A. Dunning accidentally discovered among the papers of President Johnson a memorandum that quoted Seward to the effect that the Russian Envoy, Stoekl, had paid fairly large sums to important Washington figures—to Thaddeus Stevens, $10,000; to Nathaniel Banks, Chairman of the House Foreign Relations Committee, $8,000; to John Farney, $30,000; to R. J. Walker and F. P. Stanton, $20,000 each.

Other evidence reveals that Stoekl reported to his Government that the greater part of the $200,000 which had been added to the sale price of Alaska had been used for "secret expenses." Also, Riggs Bank paid to Mr. Stoekl during this crucial period various sums in gold—$26,000; $18,000; $35,000; $45,000; and $41,000. In his request to be transferred, Stoekl wrote, "I urgently need a rest. Do not tell me to stay here in Washington because there is no other post to give me. Give me a chance to breathe for a while an atmosphere purer than that of Washington— and after that do whatever you wish with me."

In the House of Representatives, where no one knew anything about Alaska and no one wanted to, the margin of approval of the purchase was narrower. One Congressman made the comment, "That Alaska was created for *some* purpose I have little doubt. But our information is so limited that conjectures can assign *no* use to it, unless it is to demonstrate the folly which those in authority are capable of in the acquisition of useless territory." Another quoted the comment of Captain Gordon, "I would not give the most barren hills of Scotland for all I see around me."

Despite opposition in the Senate and the House, in the press and public opinion, ratification came with unparalleled speed. Little more than a fortnight passed between the first Stoekl-Seward interview and the final action of Congress. In its celerity this peaceful exchange of territory is without parallel in history. It was the first considerable part of the vast Russian Empire ever to be alienated permanently and voluntarily. Moreover, it was the first acceptance of sovereignty by the United States over any territory separated geographically from the rest of the nation. Without doubt, had it not been the current belief of most Congressmen that Canada, too, would soon be annexed, the treaty would never have been ratified.

No one understood the tremendous change in American foreign policy that the acquisition of Alaska portended. From this moment on, American hands stretched farther and farther beyond their native shores— Hawaii, the Philippines, the Canal Zone, the Virgin Islands, Guam, Puerto Rico, Yap and other bits here and there, until finally the United States even laid claim to part of Antarctica. . . .

Only the firmness and absolute power of Alexander II made possible the peaceful sale of Alaska. There was bitter opposition in Russia, particularly within the Russian-American Company. Admiral Zavoiko, the hero of Petropavlovsk, was obliged to retire from service and was banished to his estate for his refusal, as a director of the Company, to sign the release papers. The last Governor of Alaska, Prince Maxutov, was equally adamant. Baron Theodore Osten-Sacken, Russian Consul General in New York, protested the decision of the Emperor. The Russian press was indignant.

Indeed, it was a remarkable transaction—a nation that did not want to sell, selling to a nation that did not want to buy. Yet with this single event, the balance of power triangle of Russia, Britain, and the United States in the Pacific was destroyed, and overnight the United States assumed the paramount strategic position, the full significance of which may not even now be realized.

20 / ON SAKHALIN

Russian withdrawal from the Western Hemisphere did not imply a similar retreat in Asia. On the contrary, as suggested already, Russia had cut loose her ties with America, the better to be able to concentrate on the Asian continent. "Our interests lie on the Asiatic coast, and we should direct our energy thither," Stoekl, who had consummated the sale of Alaska, wrote to Foreign Minister Prince Aleksandr Mikhailovich Gorchakov in 1859.

> In that area we are in our own territory and in a position to exploit the production of a vast and wealthy region. We shall take part in the extraordinary activity that is being developed in the Pacific, our establishments will vie with similar establishments of other nations, and, in view of the solicitude which our august monarch has given to the coastal region of Amur, we must not miss the opportunity to attain in this vast ocean the high position of which Russia is deserving.*

The importance of the Amur River as an artery of eastward expansion in the days before the Trans-Siberian Railway was so great that it was natural that those favoring a strong foreign policy should clamor for Russian exploration and control of this river. But the government did not wish to endanger trade with China, and tried to restrain the zeal of its more restless subjects. These would not be restrained, however, and presented the government with faits accomplis, which the latter neither welcomed nor undid. The machinations of Captain Gennadii Nevelskoi, a naval officer of independent character and fervor, and of his superior,

N. V. Busse, *Ostrov Sakhalin: Ekspeditsiia 1853-54 gg.* (Sakhalin Island: the expedition of 1853-54), (St. Petersburg, 1872), pp. 21-25. Translated by G. A. Lensen.

* S. B. Okun, *The Russian-American Company*, p. 245.

Nikolai Muravev (later known as Muravev-Amurskii), the governor general of Siberia, to secure the Amur region remained typical of the Russian thrust east until the late nineteenth century, with a reluctant government being swept to empire on the coattails of energetic individuals.

News of the outfitting of Commodore Matthew C. Perry's American expedition to Japan smoothed the path of Governor General Muravev in selling to the Russian government Captain Gennadii Nevelskoi's plans for the occupation of strategic points on Sakhalin, which lay athwart the Amur estuary. On April 23, 1853, Nicholas I ordered the Russian-American Company to occupy the island. Entrusted with the venture by Muravev, Nevelskoi brazenly commandeered government vessels and the services of Major Nikolai Busse, who had been sent to him merely to deliver a contingent of men and supplies. Impressed against his will as commandant of Sakhalin, the polished St. Petersburg officer left a remarkable account of the occupation of the island. As Busse predicted, the Russian expedition to the island was to embarrass Vice-Admiral Putiatin in his negotiations in Japan and was soon to be recalled. Not until 1875 was Russia to gain all of Sakhalin, the southern portion in exchange for the northern Kuril Islands.

The use of the Russian bear as a bugbear with which to frighten recalcitrant negotiators into one's arms is a time-honored Western tactic. But as the following excerpt from Busse's diary shows, it is a technique no different from that of Russia, which professed to occupy Sakhalin in order to protect its Ainu and Japanese inhabitants from the Americans.

Rounding Cape Aniwa, we headed directly for Cape Kril'on, where Orlov was supposed to be waiting for us. As we traversed Aniwa Bay we were constantly surrounded by whales and whole schools of different species of fishes. It was this wealth of fish of Aniwa Bay that had attracted the Japanese, whose main food is fish, like beef in our country, which the Japanese do not use at all. When we crossed Aniwa Bay the weather was excellent at sea, but the shores remained covered with fog. . . . Toward the evening of the 18th [of September, 1853] we reached Cape Kril'on. Since it was free of fog from the northern tip for a stretch of eleven minutes, he would have heard the nine shots fired by us as prearranged. But there was no reply, and, therefore, on the 19th we used a mild head wind to tack toward the Japanese settlements. When complete darkness had descended, the captain of the vessel espied something blackish nearby, before the very bow of the vessel. Rushing on deck everyone agreed that this was land, and we cast anchor at once. We soon found that the coast was really nearby. The noise of the anchor chain must have awakened the Japanese. Lights appeared on shore about three miles from us, and the coastline loomed up. Nevelskoi posted a guard of twelve sailors on the ship with orders to watch the shore and hail any boat they might see. During supper there was argument and laughter. Some thought one thing, others another, but all looked forward with pleasure and impatience to meeting the Japanese. In the morning the ship was to weigh anchor and draw closer to the settlement, in case the Japanese had cannons and, as was their habit, should take it into their heads to meet the boats, on which Nevelskoi and I planned to go ashore, with hostility. Then the ship's battery could cover our landing with its fire. At dawn we weighed anchor. We stopped directly opposite the settlement Usunnoi (whose name I learned later). To its right two more settlements were visible; one had many buildings, and we decided therefore that it must be the main Japanese settlement. We dropped anchor about two miles from shore and prepared to land.

It was eleven o'clock. The weather was excellent. We let down two rowboats and a canoe. Nevelskoi and I, five oarsmen, and noncommissioned officer Telenev went in the first boat. We hid our guns on the bottom of the boat and took along various trifles as gifts. Lieutenant Boshniak and four oarsmen followed in the second boat. The canoe traveled alongside the rowboats, in case it would be necessary to send to the ship for something. The captain had orders in the event that we hoisted a flag to lower immediately the longboat and another boat, on which Lieutenant Rudanovskii would follow ashore with twenty armed sailors. Should a shot be fired, the ship was to weigh anchor and drawing up to about five and a half fathoms of water was to fire broadsides against the settlement. The flag of war was hoisted on the ship. When the boats pushed off, much commotion could be seen on shore. The inhabitants were hastening to the settlement to which we were going. Some seven hundred feet from shore our boats ran onto sandbanks. The savages who had gathered on shore darted into the water and ran toward us shouting and waving wooden brooms. In a minute we were surrounded on all sides. The savages gestured that they wished to receive us friendly. Some of them were uttering the word "America." We began to explain to them that we were Russians, not Americans. Nevelskoi conveyed with gestures that the Americans wanted to come to Sakhalin and that, therefore, we wanted to settle at their place to protect them from the Americans. They seemed to understand us. We produced the trinkets we had brought and began to hand them out as presents. Bronze and steel objects—small knives, scissors, little buttons, and so on—they liked very much; our cheap tobacco, on the other hand, they took reluctantly. After some time several Japanese came up to us. Their faces differed sharply from those of the Ainus.

The Japanese look somewhat like the caricatures on tea-shop signboards, only their eyes are not pulled upward so much, and they do not wear any mustaches. They shave the hair on the head, leaving a narrow strip of long hair from the back of the neck to the temples. The hair is gathered on the crown into a little braid . . . laid forward across the shaven head. . . . Their movements and manners are ridiculously feminine. The Ainus, on the other hand, are a goodlooking people. Their dark faces are masculine. They shave the black bushy hair on the front of the head, bobbing it like our peasants in the back. Their beards are full and long. Their clothing consists of robes and dogskin furcoats, with the hair facing outward. Their feet are clad in fur boots, also with the hair on the outside.

We offered some things to the Japanese who had come up to the boats. At first they did not dare to accept anything, but in the end gave in. From them we learned that their superior was at the large settlement. Getting off the sandbank we proceeded to this settlement, taking the boats all the way up to shore. The Ainus also went to Tomari and surrounded us again as we landed. A Japanese stepped from the settlement to meet us. Nevelskoi announced that he wished to talk with the superior and invited him to come to the shore. The Japanese on his part gestured that we go into the settlement. After due deliberation we decided to accept his invitation, because the Japanese seemed to have neither fortifications nor troops and thus would not be able to play on us the sort of trick they had played on Golovnin. We walked along the landing, where many flatbottomed boats lay, then turned away from shore and climbing to somewhat higher ground saw several buildings of Japanese architecture, scattered on the hillocks and in the narrow dale between them. The Japanese was leading us to the largest building. A whole crowd of Ainus was following us. As we entered the building, which looked like a menagerie, we saw seven Japanese elders of Sakhalin Island. They sat, their legs pressed under them, on straw mats, laid out on three sides of the square fireplace, in which a small fire was burning. The senior official, who was extremely fat, held the position of president. He had one sword stuck in his belt, the other lying next to him. The other six Japanese were seated, three to his right, three to his left. On the fourth side, opposite the senior official, mats had been placed for us. We lay down and began to communicate our intention of staying on Sakhalin together with the Japanese. The whole shed became crowded with Ainus. The remaining Japanese, some fifteen persons, sat down at random on a raised part of the floor not far from us. It was ludicrous to watch how Nevelskoi tried to explain to the Japanese that the Russians wanted to live in friendship with them and [with] the Ainus, and that they [the Russians] were to occupy Sakhalin to defend it from the Americans. When it seemed that the senior official and his comrades had under-stood what it was all about, we took out gifts, consisting of cloth, woolen kerchiefs, scarfs, steel products, and buttons. As we distributed these things among the Japanese, they examined them with curiosity and put them next to the senior official. Meanwhile we were served cooked fish in earthenware cups, similar to our slop bowls. The Japanese showed us how to manipulate chopsticks, which they use instead of knives and forks. We had brought along bottles of rum, of white wine, and of lemon-ade. We poured some for the Japanese. It was apparent that they liked our wines. It was going onto three, and we still had to find a place for settlement. I proposed to terminate the meeting with the Japanese to go and survey the coast. Nevelskoi began to embrace and kiss the Japanese, gesturing that the Russians would live with the Japanese in friendship; that the cannons had been brought to keep the Americans off Karafuto (the Japanese name for Sakhalin). The Japanese accepted these caresses very coldly, without comment. We got back into our boats and rode away to survey the shore to the east of Tomari.

21 / RUSSIANS ABROAD

The natives of Siberia and Alaska had neither the political organization and sense of unity nor the level of civilization to withstand the Russians. Militarily superior, the latter were usually able to dictate their terms without resort to arms. But the close association of Russians and natives in negotiation, work, and daily life left its mark on all concerned. Individually the Russian frontiersmen and settlers were simple folk, not the bearers of a superior culture. As they settled in the wilderness, they "went native" in many ways.

In their eastward expansion the Russians were aided by the general (though by no means universal) tendency to adjust to local conditions and to associate with the natives socially. The following brief excerpts from the book of an American writer and the memoirs of a Russian admiral give glimpses of Russian fraternization in America and Japan.

Japan, it should be added, had been reopened in 1854 by the pressure of the United States, Russia, and other Western powers. To Russia, with its frozen and inadequately furnished harbors, the ports of Japan were a welcome haven of refuge. There, in the benign climate of Nagasaki, they established a naval hospital and lived on shore in the little settlement of Inasa during their annual visits to Nagasaki Bay. The description of life at Inasa, translated below, dates back to 1880.

In America

The village swarmed with children, dozens of whom the Russian hunters had begotten of the Aleut women. Among those waiting Botcharov's safe return, for instance, was his half-caste son Ignatii Dimitryevich.

The hunters took mates because the women were as essential to domestic economy as they were pleasant for creature comforts. No male fingers were capable of doing the intricate sewing necessary to make waterproof *mukluks,* seagoing *kamleikas,* or the extraordinary feather *parkas.* A few trifling gifts to the girl's father cemented the alliance. The women and men were generally faithful to their chosen mates. There was little trading around.

The trouble was the strong attachment ensuing between the hunters and their offspring. One of the best characteristics of the Russian heart is its warmth for children. Shelekhov had made an absolutely unbreakable rule that no children could be taken to Russia. In the Aleut code the child belongs to its mother, not its father. Forcibly taking one away caused great anger among the natives. Because of this many a hunter eligible to return home with Delarov in spring doubted if he would ever leave.

Delarov baptized them all, the old navigator Stepan Izmailov generally standing as godfather. They made few attempts, however, to induce the adult Aleuts to accept baptism. They argued that they had always got along without religion; why give them rules which they would only disobey? Besides, it made the Russians uncomfortable to sleep with baptized women; it somehow made a sin of one of the few real pleasures the country afforded.

In Japan

As you ride up to Inasa in a boat, your attention will be drawn to a cluster of several dozen boats at the pier. These are private "carriages," hired by the month by every officer for constant communication between his ship and the shore, where his "wife" lives in the country. Then, having gone ashore, you step into a village consisting of from forty to fifty small Japanese houses, spread out in a picturesque green grove at

Hector Chevigny, *Lord of Alaska: Baranov and the Russian Adventure* (New York: The Viking Press, Inc., 1943), p. 50. Reprinted with permission of the author and of the republishers, Binfords and Mort, of Portland, Oregon.

Admiral G. Tsyvinskii, *50 let v Imperatorskom flote* (Fifty Years in the Imperial Navy) (Riga: Orient, no date), pp. 49-50, translated by G. A. Lensen.

the foot of a mountain, on the upper plateau of which there has recently been established a Russian cemetery with a chapel and a guardhouse, in which a Japanese *bonze* lives. After 5 P.M., when duty has been finished on the ships and the officers have already gone ashore, life in Inasa is in full swing. Passing by the little houses, you chance upon touching scenes: in the opened rooms (the walls in the houses are slid apart) and on the verandas young husbands, changed to light kimonos, enjoy themselves with their "wives" and conscientiously spend their honeymoons. Here the officers pass the night if they do not have to stand watch during the night, and return aboard ship in the morning by about eight o'clock. When the officer does so, the wife accompanies him on the boat up to the ship itself. Returning home, the young wife usually goes to sleep and sleeps all day until the arrival of her husband. She does not have to keep house, as there are in Inasa for this purpose two restaurants, which feed all the wives. The restaurants are maintained by two well-known Japanese women—Oie-san and Omatsu-san, who in their time were "wives" of officers now already of senior rank. Having solid patrons, they no longer become wives themselves, but run their restaurants, and feed all officers' wives. They have a large staff of very young servants (*musume*), candidates for wives of newly arriving officers, seeking "marital" happiness. For the maintenance of a wife the officer paid at that time only forty yen (Japanese dollars) a month, and for the one family cottage he paid twenty yen. And so for sixty rubles [*sic*] the officer had a house and a wife. With the departure of the ship from Nagasaki the conjugality was usually dissolved, and the wives joined the reserves of one of these restaurants, if there did not turn up immediately a candidate to take over the house and wife of the departed officer.

INTRODUCTION

The second half of the nineteenth century saw a general intensification of Western pressure on the world beyond Europe. There were two basic reasons for this: firstly, a change in the character, demands, and power of imperialism, brought about by the Industrial Revolution; and secondly, a coincidental degeneration of the ruling dynasties which had outlived their vigor. China was a case in point. Except for the United States, which acquired no special spheres of influence in China although it sought to keep the door open to all parts of the empire, the Western powers demanded territorial and economic concessions which threatened to lead to a general partition of China. Russian imperialism was no "better" and no "worse" than the imperialism of the other powers, but it was different—different in that Russian pressure came by land, rather than by sea, and affected the outlying (non-Chinese) regions of the Middle Kingdom, rather than the heartland itself. The Russian impact on China was almost exclusively commercial and military (as had been the impact of earlier invaders from the north); it was not ideological or social, not so revolutionary as that of the more industrialized and politically advanced nations which approached China by sea. Like the Chinese the Russians had an autocratic form of government; like the Chinese the Russians—officers, officials, and intellectuals alike—had a disdain for traders and capitalists. Ceremony, propriety, and honor were all-important. Only in the twentieth century, with the upheaval during 1905 and the subsequent ideological ferment and change within Russia, was Russian influence to acquire a revolutionary character.

22 / THE IDEOLOGY OF RUSSIAN EXPANSION

British imperialism was given respectability by such talented spokesmen as Rudyard Kipling. There was something noble and admirable in the concept of the "white man's burden" in the context of the nineteenth century. France's Mission Civilisatrice and Germany's militant export of Kultur also struck responsive cords in the West. After all, President William McKinley regarded it as an American duty to Christianize and civilize the "little brown brothers" in the Philippines and Ambassador Walter Hines Page in London still explained the policy of the Wilson administration in Mexico in terms of "shooting men into self-government." Russian motivations and justifications were essentially the same. To Protestants who disliked the Orthodox faith and to those who regarded Russia as "backward," the civilizing influence of Russian expansion was questionable, while Western inability to read Russian gave to Russian policy an air of enigma.

The late Andrew Malozemoff, an American of Russian extraction, gives an able overview of the ideology of Russian expansion.

Tsars, responsible statesmen, and influential generals developed ideas of Russian economic and strategic needs; but it was the Slavophiles of the nineteenth century, representing a wide stratum of cultured society, who presented and propagated ideas of imperialistic expansion in the guise of a "holy mission." The Slavophiles varied in the scope and method of their exposition; among them were historians (K. Bestuzhev-Riumin, N. N. Strakhov), writers (A. S. Khomiakov, I. S. Aksakov), and even poets (A. V. Grigoriev). Consequently their ideas reached and influenced readers of various kinds. In general, the Slavophiles stressed the religious, racial, and cultural affinity between the Balkan peoples and the Russians, drawing upon ample historical evidence to show that the Balkan peoples would like to draw closer to Russia.

After the partial liberation of the Balkan Slavs (of Serbia and Bulgaria), by the Russo-Turkish War of 1877-1878, and particularly after the anti-Russian trend of events in Bulgaria in 1886-1888, the Slavophile movement began to lay less emphasis upon Pan-Slavism. A new school of thought arose in the 1880's which stressed the idea that Russian culture was in direct contrast to the culture of Europe and must therefore develop along its own social and political lines. From that position it was but one more step to claim that Russia, with a culture midway between the cul-

Andrew Malozemoff, *Russian Far Eastern Policy 1881-1904: With Special Emphasis on the Causes of the Russo-Japanese War* (Berkeley and Los Angeles, Calif.: University of California Press, 1958), pp. 41-50. Reprinted with permission of the University of California Press.

tures of Europe and that of the Orient, had a "historical mission" to spread western culture to the Orient. The extremists of this school of "Easterners" (*Vostochniki*) considered Russian culture more closely affiliated with that of the Orient than with that of Europe and felt that it was Russia's "historical mission" to merge with the Orient by incorporating it into the Russian Empire.

Precedent and past historical experience helped to promote this imperialistic idea. Korea had sought Russian protection and even the establishment of a Russian protectorate in the 1880's. In the same period, General M. N. Prjevalskii, the most noted and respected Russian explorer of territories adjacent to Russia's Asiatic frontiers, popularized the concept that the inhabitants of Mongolia and Sinkiang were eager to become Russian subjects. In 1887 he wrote:

> The nomad Mongols, the Dungans, that is, the Mussulman Chinese, and the inhabitants of Eastern [Chinese] Turkestan, especially the latter, are all more or less possessed with the idea of becoming subjects of the White Tsar, whose name, equally with that of the Dalai Lama, appears in the eyes of the Asiatic masses as surrounded with a halo of mystic might. These poor Asiatics look to the advance of the Russian power with the firm conviction that its advent is synonymous with the commencement of a happier era, a life of greater security for themselves.

Logically and honestly, the learned explorer took cognizance of the fact that this attitude in Chinese Turkestan was due to the maladministration of the Chinese officials and the severity of their recent reconquest of Sinkiang in contrast to the relatively just rule of the Russians in Russian Turkestan, which had been annexed more than twenty years before. Furthermore, he admitted that the Mongols, in making the choice of allegiance, would gravitate to Russia only because that choice would be "the lesser of two evils." Nevertheless, Prjevalskii's views offered sound argument for an aggressive policy in Asia.

Legal support for a policy of aggression was supplied in the same period by Professor F. F. Martens, the foremost Russian authority on international law and an adviser to the Foreign Office. In two pamphlets, *Russia and China* and *Russia and England in Central Asia,* he attempted to justify Russian conquests in central Asia and to prepare a similar justification for an aggressive policy toward China by advocating the principle that "international rights cannot be taken into account when dealing with semibarbarous peoples."

The concept of Russia as a cultural missionary (*Kulturträger*) in the Orient was clearly expressed by V. P. Vasil'ev, Russia's foremost and world-renowned Sinologue, in 1883 in a public lecture at the University of St. Petersburg. After exultingly approving Russian conquests in the Caucasus and the trans-Caspian region, Vasil'ev emphasized that in contrast to Europeans, Russians advanced in the East as "liberators" of peoples oppressed by "the tyranny of internecine strife and impotency"; and he concluded: "Would it not be rather a crime before humanity were we to renounce the sacred duties designated to us and refuse to aid the 'oppressed'?"

The ideology of Russian expansion toward the East thus had many interpretations. A. Brückner, one of Russia's leading historians, defended a view that the uninterrupted advance of Russia in Asia was a benefit to world civilization, and Vladimir Solov'ev, Russia's leading philosopher, in a strangely chauvinistic article written in 1890, maintained that Russia must advance in Asia in order to defend Europe against the "yellow power," and that inferior races must either submit to the superior ones or "disappear." The gradations of the imperialistic concept as propounded by the Vostochniki and their followers are many, and their tenets are sometimes bewildering. Because of their popularity and ubiquity in Russian cultural and official circles, the Vostochniki represented a powerful ideological support of renewed Russian interest in the Far East.

Probably the most influential early exponent of Russian expansion in Asia was Prince Esper Esperevich Ukhtomskii. His noble descent and enormous wealth assured him a prominent position in high society. As a publisher and editor of the St. Petersburg *News (Peterburgskie Vedomosti)* Ukhtomskii maintained a policy of printing liberal and at times radical views in curious juxtaposition with his own chauvinistic ideas. In 1889 he traveled in Russian central Asia as a member of the Bureau of Foreign Concessions and returned aghast at the Russians' lack of interest in their Asiatic possessions and their opportunities. He thereupon began to advocate Russian imperialism in the East.

In 1890-1891 Prince Ukhtomskii accompanied Tsarevich Nicholas on a voyage to the Far East in the capacity of tutor and lecturer on peoples and territories visited by the future monarch. On his return he wrote an account of that voyage which was published in de luxe editions in England, France, Germany, and Russia, possibly to propagandize the awakening of Russian interest in the Orient. Through the medium of his newspaper, pamphlets, and articles in European periodicals, Ukhtomskii propagated the already familiar theme that because of their kinship with the Orient the Russians would succeed in subjugating the East "by the secret powers of emotional sympathy." He expressed the quintessence of the ideology of the Vostochniki thus:

Asia—we have always belonged to it. We have lived its life and felt its interests. Through us the Orient has gradually arrived at consciousness of itself, at a superior life. . . . We have nothing to conquer. All these peoples of various races feel themselves drawn to us, and are ours, by blood, by tradition, and by ideas. We simply approach them more closely. This great and mysterious Orient is ready to become ours.

In June, 1904, when Russia was already suffering initial defeats at the hands of Japan, proving the inadequacy of her preparations for a grandiose imperialistic role in the Far East, Ukhtomskii broke out in expressions of blatant and unabashed chauvinism. He forecast that Russia would defeat Japan and compensate herself for the expenses of the war by taking a large section of China. This would lead to a Russo-Chinese war in which the Chinese would be conquered. The English would then intervene, and Russia would have to drive the English out of India.

Ukhtomskii had many critics who lampooned him with derisive remarks. He was labeled a "superpatriot" and a "faddist," and contemporary critics sarcastically attacked his "yellow Russia" (*zheltorossiia*). But despite his weakness for collecting Buddhist statues, his vague and bewildering expositions, and his occasional glaring errors in predictions, he was a practical statesman. He had traveled in and read widely about the Orient. He remained a close friend of Nicholas II and became an assistant to S. Iu. Witte, whom he greatly admired. He was a known proponent of the Russo-Chinese alliance which eventually materialized. In 1896 and again in 1900 he was entrusted with special secret missions to the Far East. In 1896 he became the first chairman of the Russo-Chinese Bank and a director of the Chinese Eastern Railway, agencies which were then the spearheads of a practical Russian policy of expansion in the Far East.

Until the beginning of the construction of the Trans-Siberian Railway, the Vostochniki were prominent only as theoreticians. The decision to construct the railroad opened an enormous range of real opportunities to the Vostochniki, who found an influential and unexpected protagonist in S. Iu. Witte, the able Russian Minister of Finance.

Witte rose from humble origins to a position of enormous power. He started as a clerk on the Odessa railroad at a salary of forty-five rubles a month and eventually was appointed to posts in which he disposed of almost half of the budget of the Russian government. He was a self-made man, struggling to the top by dint of his ambition, perseverance, keenness, and ability to make and utilize friends. Good fortune also played some part in his rise to power. He enjoyed the patronage of Alexander

III, although this came to him more as recognition of his services than as a mark of favoritism. Witte had had a limited education and was uncultured, but his keen interest in economic and cultural questions rapidly matured him and gained for him the friendship and admiration of Russia's leading businessmen and many statesmen. The noted American engineer and financial expert John Hays Hammond, whose personal dealings with many prominent men in all parts of the world qualified him to make comparisons, ranked Witte with Cecil Rhodes as a "constructive business genius, empire builder, and statesman." . . .

Witte showed no interest in the Far East before 1892. In his early years he was a Slavophile; later he became a "Westerner" in that he exhibited a keen desire to see Russia catch up with the industrial progress of a western Europe. However, after his appointment to the position of acting minister of communications (February 27, 1892) and acting minister of finance (September 11, 1892) his thoughts turned to the Far East and the benefits that could be derived by Russia from the national and international significance of the trans-Siberian railroad. At the time, this was an enormous undertaking for a backward industrial state. It fitted in with Witte's plan to encourage heavy industries. It promised to create an outlet for the grain of western Siberia and in many other ways strengthen the economic position of Russia.

But Witte saw far greater implications in the building of the railroad. In a report of November 18, 1892, on "Measures for the Construction of the Great Siberian Railroad" he described the basis for Russo-Chinese economic unity. He argued that the production of tea in India and Assam had undermined the Chinese tea trade, which in time would collapse in the face of this new competition. With the completion of the trans-Siberian railroad, rapid transit of Chinese tea to Europe would give China a new opportunity to export this product and at the same time permit Russia to compete with England in China in the sale of cotton, wool, and metal goods. The railroad would also permit Russia to maintain a fleet in the Far East which "could be considerably strengthened, and which in case of political complications in Europe or in the Asiatic East would acquire an especially important significance in dominating all commercial movements in the waters of the Pacific."

It has been suggested that Witte sponsored Russian interests in the Far East to avoid complications in the West and to secure a period of peace for Russia. But it seems more likely that Witte, often called an "opportunist," first saw in the construction of the trans-Siberian railroad a possible means of achieving his economic policies. In the period 1892-1903 he also continued to show interest in railroad developments in central Asia, in plans to open an ice-free port at Murmansk with a railroad connection with St. Petersburg, in the building of the naval port at Libau, in the creation of a large navy, and in other projects in line with the promotion of Russian heavy industry. . . .

To promote the progress of the trans-Siberian railroad Witte chose a powerful ally. In 1893, by a master stroke which greatly influenced his relations with the next ruler, Nicholas II, Witte persuaded Alexander III to appoint the Tsarevich president of the Control Committee of the Trans-Siberian Railway. The Tsar argued that the Tsarevich was too young and immature for such a post. However, the Tsarevich became the president of a committee created by Witte for the express purpose of "avoiding all barbed wires in relations with other ministers" in Witte's main enterprise, on which Witte was the authority and in which he was the "leading spirit." Furthermore, Nicholas when he became Tsar retained the presidency, in accordance with his own wish, and became directly affiliated with the Russian railroad penetration of Manchuria.

The character of Nicholas II and his role in determining the course of Russian policy is still obscure. Most of his private letters and annotations of official papers were too brief to reveal clearly his ideas on the affairs of state. Writers who have analyzed his character, with an attempt to be scrupulously fair, generally have portrayed him as being continually torn between an urge to accept the views of his advisers and a desire to assert his own views. This analysis may explain his unpredictable behavior in violation of Russia's international commitments, such as his sudden expression of friendship toward the German Emperor at the meeting at Björkö in 1905 and his unexplained, sporadic personal interference in Russian Far Eastern affairs.

Nicholas II lacked consistent determination and accepted the guidance of such dubious advisers as K. P. Pobedonostsev, E. E. Ukhtomskii, and his favorite uncle, the reactionary Grand Duke Sergei Alexandrovich, as well as of the more modern and practical Witte. Maturing under the influence of a sycophantic court, and urged toward the assertion of his own will in the affairs of state, the young Tsar grew impatient with the intelligent opposition which hindered his will. Nicholas II not only had a mind of his own but could claim to be an authority on the Far East by reason of his personal observations and impressions during the voyage of 1890-1891. It can hardly be asserted that the saber blow he received in an attempt on his life by a Japanese fanatic while in Japan passed without impression. Though the Russian government was satisfied with official apologies and the expressions of regret from the Japanese Imperial family for the unforeseen occurrence, the visit of the Tsarevich to Japan was hastily and impolitely concluded, and in later years Nicholas II carried a visible scar and suffered severe headaches as mementoes of the occasion.

The aggressive views of the early Vostochniki matured into a policy which received ministerial and imperial sanction under Nicholas II, without which it could not have attained fruition. Imperialism had become popular, and its aims seemed possible of attainment. An able observer of Russian affairs with understandable exaggeration and in a slightly humorous vein wrote in 1896: "There is not a graduate of the Corps de Pages, an Officer of the Guards, nor an employee of the Foreign Ministry, it is asserted, who is not firmly convinced that all Asia, including, of course, India, is part of Russia's birthright, and that the policy of the Tsardom should be shaped in accordance with these great expectations."

23 / RECOLLECTIONS OF AN AMUR COSSACK

The rôle of such eminent statesmen as Muravev and such noted naval officers as Nevelskoi in advancing the Russian flag has already been described. These men were, of course, the instigators, the planners and leaders, one may even say the driving force behind Russia's eastward expansion in the nineteenth century. But their success depended on the exertions and stamina of their subordinates. The following selection is taken from an eyewitness account of the dangers and hardships which confronted the common soldiers and settlers, who gave substance to the visions of their superiors.

1856. With the opening of navigation, an increased number of different vessels began to follow one another down the Amur River with provisions. They were navigated mostly by line soldiers and foot Cossacks. . . . In Mariinsk there was the headquarters of all the Amur forces. There were Cossack barracks, several small houses, and two small magazines. From Mariinsk I was . . . sent out on a boat with six Cossacks of the First Composite Troop . . . with mail. We were given . . . 100 silver rubles per person for the trip. Some two days before us the Thirteenth Line Battalion had left there on boats, under the command of Lieutenant Colonel Obleukhov. Toward the end of June or the beginning of July there were to depart from there too: half the First Composite Amur Foot Battalion and part of the Fourteenth Line Battalion, while the First Composite Amur Cossack Troop did not yet have instructions to return, though this was expected. We overtook the Thirteenth Battalion some

Roman K. Bogdanov, "Vospominaniia amurskago kazaka o proshlom, s 1849 po 1880 god" ("The Recollections of an Amur Cossack about the Past, from 1849 to 1880"), *Priamurskiia Vedomosti* (1900), No. 341, pp. 17-19, and No. 342, pp. 14-17. Translated by G. A. Lensen.

ten or thirteen miles above Mariinsk. The soldiers did not know at all how to tow and needlessly overexerted themselves, and thereby only exhausted themselves. . . .

The heat was terrible. All the provisions were spoiled. We ate only millet, buying it en route from the Goldi and the Manchurians. Arriving in Aigun with the thought of obtaining provisions, we were unable to purchase them from the inhabitants. I wanted to appear personally before their [Manchu Chinese] governor, but was not admitted. Our boat was taken away, the Cossacks and I were put into an abominable building, and a strong guard of almost thirty soldiers was mounted. They even wanted to tie us up, but among the guards there was found one who knew Tungus, which the Cossacks and I spoke a little; somehow we persuaded them not to bind us. We sat under this guard for almost twenty-four hours without any food or freedom. The day after our arrest there came up to the guardhouse an official, from among those who traveled along the Shilka and Amur for the inspection of the frontier and who had partaken in Ust-Strelka of the hospitality of my father's house, recognized me and ran to report to some colonel, who was in a position to beg the governor to condescend [to look into] our condition. About two hours after the departure of my acquaintance, some official, several soldiers, and my acquaintance appeared at the guardhouse. They ordered me to get dressed and to go to their governor. My acquaintance advised me to present several coins to the colonel and to give no less than twenty as a gift for the governor. When reaching the governor, I was to get down on my knees and bow, lest we be sent to Peking. There was nothing left to do, but to give in to circumstances. I handed ten silver coins to the official who had come after me. Upon coming to the governor, who was sitting with his legs folded under him, on his stove, I had to kneel and bow. My acquaintance, acting as interpreter, spoke at length. He too was kneeling and bowing to the authorities. Then he told me in Tungus that I should rise and hand the coins to the governor. When I had done so, the governor gestured that I sit beside him. Without much delay, he announced through my acquaintance that in return for the hospitality my father had shown his subordinates in Ust-Strelka, he acceded to my request for free passage along the Amur by boat and ordered that we be supplied with the necessary provisions. We received millet, pork, millet flour, and oil, and the governor had an official accompany us without charge. . . .

On the second day after leaving Aigun we came to the place where there is now a monument in commemoration of the first stopping of Count Muravev-Amurskii. Across from this place, on shore, in a tent, there lived the Captain of the Transbaikal forces, Travin, who had just arrived with several Cossacks from his unit. The place was called the Zeiskii Post. It was the duty of these Cossacks to guard the provisions, delivered there for the forces that were to return from the mouth of the Amur. According to Travin, a post had been established also at the mouth of the Kumara, my father having accompanied the Cossacks there to choose a site and establish the Kumarskii Post. We rested at Zeiskii Post for twenty-four hours and then, taking along provisions for ten days, we moved on. The provisions lasted somehow till Kumarskii Post (now Kumarskaia Station). There, too, Cossacks and a sergeant, Vissarion Perfilev, guarded provisions for the same purpose. They had made mud huts. Next came Kotomandskii Post, where the previous year the steamer *Shilka* had run aground. At all these points we took provisions for eight to ten days and in mid-August returned to Ust-Strelka, almost ninety days after leaving there.

The Transbaikal foot Cossacks and the line soldiers of the Fourteenth Battalion went past Ust-Strelka on boats; those behind, who left Mariinsk later, went on foot.

The eyewitnesses Cadets Malkov and Komarov, whom I saved from starvation, told me the following: Lieutenant Colonel Obleukhov, just before being sent to the Amur with the battalion, had married the daughter of the rich Verkhne-Udinsk merchant Kurbatov. According to them, grieved by the separation, Mr. Obleukhov frequently raved about a prompt reunion with her. He lay awake entire nights, and would fall asleep in the morning with orders not to be disturbed. As a consequence the whole battalion had to wait for the commander to wake up and was not allowed to move on. Furthermore, they said, they had to spend two to three days at the same overnight stop: on the road there were held feasts in honor of the birthday of his wife, father-in-law, and mother-in-law, and likewise there were celebrated all state and church holidays by staying in one place. Before one could notice, the whole summer had passed in these festivities and stops.

The higher authorities thought that the Thirteenth Battalion had passed on the Amur on boats during the navigation season. According to the calculations of the governor general [who did not personally travel on the Amur that year], it was to take on provisions for not more than eight or ten days at the posts. Assuming that flour would be delivered to the posts, the other units were sent off, as mentioned above. These units overtook the Thirteenth Battalion, some of them still below Aigun, and took the provisions at the posts. The flour was not delivered from the upper reaches of the Amur, as the barge with the flour, commanded by Second Lieutenant D. O. Preshchepenko, ran aground some thirteen miles below Albazin, opposite what is now Voskresenskaia Village. Those who did not know the details thought that this was a stroke of good fortune and said that the barge, by running aground, greatly helped the starving and by this accident saved many lives. On the contrary, the barge mishap caused a catastrophe. Had the flour been supplied in time to Kumarskii Post, where there were already baking ovens, it is likely that no one would have starved to death.

Between Kotomanda and Ust-Strelka there were almost no dead soldiers, because flour had been left at this post and baked into bread in good time, and passing soldiers were duly supplied with sufficient rations for so-and-so-many days. Before the arrival of Lieutenant Colonel Obleukhov to Ust-Strelka my father had learned from the Manegrs that downstream soldiers were dying from hunger and even ate each other. Details were requested. He reported about everything by special messenger to the chief of the Transbaikal Cossack forces in Chita, and meanwhile in Ust-Strelka outfitted a transport of twenty-four Cossack horses and, supplying it with the provisions and warm clothing that could be found in Ust-Strelka, sent me with six Cossacks to meet the starving men and give them food. The lieutenant colonel arrived in Ust-Strelka on the day of our departure. This was toward the beginning of December. Just out of Ust-Strelka we began meeting weary soldiers. There were many of them at Kotomanda; they were resting and supplying themselves with provisions for Ust-Strelka. Between these two places, a distance of almost 130 miles, there were no dead. Near Albazin we met the First Composite Troop. Below Albazin, near the stranded barge with flour, there were several corpses. According to Preshchepenko, the starving soldiers had gorged themselves on flour and died. Below this barge we saw heart-rending scenes: starving soldiers, wearing only overcoats and hats, walked through the bitter cold [−35°R or −47°F], half-dead, disfigured by the frost, blackened with smoke, so that one could not recognize them. In short, one could not tell a close acquaintance. Their hands and feet were disfigured by frost. In spite of all this the soldiers dragged their rifles and packs. If one met soldiers who could barely move their legs and advised them to discard their ammunition, they replied that they would be court-martialed were they to lose government property. Along the shores one could see bonfires that had been started by those who had come first and that were being kept up by those who followed, though the latter had no axes. I do not know how they got along without them.

Beyond what is now Permykinaia Station we began to meet ever more frequently dying soldiers along the road and at bonfires. On an island below the present Vaganovskii postal stop there were many corpses who had died in different positions and had perished mostly, one must assume, from hunger. The hind parts of some of the corpses had been cut off. On this island we found some twenty or twenty-five survivors, who because they had no boots or for other reasons had not been able to go on and had remained here, living on human flesh and waiting for death. Noncommissioned officer Bezobrazov, who had traveled with me with the mail, and Cadet Komarov, a Transbaikal native, both of whom I knew from before, were among these men. Bezobrazov admitted that he had eaten human flesh; Komarov denied having done so. He claimed he had subsisted on straps and leather from packs and various discarded footwear. He told us of an incident that happened to him some days before our arrival: There were no less than fifty people on the island. Almost all of them ate the flesh of dead soldiers, which became repulsive to them all. One evening they decided to cast lots to tell which one from the artel was to be butchered alive in the morning. Fresh meat might be pleasanter to eat. The lot fell on Komarov. From despair that there would be no mercy Komarov did not sleep all night, prayed to God to save him from this death, and almost beside himself went into the woods to die from hunger to avoid being eaten. It had just began to get light and he had run from the island to a channel, opposite which there was a large cliff, when he saw in the channel under the cliff a wolf and a roe deer that had fallen to death from the cliff. Not believing his eyes, Komarov began to call his comrades. Those who could walk followed his shouts. Those with sufficient strength cut the animal into pieces and left the island; those who could not go any further remained on this island to wait for death. Thus Komarov escaped a violent end.

We provided Komarov with warm clothing and took him with us to Ust-Strelka. We traveled some ten miles beyond the island, but did not find anyone. The corpses, insofar as possible, we buried in the ground; the rifles and all government property we gathered together and brought to Ust-Strelka, whence they were sent on to the headquarters of the Thirteenth Battalion. On the way back we picked up and transported all who for various reasons could not walk by themselves and those who were sick. The commander of the battalion did not wait for the soldiers in the rear, and had left for Shilkinsk, though he did leave an officer to send them on.

Malkov narrated the following: The colonel and the officers, seeing the inevitable death of the entire battalion, bought and forcibly took horses from the Manegrs, and deserting the battalion rode ahead. It was for this reason that there was not a single officer among the soldiers who had starved to death. Malkov, a Kiakhta native of the Transbaikal region and son of a local clergyman, had been found by us below the Ignashinaia Station, near wind-fallen wood, covered by snow; only his legs were sticking out. When he was dug out from under the snow, he was partially unconscious. Warm oil was forcibly poured into his mouth and in a few minutes he regained consciousness. But his legs were frozen up to the knees, and when he learned this he complained that we had not let him die in peace. At Ust-Strelka Malkov was carried to the billet. The first thing he did was to ask for paper and ink and wrote a letter to his father, giving it to my father for mailing. It developed that Malkov was a relative of ours and the fathers were closely acquainted. There was a doctor in Ust-Strelka. After the letter had been finished, the doctor advised Malkov to put his feet into water with ice, poured into a tub. Malkov asked that both his legs be amputated, but the doctor had no surgical instruments. Several minutes after immersing his legs in water, Malkov felt a strong pain in his legs that was driving him absolutely out of his mind. He yelled without letting up. By morning the inflammation increased and the poor young man died in terrible agony. He was between twenty-two and twenty-four years old. My father buried him in Ust-Strelka in the cemetery with due honors.

Komarov soon recovered from illness and exhaustion and together with the other men of lower rank was sent to the headquarters of his battalion and at present, it seems, is still alive, but I do not know where he is. We returned to Ust-Strelka toward the end of December. We had saved some 150 men from starvation and had brought back about seventy on horses.

The First Composite Amur Cossack Troop departed from Mariinsk about mid-September, left the boats at Khingan, and from there proceeded on foot; they made hand sleds and two at a time dragged their belongings to Aigun. The Chinese governor on the persistent demand of the commander of the troop, the acting army Sergeant Major Pavel Ivanovich Belomestnov, authorized the purchase of the required number of horses and the necessary provisions for the trip in Aigun, because they could not hope for regular provisions, calculating that the outfits up ahead had taken everything. The Chinese government also provided an officer guide to the mouth of the Kumara River as well as a paper authorizing free travel along the right bank too (the left bank, since the establishment of military posts on it, was regarded as the property of Russia). From Kumarskii Post they went along the Kumara River, the tributary on the right of the Amur. . . . The Cossacks got onto the

Amur near the Beketovskii settlement, at the mouth of the Silerka River. In spite of all the uncomfortable conditions of autumn travel the Cossack troop, though it was short of food and ate the flesh of stray and superfluous horses, safely reached Ust-Strelka toward the end of December. . . .

In the fall of 1856 the orders of the governor general of Eastern Siberia concerning the assignment of Cossacks for migration to the Amur were circulated among the troops of the Second Cavalry Brigade of the Transbaikal Cossack forces. They stated:

> To call for a certain number of volunteers for migration to the Amur; if there will be few volunteers, to name one person each from the wealthier and larger families and have them cast lots. They are to be told that they will be provided with rafts and barges for the transportation of themselves and their families and all their belongings as well as with the assistance, en route, of soldiers and Cossacks going to serve on the Amur. Upon arrival at the place of new settlement they will be exempt from service for a period of two years, will be given two years' maintenance according to their status, the field Cossack getting full maintenance, the other members of the family half the provisions. Furthermore, every Cossack will receive at the same time an allowance of fifteen rubles, and the wood on which they will float will be put at their disposal. If a rich person, chosen by lot, will not want to migrate himself, he may, with the permission of the nearest command, send a substitute for himself, upon giving him a horse, a cow, and everything necessary for farming.

The Cossacks of the Fifth Ust-Strelkovnaia and Sixth Gorbachenskaia had the right to migrate on the Amur to the places nearest Ust-Strelka: they must travel there at their own expense; at the place of new settlement they will enjoy all the above-mentioned rights.

In the spring of 1857, with the opening of navigation, a large number of different vessels began to travel on both rivers [the Argun and Shilka] again. . . . The governor general [Muravev-Amurskii] himself also arrived on a launch. He personally ordered me to take the draft letter about the perishing of the soldiers and to prepare to travel with him to the Amur as assistant clerk of the field office. . . . In the evenings the governor general himself frequently rode with me on the boat to inspect in what order the unit [of transport vessels and barges carrying troops, Cossack families, women exiles and supplies] moved and stopped. He greeted the soldiers kindly; on overnight stops [he] often shared with them their meager meals, ate and praised the mouldy rye biscuits. . . . The general was the soldiers' friend. Sometimes I heard nothing but kindness toward them. The officers, particularly of his suite, on the other hand, he could barely tolerate, and did not let pass without comment the slightest derelictions and demanded from everyone energy and good judgment. Riding on the longboat, he himself designated the Cossack villages and gave them names which they bear to this day. All this was immediately recorded in the travel journal. Names were given in honor of his associates and in memory of former Amur heroes.

In Albazin we stopped during the day. The general with his suite stepped ashore near the old citadel (as he called a place surrounded by an earthen wall), where, in 1854, there had been erected a wooden cross in memory of those who had perished at Albazin. Later he ordered that a church be erected here. . . . Traveling from Albazin, he often rode with me alone in the boat and questioned me in detail about the soldiers who had died; he gave me strict orders and made me promise on my word not to tell anyone about this until his death. I have carried this order out absolutely. In Tolbuzinskaia, having named the village in the evening, he ordered me, early in the morning, without waiting for the unit to pass by, quietly to take a teapot and bread and travel ahead with him in the boat. He wanted to see the place, where the many soldiers were buried. We got there long before the arrival of the whole unit. The general walked about the island and pondered something in silence. He was in a most dismal mood and had said nothing almost since morning. Then he himself began to collect bones (some of the corpses must not have been buried or else must have been pulled out of the fresh graves by wolves, and the bones scattered), and ordered me to bring from the boat an oar and an ax and, having pointed out the place, made me dig a hole. When all the bones had been collected, he put them in the grave with his own hands and covered them with earth. Meanwhile, on his order, I made a small cross, which we placed above the grave. Then he ordered me to kneel and to pray for those who had died without fault; he himself also stood on his knees, kept crossing himself and whispering something about himself. Tears appeared in his eyes. Having bowed to the ground and getting up on his feet he uttered: "Forgive me, you have died innocently. I am not guilty in your death."

24 / IN THE NAME OF THE KING

British humiliation of Manchu China in the so-called Opium War (1839-42) was a green light for renewed Russian expansion in Inner Asia. The decline of Manchu power made possible, if it did not invite, the enlargement of the Russian Empire at China's expense. In 1858-60 Russia acquired the Maritime Territory, in 1864 the Tien Shan region south of

Walter C. Hillier, *Confidential Prints* of the Foreign Office, Great Britain, F.O. 405-71, pp. 3-5, 19-20, 23, 28-29.

Lake Issyk Kul. Attempts were made also to spread Russian influence, if not control, in Kuldja and Sinkiang.

While Russian activity in Inner Asia was relatively sheltered from Western eyes, Russian measures in Korea aroused more than their share of international alarm. Considering that Russia had shared a common frontier with Korea since Russian acquisition of the Maritime Province in 1860, her interest in the peninsula had actually germinated surprisingly slowly. The first treaty between Russia and Korea was not signed until 1884, eight years after Japan and two years after the United States had done so. But by this time there had developed a general scramble for influence and territory in the Far East, Russian expansion becoming enmeshed in a balance-of-power steeplechase.

The Sino-Japanese War of 1894-95 had knocked out China as master or mentor of Korea. But the ruthlessness of Japanese efforts to dominate the country, including the murder of the Queen and the virtual imprisonment of the King in his own palace, played into Russian hands. One night King Kojong escaped and sought refuge in the Russian legation. In a series of confidential dispatches Walter C. Hillier, the British Consul General in Seoul, informs his government of the momentous events.

Seoul, February 12, 1896.

My telegram of yesterday's date, which I sent to Chefoo for dispatch by favour of a Russian vessel of war owing to the interruption of direct telegraphic communication viâ Japan, will have acquainted you with the fact that the King has now placed himself under the protection of the Russian Legation.

In order to furnish you with a connected narrative of the events which have led up to this unexpected denouement, I should mention that on the afternoon of the 6th February the Russian war ship "Admiral Kornilov" arrived at Chemulpo. On the morning of the 10th I received a telegram from Mr. Wilkinson reporting the departure of four Russian officers and 100 sailors, with one field-piece, for Seoul. As the guard in the Russian Legation had been increased a few days before to forty men, I was at a loss to understand the reason for this sudden and apparently uncalled-for reinforcement, so I went round to see M. Waeber [the Russian Minister] and ask him if he would mind giving me some explanation. He told me that M. de Speyer [the Russian Agent Provisione] and himself were impressed with the gravity of the situation. The so-called insurgents were increasing daily in number, they had defeated the Government troops, who were now in retreat, and they had arrived within striking distance of the city. The Japanese Government had declared a policy of non-intervention in Corea, and if, as was quite possible, the insurgents marched upon Seoul, the Japanese troops would have quite enough to do to look after their own people, whilst under any circumstances he did not wish to be beholden to Japan for assistance. If anything happened he would be only too glad to afford protection to British residents, but he strongly urged me to lose no time in getting up a guard for myself, adding that he had offered similar advice to the United States' Minister.

M. Waeber's remarks were subsequently indorsed by M. de Speyer, who told me that he had reason to believe there would be some startling events in Seoul before long. I then went to see Mr. Sill, and we agreed that, from our own point of view, MM. Waeber and de Speyer were taking a rather exaggerated estimate of the situation, but that, as a measure of precaution, we would ask the Commanders of our respective vessels of war at Chemulpo to be ready to send guards on demand.

MM. Waeber and de Speyer were dining with me on the evening of the 10th, as was also Mr. Komura, when the two former repeated their advice that it would be advisable to call up a guard, and yesterday morning I was surprised to hear, about 9 o'clock, that the King and Crown Prince were in the Russian Legation. Shortly after I received a despatch from M. de Speyer, copy of which is inclosed, informing me that the King and Crown Prince, considering that their stay in the Palace was attended with serious danger to themselves, in view of the present political situation, had taken refuge at the Russian Legation. About 10 A.M. M. Waeber came to see me, and told me that the Minister for Foreign Affairs had been dismissed and replaced by Yi Wan-yong, an English-speaking Corean, who was one of the persons that sought asylum in the United States' Legation after the murder of the Queen, and that I should probably be invited to see His Majesty in the course of the morning. I asked M. Waeber how the King got to the Russian Legation, but he parried the question, and to this moment I have been unable to ascertain how His Majesty managed to evade the sentries at the gates, or, at any rate, to pass through unchallenged. All that is known so far is that the King and Crown Prince arrived in the Russian Legation at 7:30 A.M. yesterday morning in two Corean ladies' chairs, a lady being seated in front of each chair with the King and Crown Prince huddled up behind them.

In due course I received a Circular letter from the new Minister for Foreign Affairs, sealed with the Royal seal, his own not having yet been delivered to him, informing me that His Majesty would be glad to see my colleagues and myself at the Russian Legation at noon. We all assembled at the Russian Legation at the appointed hour, except Mr. Komura, who arrived after we had left, and we were received by M. de

Speyer, who told me that he regretted he had not been able to be more explicit on the previous evening, but that, as I now saw, he had reason for his warning that there was "something in the air." He added that the state of affairs in the Palace had become so intolerable that the King had thrown himself on Russian protection, which could not be withheld, and he went on to tell me that the escape of the King had been managed very quietly, and that since his arrival the Legation had been besieged by high officials who had come to offer their congratulations and assure the King of their approval and allegiance. He also said that he hoped it would not be many days before His Majesty was back in the Palace again, for the soldiers and police were perfectly loyal to him, but that in view of eventualities he still hoped I would send for a guard. The hall was filled with Corean officials, notably Yi Pom-chin, ex-Chamberlain, who has been hiding in the Russian Legation since the 8th October, and is the individual who was supposed to have escaped to Shanghae in a Russian man-of-war. I also noticed Pak Chong-jong, formerly Prime Minister, who was dismissed on the 8th October last, and An Kiong-su, late War Minister, who was also dismissed on that date and recently condemned to imprisonment for being concerned in the abortive plot of the 28th November. These men are all members of the new Cabinet, a list of the names of whom, as far as they are at present nominated, I beg herewith to inclose. We were shortly afterwards invited into the room which was occupied by the King. MM. Waeber and de Speyer had already, they said, seen His Majesty, and therefore excused themselves from accompanying the Representatives of the United States, Germany, France, and myself.

His Majesty told us he had invited us to see him in order to explain that his position in the Palace had become so dangerous and intolerable that he had decided to place himself under the protection of the Russian Legation, and he hoped that we would support the Russian Minister in affording him asylum and assisting him in his difficulties. To this remark an answer was returned by Mr. Sill to the effect that he begged to express his satisfaction at the safety of His Majesty, and to assure him of his sympathy and devotion. My other colleagues and myself confined ourselves to expressing our satisfaction at finding His Majesty and the Crown Prince in good health. We then took our leave, informing the King, in reply to a question when he would see us again, that we should be ready to obey his summons at any time he might wish to see us.

After leaving the Russian Legation, I learnt that Proclamations, signed and sealed by the King, had been posted in the streets, one of which announced that the King had sought asylum in the Russian Legation, and had appealed to the foreign Representatives for protection, that the people were not to excite themselves, and that an amnesty would be granted to all but the leaders in the recent revolutionary acts, Cho, Minister of War, and some five other officers, mostly military, being mentioned by name, whom the people were called upon to decapitate at sight and to bring their heads to His Majesty at the Russian Legation. . . .

Seoul, February 15, 1896.

I had the opportunity of a short conversation with M. de Speyer the day before yesterday, and, though he was reticent as to the nature of the instructions he had received from his Government, and was evidently averse to telling me what share he and M. Waeber had taken in the arrangements for the flight of the King, which must have been agreed upon several days before it took place, he was frank enough in his professions with regard to the policy which M. Waeber intended to pursue. . . .

M. de Speyer told me that the only object he had in view in affording asylum to the King was to secure His Majesty's emancipation from the thraldom and terrorism to which he was subjected by his late Cabinet, with the approval and support of the Japanese Legation. A termination had to be put to the insupportable arrogance, tyranny, and incompetence of Japanese dominion, which an experience of eighteen months had proved to be a signal failure.

The time had arrived when the actual independence of the King had to be asserted, and Japanese power in this country broken. It had been broken, in M. de Speyer's opinion, and could never be allowed to be restored, but the share taken by the Russian Legation in accomplishing this necessary object could, or should not, offend the susceptibilities of Japan.

The Japanese Government preferred not to interfere in the internal administration of Corea, and to give the King a free hand. In the exercise of this freedom, His Majesty had fled from the machinations of a traitorous Cabinet, and had asked for asylum in the Russian Legation, which had naturally not been refused.

At this point Russian responsibility ceased. Neither he nor M. Waeber had interfered, nor would interfere, in the slightest degree in the arrangements which the King had made, or might see fit to make, for securing his independence and ruling the country with Ministers of his own selection. Advice would be given if solicited, but it would not be intruded.

The barbarities inflicted upon the two Cabinet Ministers were a regrettable episode, but the new Ministry was rapidly falling into place, and he confidently expected things would run smoothly before very long, and that the King would shortly return to the Palace. . . .

M. de Speyer has, I venture to think, not been long enough in this country to realize, as every one else must realize, that, having saddled themselves with the King, and having acquiesced in the complete change of front which he has effected in virtue of Russian protection, it would reduce matters to a more hopeless condition than ever if he and M. Waeber now leave His Majesty to his own devices directly he quits their protection. It is reported that His Majesty will move into the building adjoining this compound in the course of a few days, and M. Waeber has announced that the Russian guard will not follow the King there.

It is the general opinion that, so long as the Japanese retain their garrison here, and it would not be safe for them to dispense with it, the King will not move back to the Palace, and the opinion is equally prevalent that the King will not be safe even in the quarters he proposes to occupy if he is left to the protection of his own troops alone, who are a crowd of coolies dressed up in uniform, are devoid of the most elementary knowledge of their duties, and whose loyalty can be corrupted at the cost of a few dollars per head.

The fatality of a policy of non-interference cannot have been overlooked by M. Waeber, who knows this country too well to imagine that it would be wise or safe to withdraw protection from the King now that he has gone so far. . . .

Seoul, February 22, 1896.

For the last day or two there has been less talk of the immediate departure of the King from the Russian Legation. He will remain there, it is now said, until a reply has been received by the Russian Chargé d'Affaires to certain questions which have been referred by him to his Government for instructions. . . .

Considerable confusion, as might have been anticipated, prevails in the public offices. Business is more or less at a standstill, and the new Ministry, unacquainted as they are with any form of official routine, and especially that created under the auspices of Japanese officials, must take time to reduce matters to order, even if they ever succeed in doing so. The new Minister of Finance is a young man in the last stage of consumption, and chaos in his department appears to reign supreme. The Japanese military instructors have withdrawn, and it is difficult to say who is in charge of the undisciplined rabble that go by the name of the "Imperial Guards."

Another unsatisfactory feature of the recent upheaval is the return of the American element to the Palace *entourage*. General Dye and "Colonel" Nienstead, whose services as "military instructors" have been conspicuously inefficient in past years, and who had been ousted by Japanese, are now back again manœuvring for a renewal of contracts, one of which has expired and the other has only a month to run, while Mr. Greathouse, the Adviser to the Foreign Office, who is engaged from month to month, and is not a desirable, I am tempted to say reputable, agent, is also much in evidence at present. A fourth American is General Legendre, who styles himself "Adviser to the Royal Household." Not one of these gentlemen is regarded with favour by their own Minister, or, indeed, their fellow-countrymen, but no one likes to thwart their efforts to make a living out of the Coreans or to oppose their attempts to obtain a renewal of their contracts. . . .

Seoul, March 2, 1896.

The political situation remains much as it was at the date of my last report. The King displays no intention of leaving the Russian Legation, though his continual residence there is causing a good deal of dissatisfaction amongst the gentry and trading classes, by whom several meetings have been held at which resolutions were passed and forwarded to His Majesty, requesting him to return to the Palace. The popular dissatisfaction is encouraged by the Japanese local newspapers, which suggest, in thinly veiled language, that the desertion of his Palace by the King is an insult to the country, and may bring about a usurpation of the throne during his absence, for which there are precedents in Chinese history. The Cabinet Ministers as well as the King are evidently afraid to venture beyond the protection of the Russian Legation, for, with the exception of the Minister of the Household, a cousin of the King, who goes home occasionally to sleep, the other Ministers spend their whole time in one of the rooms of the Legation building adjoining the King's apartments, or in a house in an American missionary compound adjacent to the Russian grounds, which has been rented by two of their number. The control of affairs is now practically in the hands, not of the Prime Minister, who appears to be a timid and incompetent person, but of Yi Pom-chin, the man who has so long been in hiding in the Russian Legation. This officer, who bears an indifferent reputation, is by no means popular and is addicted to strong drinks, now holds the dual appointment of Minister of Justice and Chief of Police, and commenced his *régime* with a wholesale crusade against his enemies and others suspected of complicity in the outrages of the 8th October [the attack on the Palace and the murder of the Queen].

A list of no less than 140 names of persons to be arrested was drawn up by him, and there was quite a panic in the city for a couple of days, as no one knew whose turn was coming next. Matters were assuming so serious an aspect that my colleagues and myself came to the conclusion that some steps ought to be taken to mark our disapproval of a policy of wholesale vengeance which, apart from the humanitarian point of view, was not only dangerous but a breach of the distinct promise, contained in the King's Proclamation of the 11th February, that only the principals in the affair of the 8th October would be dealt with. M. Komura, the Japanese Minister, was anxious that a meeting of the foreign Representatives should be held and a joint and personal protest should be submitted to the King, but before summoning a meeting of his colleagues, Mr. Sill, after consulting with me, decided to speak with M. Waeber on the subject and see if he could not induce the latter to use his influence to put a stop to these wholesale arrests. M. Waeber and Mr. Sill then came to see me, and the former deprecated any immediate action on the part of the foreign Representatives. He said that the King had determined to get to the bottom of the plot of the 8th October, and with that object a number of witnesses had been summoned to give evidence. He had received the most positive assurances from the Minister of Justice that these witnesses should be treated humanely, and that when their testimony had been taken they should be released, and he suggested that we should wait a few days before intervening and so give the Minister of Justice an opportunity of making his promises good. He also undertook to renew his injunctions to the Minister to see that the proceedings were conducted in proper order, and to suggest to him that a proclamation should be issued reassuring the people and reiterating the King's promises of immunity for all but ringleaders. This proclamation has not been issued, but the warrants already out were evidently recalled, for the number of people arrested was limited to thirteen, and a further concession to foreign opinion was made by an invitation to Mr. Greathouse to be present at the examination of witnesses, which is now proceeding, in order to see that they were not maltreated. While the presence of Mr. Greathouse at the formal sittings of the Court will not prevent the application of torture to witnesses outside of the courtroom, and Mr. Greathouse's information will be limited to the amount that his interpreter is permitted to give him, his presence will have a reassuring effect on the public mind, and will, it is hoped, prevent any flagrant acts of cruelty, the traces of which would be noticed by him. M. Waeber gave us to understand that he was anxious to obtain all the evidence he could with regard to the events of the 8th October and the subsequent treatment of the King, in order to show that His Majesty had good cause for his flight to the Russian Legation, and under these circumstances we all decided to refrain from intervention so long as the inquiry appeared to be conducted in a legitimate manner. That the King is now enjoying greater peace of mind and a sense of personal security, to which he has long been a stranger, is testified to by all who have seen him lately. I am told that His Majesty looks a different man to what he did a few weeks ago; that he has put on flesh, is cheerful in manner, and has lost the hunted and anxious look that was previously noticed by all who came in contact with him.

M. Waeber continues to disclaim any responsibility for the acts of the Government, but there are indications that he is proffering advice to the King and his Ministers. Rightly so, in my opinion, for it is absolutely hopeless to expect that the King, or any Minister he may select, can govern the country without foreign advice, enforced, if necessary, by insistence. . . .

25 / THE TRANS-SIBERIAN RAILWAY

Nothing so symbolizes the coming of the machine age to Siberia as the Trans-Siberian Railway, which formed an iron link between Europe and Asia, revolutionized the settlement and economic development of the eastern regions, and threatened to upset the whole balance of power in the Far East in Russia's favor.

The longest railway in the world, the Trans-Siberian was constructed between 1891 and 1915, with the 1890's bearing the brunt of the work. The excitement and magnitude of the undertaking are brought out in a French traveler's observations, penned at the turn of the century.

The great difficulties of constructing the Trans-Siberian Railway were mainly due to its abnormal length. Whereas the Americans had only 2,000 miles to cut in creating their line between the Mississippi and the Pacific, the Russians thirty years later had to lay down more than 4,000 miles of rail in order to reach the same ocean from the Ural. Otherwise their difficulties were very much less formidable than those which at times nearly baffled even the ingenuity of the Americans. Happily there are no Rocky Mountains or Sierra Nevada in Siberia to traverse at a great height, but only comparatively low ranges like the Yablonovoi, or "Apple-Tree Mountains," so called from their rather dumpy shapes. Then, again, although Siberia is at present not more densely inhabited than was the Far West from 1860 to 1870, it contains no such desolate regions as the

Pierre Leroy-Beaulieu, *The Awakening of the East: Siberia—Japan—China* (New York: McClure, Phillips and Co., 1900), pp. 67-70.

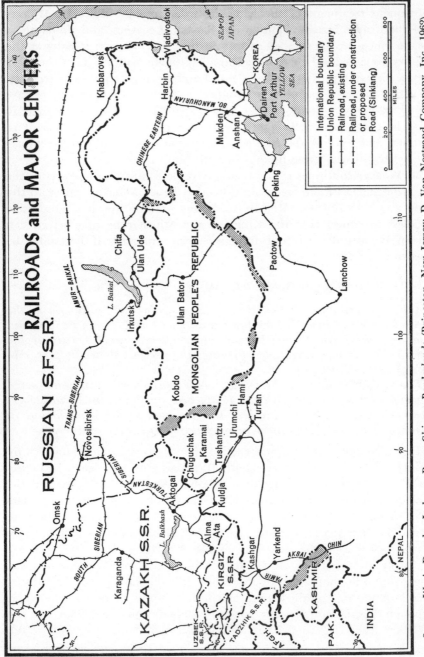

Source: W. A. Douglas Jackson, *Russo-Chinese Borderlands* (Princeton, New Jersey: D. Van Nostrand Company, Inc., 1962), p. 46. Reprinted with permission of the publisher.

plateaus of Utah and Nevada. It may, therefore, be safely affirmed that from the engineering point of view the task was a comparatively easy one, although the line has to pass over an exceedingly varied country after leaving the Ural, and through interminable plains, to reach the undulating regions between the Obi and the Yenissei, where it ascends a chain of hills at an altitude of not less than 2,000 feet on the road from the Yenissei to Irkutsk. On the eastern shore of the Baikal the railway gradually ascends to an altitude of not less than 3,500 feet above the level of the water, whence it descends in rapid zig-zag into the valleys of the Ingoda and the Chilka, cuts the abrupt spurs of some very high mountains, and passes into marsh-lands where, by the way, the engineers have had to overcome their greatest obstruction, mainly due to the unstable condition of the soil. When, therefore, we take into consideration that between the Amur and the Ural there is not a single tunnel, we may safely conclude that, if it were not for its enormous length, this now famous line has not been from the engineering point of view as arduous an undertaking even as have been, for instance, some of the much shorter lines nearer home, across the Alps and the Cevennes.

The bridges, on the other hand, are very remarkable and numerous, and some of them required great skill in their construction, since they span the more important rivers of Siberia, which, with the exception of those in the basin of the Amur, invariably flow due north. There are four principal bridges, of which two cross the Irtysh and the Obi respectively, each 2,750 feet in length; the other two span the Yenissei and the Selenga, and are about 3,000 feet in length. These four bridges were exceedingly costly, necessitating the erection of stone piles of prodigious strength, capable of resisting the shock of the enormous masses of floating ice. The minor bridges, some of them 700 to 900 feet in length, are very numerous, but, beyond the difficulty of fixing them firmly a great distance on either side of the rivers, owing to the marshy nature of the soil on the immediate banks, it needed no superlative skill on the part of the engineers who superintended their erection.

Altogether the most remarkable feature of the line will be the manner in which the trains are eventually to be transported across the Baikal, the largest lake in Asia. In America and in Denmark the system of running a train on to a monster ferry-boat, crossing considerable expanses of water, has now been in practical use for many years; but the distances hitherto have never exceeded seventy miles. The Toledo, Ann Harbour, and Northern Michigan Railroad possesses a service of ferry-boats that convey the trains across Lake Michigan, a distance of about seventy miles. The *Père Marquette,* the biggest ferry-boat in the world, so-called in honour of the celebrated Jesuit missionary and explorer, is 344 feet in length by 54 feet in width, and possesses four lines, whereby it can carry thirty freight cars and sixteen very up-to-date passenger corridor carriages. The difficulties to be surmounted with respect to Lake Baikal are happily less than those to be encountered on Lake Michigan. The distance from shore to shore, to begin with, is considerably less. Between Listvenitchnaya, otherwise the "Larches," to Misofsk is only forty miles. Notwithstanding the excessive cold, the Baikal does not freeze until quite late in January, on account of its great depth, 4,200 feet, of which 2,900 feet are below the level of the sea, forming a prodigious volume of water which takes a very long time to freeze, and an almost equally long time to thaw, for its temperature rarely rises, even in summer, above 5° C. During eight months of the year Lake Baikal is free and navigable, and it is believed that two crossings a day, always in the same channel, may eventually reduce the thickness of the ice in winter.

The building of these enormous ferry-boats has been entrusted to a well-known American firm.* They are to be larger than the *Père Marquette*, and provided with special contrivances for cutting the ice as they force their passage through it, and they are, moreover, intended to go at the rate of thirteen and a half knots an hour in free water, and four knots when cutting through the ice. The passage will take nine hours in winter and about two and a half hours in summer. Unfortunately, storms are very sudden and frequent on Lake Baikal, and, moreover, in summer travelling is often impeded by dense fogs, and it occasionally happens that boats are detained for hours and even days at a time before they dare venture across. It will certainly be very unpleasant for the passengers to be kept for many hours at Listvenitchnaya or Misofsk waiting for the weather to clear. However, they can take heart of grace; for not so very long ago they might have been detained for days at some out-of-the-way post-house, in company with a regiment of most unpleasant and unnameable bedfellows!

The difficulties of obtaining workmen for building this railway were not so great as might have been expected, thanks to the nomadic habits of the Russians, who think very little of leaving their wives and belongings at home, and going hundreds, even thousands, of miles away in search of employment. Then, again, there were already a considerable number of workpeople to be obtained on the line itself; for, as already stated, the population of Siberia is concentrated on the old postal-road,

* The author is misinformed here. The *Baikal,* the great ice-breaking, train-carrying steamer, and the *Angara,* a smaller passenger-boat, have both been designed, constructed, and set up on Lake Baikal by Sir W. G. Armstrong, Whitworth and Co., Ltd., of Newcastle-on-Tyne.—H. N.

which runs in many points parallel to the railway. Convict labour was not greatly used, and when it was it proved unsatisfactory, and was soon more or less abandoned. The line, however, has taken an unusually long time to finish, because the only season during which work can be carried on in Siberia lasts but six months; but this probably proved attractive to the Russian and Asiatic workmen, as it gave them ample time, when the ground was thickly covered with snow, to return to their cabins and indulge in those day-dreams so dear to them and to all Orientals.

It is difficult to estimate the exact cost of the line, but it was at first reckoned at over £40,000,000 sterling,* of which unfortunately a considerable percentage was absolutely wasted, if not worse. Grave charges have been brought against a great number of people in connection with this line, and doubtless with reason; for it must not be forgotten that the notions of honesty entertained in Asiatic Russia are apt even now to be distinctly Byzantine. However, be this as it may, Russia can be congratulated upon having completed a brilliant achievement, which no other nation, except perhaps England or America, would have dared to undertake, especially in so short a time.

26 / THE TAKING OF PEKING

In the last year of the nineteenth century the endurance of the Chinese people reached the breaking point. Years of humiliation at the hands of foreigners, from Manchus to Westerners, swelled up in a sudden outburst of violence—the Boxer Rebellion. Missionaries were massacred and the foreign legations besieged. Deftly deflecting the onslaught from itself toward the Westerners, the Manchu government made common cause with the Boxers. An international expedition had to be launched to rescue the families bottled up in the diplomatic quarter of the capital city.

By virtue of her geographical position Russia was able to rush to the rescue with the largest number of troops. In Manchuria she bore the brunt of the battle singlehandedly. Once the Chinese forces had been crushed and the siege lifted, the presence of such a large number of Russian soldiers and especially their apparent entrenchment in Manchuria assumed a different color in the eyes of Western and Japanese observers. But in the fateful days of August 1900, everyone but the Boxers and their supporters were glad to see them.

On July 31, the Russians had received word that the situation of the beleaguered Europeans was desperate, that the Chinese were about to

---

D. Iancheftskii, "Vziatie Pekina," *Priamurskiia Vedomosti* (1900), No. 351, pp. 14-17; No. 353, pp. 12-15. Translated by G. A. Lensen.

* The official estimate of the total cost of the railway is over £80,000,000, of which over £50,000,000 were spent by the end of 1899.—H. N.

*mine the approaches to Peking, and that the Japanese, with whom the
Russians worked closely throughout the campaign, had started toward the
capital city; so the Russians decided to launch their offensive that very
night, twenty-four hours ahead of schedule. In the early morning hours of
August 1, the vanguard, under the command of Major General Vasilevskii,
approached Peking. The 7th Company of the 10th Regiment, commanded
by Captain Gorskii and armed with two machine guns, led the way, followed by three companies of the 2nd Regiment, four cannons, and the
Cossacks. D. Iancheftskii, from whose eyewitness account this selection
has been translated, was ordered to show the way and to lead the company
to the gates of the city.*

We advanced in the semidarkness, along the granite road, stepping
into puddles and holes. We crossed the last bridge and were in front of
the locked gates. To the right and left there were tents. The sentries
slept beneath the open sky. Others slept in the guardhouses. Within a
few minutes, all the guards, fully or half asleep, were bayoneted by the
riflemen. As the bridge was not mined and the gates were protected
merely by the guard, who slept below and had been slaughtered, General
Vasilevskii ordered two cannons to be rolled up and placed side by side,
some fifteen feet from the gates.

The great and glorious hour had come, when Russian heroism shone
again. Before us lay the centuries-old gates of the ancient sacred city.
We did not know what might would meet us on the gigantic walls of
Peking, which at last were in front of us. But we knew that behind these
formidable gates and walls, which no gun could penetrate, there were
Europeans with their wives and children who had already languished
there for two months and who must be liberated at any cost and as soon
as possible. Every day and hour of delay could prove fatal for them or us.

General Vasilevskii ordered the gates breached. The deathlike ominous
silence, which reigned over the sleeping city, was shattered by a shot,
another, a third, but the gates did not open. The cannons fired one shell
after another.

Clearly the orders of Second Lieutenant Ivanov resounded: "First!"
"Second!" For some twenty minutes the thunder hung over the gates.
Because of the clouds the moon faintly illuminated the two cannons and
the gunners and riflemen who stood next to them and fired at the walls.
Roused from their sleep, the Chinese soldiers began to fire from the
walls, but, in their fright, could not find their target and the bullets
flew far away. The thunder and lightning of the artillery pieces, the
sharp salvos of our riflemen, the disorderly firing of the Chinese, and
the dreadful roar of the Russian machine guns in the lunar twilight, the
gates blackened by centuries, and the grandiose walls of the millennial

capital—such was the picture of the first storm of Peking by the Russians.

At exactly 2 A.M. the riflemen and gunners gave a rousing cheer—a shell had knocked down the bolt and opened the gates. General Vasilevskii bravely led the way through the gates, beyond which there was a paved courtyard and a second pair of half-closed gates, which led to the street.

The gates of Peking were forced by Russian weapons. The tower above the gates was deserted by the Chinese guards and on it there was raised the Russian flag, which as symbol of victory and liberation was the first to wave over the wall of the capital of the Emperors of China.

The 2nd Company of the 2nd Regiment was sent at once to occupy the wall which bordered unto the gates; the 1st Company of the same Regiment was left to guard the gates. Second Lieutenant of Artillery Ivanov was dispatched to General Linevich, commander of the Pechili detachment, with a report on the taking of the gates and the state of affairs. It was 3:30 A.M.

The gates of the Chinese city were taken. It remained only to break through the inner gates to enter the Tartar city, where the European missions were located. The commander of the detachment, General Vasilevskii, ordered the 7th Company of the 10th Regiment and two cannons to advance against the Tartar city. It was necessary to go along the Tartar wall, at a distance of thirty to fifty feet. The brave troops of [General] Tung Fu-hsiang scattered on the whole wall and, hidden behind the loopholes, began to fire at Gorskii's courageous company from their large ancient muskets. Within several minutes all six horses of one cannon were killed and some fifteen gunners were wounded. The brave Captain Gorskii was wounded by one bullet in the arm and by another in the left side of the chest. Second Lieutenant Piunovskii was wounded in the arm. Several wounded riflemen lay already behind the rampart. Since it was impossible to advance under such fire, General Vasilevskii ordered to withdraw the company and the guns. But this was not so easy: from the height of the wall, some sixty feet up, the Chinese soldiers shot point-blank at the riflemen passing below. One cannon was successfully pulled away with the assistance of additional horses, but the other could not be removed, as its horses and crew had been killed and it was risky to send more horses, since it was getting light and such large targets as horses could be seen all too well. The Chinese shot from every loophole. The terrifying deep-toned roar of the ancient Chinese cannons emanated from one of the towers. It was a picture at once dreadful and splendid. The ancient walls and towers of Peking were illuminated by small arms and artillery fire. But this was the last illumination of the ancient city, costly for the Russians, who with Russian bravery took the impregnable walls, as well as for the Chinese, who stubbornly defended their strongholds. But Peking fell with every hour.

Upon hearing the first shots of the Russians and learning that the gates had been forced and the wall occupied by Russians, the Chinese Empress, the Emperor, and Crown Prince fled at once from Peking westward, to Shensi Province.

Under the fierce fire of the fortress bullets, the riflemen heroes of Gorskii's company dragged the stranded cannon back by hand. The weapon was saved, but the sergeant major was killed and several riflemen were wounded.

It was 4 A.M. It had become light. Inside the besieged missions, which the Chinese had bombarded especially heavily during the night, it was guessed as soon as the Russian shooting was heard that this was the liberators' firing.

Alarm spread on the walls of Peking. The brave soldiers of Tung Fu-hsiang rushed to the southeastern corner of the Tartar city, whither the Russians had penetrated, and opened up on the courageous detachment of General Vasilevskii with a murderous fire from every loophole and from the enormous four-tiered tower, also located there, which rose some sixty-nine feet above the wall we had taken. The Chinese soldiers took up position in this huge, clumsy four-cornered tower and shot from all windows. They saw our wall as if it were in the palm of their hand and fired a burst of large lead bullets at anyone who emerged from behind cover. The towers and walls of the Tartar city pounded us from the west.

At about 5 A.M. hordes of Chinese started running across the wall from the eastern side and attacking us. In spite of enemy fire, General Vasilevskii had a machine gun pulled up onto the wall, and it showered the oncoming hordes with bullets so accurately and incessantly, that they soon withdrew. The machine gun protected us from the eastern side. But from the west we continued to be exposed to fierce bombardment from the ancient fortress guns—from the tower as well as from the wall.

Thus the advanced detachment fought off [the enemy] until 7:30 A.M., losing wounded and dead, when cannon and small-arms fire was heard from the suburbs surrounding Peking on the eastern side. This was the advance of our main forces under the command of General Linevich. Upon receipt of General Vasilevskii's report that the gates had been taken, the commander of the detachment had ordered an immediate offensive by all our main forces, with the 2nd and 3rd Companies of the 10th Regiment as vanguard, commanded for the last time in his life by

Colonel Antiukov, followed by four fieldpieces of the 3rd Battery of Lieutenant Colonel Meister, half of the 4th Company, and the 5th and 8th Companies of the 10th Regiment, with the 2nd Battery and the 9th Regiment in reserve.

As the vanguard moved into the suburbs of Peking, the first shot was fired from the observation tower over the heads of General Linevich and his staff. The soldiers left the road and deployed in combat formation.

Our troops scattered through the narrow streets and began to shoot at the walls and towers of the great city. But as our forces took up position in the entrance corner, occupied by the advance detachment, their situation proved very difficult. The Chinese fired at them from both walls, forming a corner, and from the high tower, at a distance from four hundred to six hundred paces. The tower wrought particular damage. General Linevich, who was all the time in the front line and personally observed the course of battle, ordered Colonel Modl, the commander of the 2nd Company, to take half his men and reconnoiter the approaches to the tower. Two riflemen were killed, yet no entry to the tower was found: it could be taken only with assault ladders, with heavy losses. Then Second Lieutenant of Artillery Ivanov placed two cannons on the street, behind the wall that was in our hands, and from behind its cover lopped shells at the formidable tower. As long as the artillery fired, the tower was silent, but then resumed its extermination of Russians.

Two fieldpieces of the 3rd Battery were dragged by the 4th Company by hand through the narrow streets and were placed on the left flank of the position. The 3rd Company, having run across the bridge, occupied the front houses. Half the 4th Company remained to cover the guns, while the 2nd Company took up position on the extreme-left flank. All these forces began to shoot at the walls, the four-tiered tower, and the observation tower.

It was 8 A.M. General Linevich, Colonel Antiukov, Captain Iaroshevich, and Cornet Pikov sat together, under cover of the rampart. The general had scarcely gotten up to walk to his tent to write a paper, when a shell flew by, tore a soldier to pieces, and with a fragment killed Antiukov, the commander of the 10th Regiment, on the spot, the flying shell fragment striking him in the head. The valiant colonel, beloved not only by his regiment but by all of Port Arthur Society, fell silently into the lap of Captain Iaroshevich, who sat beside him. Death was instantaneous. The colonel was killed at his post, facing the enemy. May he be remembered forever!

The walls and towers continued to pound our forces. Wounded and dead were being carried out all the time. General Linevich ordered another two fieldpieces of the 3rd Battery to be rolled out and this was done by riflemen of the 5th and 8th Companies by hand; the 2nd and 3rd Companies shot at the enemy from the left flank, the cannons fired from the middle; the 5th and 8th Companies used bayonets to drive Chinese out of houses from which they were shooting.

The morning was burning hot. Our soldiers were worn out from thirst and exhaustion, but staunchly and manfully carried out their duty. For a whole week now they had not drunk, eaten, slept, and rested properly. Having covered some eighty miles by forced march, without a single day of rest during the past week, these heroes in white shirts, turned brown on the road, with dusty and sunburned faces, covered with sweat and blood, now moved to take the impregnable walls of the Chinese capital.

The four cannons of the 3rd Battery, which had covered themselves with glory already during the taking of Tientsin, continued to pound the Chinese on the walls to the right and left of the gates, which had been taken by us. Our shrapnel exploded directly above the heads of the Chinese and forced them to halt their gun fire.

It was about 10 A.M. The position of the unit which had taken the gates and the wall was not easy. Everywhere the large lead bullets of the Chinese muskets smashed into the wall with sharp impact. The 4th and 5th Companies of the 2nd Regiment and half of the 7th Company of the 10th Regiment took up position on the wall and at the gates. Several wounded riflemen already lay on the wall. The Chinese sat behind their loopholes and showered our riflemen with bullets. Our riflemen, taking cover behind Chinese loopholes, tracked the Chinese and knocked out a few.

At 10 A.M., the commander of the advance unit, General Vasilevskii, walking on the wall, from where he commanded his troops, collapsed wounded, shot through the right side of the chest. Two riflemen who rushed to pick up the general, were wounded at once. Two others followed suit and one was wounded. Eventually the general was moved and stretched out on the wall under cover of the loopholes. The Chinese probably saw everything well and directed violent fire on the place where the general had been wounded. There was no chance of carrying the general from the wall down to the houses where a dressing station had been established. All one had to do was to cross an exposed stretch of the wall, some twenty paces in length, but it was showered with a hail of bullets; some ten wounded men lay here already. The fearless doctor of the 2nd Regiment, Peterson, having dressed that difficult morning fifty persons under fire, safely ran across this fatal ground and bandaged the wounded general. Fortunately the wound had been made by a small caliber bullet, either a Mauser or a Mannlicher. The pulse was completely normal, so that one could hope for his recovery. Suffering severe pains from the fresh wound, burned by the hot sun, and shot at with bullets, the general lay on the stones above the very gates through which he had broken with his detachment just before this and through which he had stepped first.

The staff interpreter, the Swede Mr. Munde, who was well versed in Chinese and in modern languages and who had been the interpreter of General Seimura, two doctor's assistants, and I remained all the time near the wounded general. The stone battlement, one man high and about four and a half feet wide, was our only protection. The moment anyone leaned out, he drew a hail of bullets. Twice we tried to carry the general through: first one of the doctor's assistants was wounded and expired half an hour later, then the other doctor's assistant was wounded in the arm and in the leg. Only after about three hours did we succeed in carrying the general down from the wall.

It was 10:30 A.M. when the commander of the detachment ordered a battalion of the 9th Regiment to move from the reserves to reinforce the detachment. Meanwhile Lieutenant Colonel Kolin, the commander of the 1st Battalion of the 10th Regiment, reconnoitered the bridge and under Chinese fire rode through the gates taken by us and back to the main forces. It was 11 A.M. The fire of the Chinese died down and white flags appeared on their wall. The commander of the detachment with the staffs of the 2nd, 3rd, 5th, and 8th Companies of the 10th Regiment immediately moved forward to the gates. Seeing this movement, the Chinese soldiers put away the white flags they had hoisted and treacherously resumed their fire.

Without let-up our guns continued to shower the Chinese wall with such a hail of shrapnel and grenades that the Chinese muskets and cannons gradually fell silent. In different places white flags appeared.

At noon the commander of the detachment and his main forces entered Peking. But the passage across the bridge to the gate was still dangerous. Notwithstanding the white flags, shots were fired from various corners of the wall and from the towers.

Upon learning that we had broken through the gates of Peking that night and that we were storming its walls, the Japanese spurred on their troops, which moved almost parallel with our main forces. At about 9 A.M. they advanced to the Chihwa-men gates and mounted an attack against that part of the city. The Chinese, who had expected a foreign attack from this direction, had prepared for a desperate defense and met their old enemies with the heaviest possible salvos of musket and artillery fire. Several Japanese daredevils together with Captain Bolkho-vitinov of the General Staff tried to get up to the gate to plant a mine under it, but all of them, except the captain, were mowed down. An hour later General Yamaguchi requested General Stoessel to order our artillery to bombard the Peking wall between the observation tower and the Chihwa-men gates, as he would attack the Peking gates with six battalions. Major General Stoessel, commander of the reserve column, immediately ordered the 2nd Battery into action. The battery took up position first about 4900 feet then about 700 feet from the wall. The commander of the battery, Captain Second Grade Skrydlov, zeroed in most accurately, and from 10 A.M. until 5 P.M. shelled the Chinese. Had the Russians not deflected the main Chinese forces to their gates the night before and had our 2nd Battery not supported the left flank of the Japanese with heavy fire, the latter would hardly have succeeded in tak-ing the gates. Only late in the evening, when our forces had already en-tered Peking and part of the Japanese forces had also passed through our gates, did the Japanese finally break through the so-called Imperial (Chihwa-men) Gates, which they had chosen to storm. Captain Bol-khovitinov of the General Staff was of great service to the Japanese dur-ing the assault, as he rode back and forth under fire with messages from General Stoessel to General Yamaguchi.

The Americans entered Peking only with our help. They came up to the walls of Peking at about 11 A.M. and, instead of storming the gates assigned to them with the aid of their artillery, asked our 3rd Battery to make a breach in the wall for them. Grenades from the battery of Lieutenant Colonel Meister soon crumbled part of the wall so that the Americans could clamber up, but they encountered no enemy whatsoever, as he had been chased away still early in the morning by our riflemen and machine guns. The Americans then wanted to raise their flag on the wall, but seeing the Russian flag on the gates, set out to find another place. To their disappointment this whole side had already been taken by the Russians. Then the Americans entered Peking under the cover of our guns.

While the Russians and the Japanese were fighting to the death with the Chinese and were storming the walls under heavy fire and while the Americans were bravely climbing the walls already taken by us and searched for a place to raise their flag, the English very prudently climbed under the walls, and by way of a dried-up riverbed entered the Chinese city of Peking. Then, without fighting, they crossed the empty city and climbing through under the wall of the Tartar city arrived at 2 P.M. to protect the English Mission. English sepoys were the first heralds of liberation.

At about 2 P.M., along the whole eastern Tartar wall, which was being pounded by our batteries, the red battle flags of the Chinese gave way to white ones: the Chinese surrendered and Peking fell. Only from the corner tower, which had cost us so many casualties, did die-hard soldiers of Tung Fu-hsian continue to shoot until evening, when the Japanese took this tower.

Having safely entered Peking under enemy fire at the head of his troops, Lieutenant General Linevich ordered a brief rest. There was no thought of a meal; the men recharged their energy with biscuits and fresh water.

At 2 P.M. the joyful tidings of freedom spread through all the missions. At 3 P.M. Ensign Den, who had been in the Russian landing party in Peking from the battleships *Navarin* and *Sysoi Velikii*, made a brief sortie along the wall and drove the Chinese from the Tsienmen Gates and opened them to the American forces, who had approached from this side. Then Lieutenant Baron Raden, commander of the landing party, appeared with the rest of the men and chased the Chinese farther away, till the next gates. Five Chinese cannons and ten flags were the trophies of the Russian landing party.

At 4 P.M. General Linevich and his staff entered the Imperial Russian Mission. It was found intact, with all its members well. All the other besieged Europeans proved also whole and well.

For a long time the loud and joyful hurrays of the liberated and the liberators resounded through all the missions. . . .

27 / THE UNPOPULAR WAR

Russian reluctance to withdraw from Manchuria and her unwillingness to assent to Japanese domination of north Korea, with which she shared a common boundary, conflicted with the continental ambitions of dynamic Meiji Japan. The Russo-Japanese War which broke out in 1904 was a great and costly struggle, which exhausted both sides. It gained Japan much glory and punctured the paper tiger of white supremacy. But the most striking feature of the war, in the context of this book, was the apathy of the Russian public and the lack of fighting spirit of the Russian soldier. On December 6, 1941, the American people were divided and reluctant to do battle. The Japanese onslaught galvanized the nation into firm and united resistance. Not so in Russia. The Pearl-Harbor-like sneak attack on Port Arthur did not arouse fervor or unity. To be sure, there were patriots and heroes, men who fought and died gallantly, but gen-

erally speaking the heart of the nation was not in the war. Liberal intellectuals and businessmen welcomed military reverses in the expectation that they would force the autocratic government to make political concessions at home; radicals sought to hasten reform by revolutionary agitation. To a large extent, in the Russo-Japanese War, Russia defeated herself.

As long as Russia had pushed across the continent, her expansion had seemed necessary, for the Eurasian plain formed a natural unit. Korea and regions beyond the outer fringes of the empire, on the other hand, failed to hold the public interest. In fact, involvement there became associated with the "private" machinations of the Imperial family and irresponsible adventurers. The sacred soil of Mother Russia did not seem threatened.

The following selections from the memoirs of a Russian surgeon and a Russian naval officer illustrate the dual defeat of Russia—by its own subjects and by the Japanese.

Weary Warriors

The Army was in a gloomy and sombre mood. Hardly any one looked for a victory. The officers tried to give themselves courage, figured out by how many thousand bayonets our army increased each month, and put their hope in the Baltic Squadron and Port Arthur. Port Arthur capitulated. Nogi's delivered army moved for a union with Oyama. The morale kept falling, and peace was desired; but the officers said:

"How can we return home? We might just as well take off our uniforms, for it will be a disgrace to appear in the streets!"

There were a considerable number of officers who would not even listen to peace. They had their peculiar military "honor," which demanded a continuation of the war.

The soldiers had no such "honor"; they could not comprehend the war at all, and in vain tried to get some explanation for it.

"Your Honor, what is this war about?" a soldier would ask an officer.

"It's the Japs' fault! We didn't want it! They attacked us first!"

"Yes, sir. But why should they attack us without any cause?"

Silence.

"They say that this war is about Manchuria. What do we want with it? We would not like to live here, if it were given to us! As we were travelling through Siberia, we saw a lot of land, there is no end to it!"

The position of those who desired "to uphold the spirit of the Army" was becoming exceedingly difficult. It was impossible to discover anything which would fire the soul with the desire for heroism, with the desire to struggle for something high and glorious.

V. Veresáev, *In the War,* trans. Leo Wiener (New York: Mitchell Kennerley, 1917), pp. 204-207.

At the staff of the Commander-in-Chief they published a special little paper, *The Messenger of the Manchurian Armies.* This paper, whose problem it was to play the rôle of a Tyrtæus of the Russian Army, was amazing for its incapacity, its lying, its absence of fire and inspiration. The governmentally over-sweet phrases about faith, Tsar, and country, about the honor of the native land, endless and heedless boasting,—that was to feed the spirit of those who were participating in a titanic struggle, where the cannonading caused the clouds to gather in the disturbed air, and where whole plains were covered with bloody carpets of corpses. I shall have to quote this truly remarkable paper more than once.

This is the way the patriotic authors wrote in pamphlets which were scattered in great numbers among the soldiers. Before me lies an elegantly published book, with pretty illustrations, bearing the title: *In Besieged Port Arthur, or the Heroic Death of Private Dmítri Fómin.* The story begins as follows:

" 'No, Brother Jap, you can't get out of my embrace! You will now taste Russian cabbage soup and porridge,—it's an A-1 dish!'

"Thus thought Private Dmítri Fómin, sitting in his lurking place with his gun primed, and watching a Japanese scout.

"The Japanese is crawling over the rocks, in danger of falling down at any moment. 'It isn't easy for the Jap, either,' thought Fómin, 'for he, too, carries out the commands of his superior.' Indeed he was sorry for the Jap. At any other time Fómin would have helped him to reach the top, but now, since he was ready to carry out the commands of his own authorities and to do their will, he impatiently waited for the Japanese to get close enough to him so that he could suddenly throw himself upon him and capture him."

Poor Russian Army, poor, poor Russian people! So this was to fire them with the desire to struggle and do heroic deeds,—the wish to do the will of the authority. But the patriotic author is wrong in assuming that the Japanese only "carry out the commands of their superiors." No, this fire does not heat up the soul and inflame the heart! The souls of the Japanese burned with a glowing fire, they were eager for death, and died smiling, happy, and proud.

Nemírovich-Dánchenko says that once, during a private conversation, Kuropátkin remarked: "Yes, one must admit that, at the present time, wars are not waged by governments, but by nations!" Anybody who had eyes and ears, had to admit that. Those times, when the Russian "saintly cattle" crawled up the Alps after Suvórov, astonishing the world by their senseless heroism—those times have gone irretrievably.

Every day they brought wounded men to our hospital. There was an amazing number of men who were wounded in the hand, especially the right hand. At first, we took this to be accident, but the unusual regularity of such wounds soon attracted attention. The surgeon's assistant comes and reports:

"Your Honor, we have brought five wounded men."

"Are they wounded in the hand?"

"Yes, sir," answers the assistant, restraining a smile.

You ask a soldier under what conditions he was wounded. He is embarrassed and confused. "I stretched out my hand for a blade of grass," "I put out my hand to get the cartridges from the breastwork." To the Sisters, in whose presence they were less embarrassed, they told outright:

"This is the way it happened. I just raised my hands and shot, and it hit me in the hand. If I had put out my head, I would have caught it in the head!"

The Chief Commander of the Rear writes in one of his orders:

"A large number of the rank and file have been received at the hospitals, who have wounds on their fingers. Of these there are twelve hundred who have only the index finger wounded. The absence of the index finger on the right hand frees a man from military service. Hence, considering the fact that the fingers are well protected during the firing by the trigger-shield, there is reason to assume an intentional injury to the fingers. In view of the above, the Commander-in-Chief has ordered an investigation, so as to bring the guilty persons before the law."

The soldiers lived merely in the expectation of peace. The expectation was impassionate, tense, with an almost mystical faith in the nearness of the desired and delayed "peace-making." The moment "Hurrah!" was heard at the station the soldiers of all the surrounding units became excited and in agitation asked:

"What is this? The peace-making?"

The Tsushima Debacle

The recollections of the battle in their disordered sequence rise up before me like some horrible nightmare. It is beyond my power to give a full and coherent account of these terrible events. No human being is able to grasp and co-ordinate such complex impressions. Our fleet was smashed to pieces, and when darkness fell and the battle—which lasted for seven hours—ended, our vessels had been scattered to the four winds by the enemy. Therefore, I can only try to describe the things that I

Captain Nicolas Klado, *The Battle of the Sea of Japan,* trans. J. H. Dickinson and F. P. Marchant (London: Hodder and Stoughton Publishers, 1906), pp. 159-70.

myself witnessed; flashing as they did one after the other before my eyes as in some portentous and swiftly moving dream.

By morning we arrived at the narrowest portion of the Korean Straits between Tsushima and Kiu Shiu. My servant woke me with the words "The Japanese ships are in sight." The day was bright, but a thick mist enveloped the horizon all round. The wind was from S.W., with a strength of between 4 and 5, and there was a swell on the sea. At nine o'clock, at a distance of from fifty-five to sixty-four cables, we could make out the dim silhouette of a grey Japanese cruiser. They told me that earlier (at 6:30 A.M.) three ships had been sighted, and that the *Oslabya* had by signal asked for permission to engage them, but that our Admiral had refused and the fleet had continued on its course. The cruiser meantime had been following us, always at the same distance, sending off frequent messages by wireless telegraphy, which we of course could not decipher. We were advancing in two columns. The starboard column consisted of the battleships *Kniaz Suvorov* (flying Rozhestvensky's flag), *Imperator Alexander III, Borodino, Orel, Oslabya* (flying Felkersham's flag), *Sissoi Veliky, Navarin,* and *Nakhimov.* The port column was composed of the battleships of Admiral Niebogatov's squadron. Four transports, the *Irtish, Anadyr, Kamtchatka,* and *Korea,* with the auxiliary river tugs *Rus* and *Svir,* followed astern of the battleships, and were protected by our cruisers and scouting vessels. The cruisers *Zhemtshug* and *Izumrud* were in advance of the leading vessels four points to starboard and port respectively, and at a distance of about ten cables. Our duty was to warn off any steamers or junks we might meet. We fell in with some coasters and a small Japanese steamer, the latter on a course at right angles to our own. We fired a shot across her bows, and she thereupon turned away from us and stopped. The poor Japanese on board her were dreadfully frightened, being convinced that we were about to sink them. They had already begun to lower a boat to save themselves, but it was dashed against the side, owing to the heavy swell, and swamped. We passed on, leaving the peaceable little steamer unmolested. During the dinner hour, as a measure of precaution, our transports were ordered to steam between the two columns of battleships. During the morning several alarms of battle, as when the Japanese cruiser appeared and the steamer was met with, served to heighten one's tension of mind. Dinner itself was at the very beginning interrupted by a fresh alarm. At 11:20 two Japanese cruisers were observed ahead, and three more on our port beam. On our right, the Japanese ship previously sighted continued her course, parallel with us as before. A milky fog hung over the horizon, so that we could only with difficulty make out, by the aid of the range-finder, that their distance from us was some fifty to sixty cables. They must have been fast third-class cruisers of the "Nitaka" type, forming part of the enemy's light scouting division. We gave them one shot from our forward gun, but could not well see where the shot fell. Our battleships also fired a few shots, until the Admiral signalled "Cease fire." The strong swell and the mist on the horizon made such long-range shooting quite useless.

And now the outlines of these cruisers were swallowed up in the fog, and we went below to continue our interrupted dinner. The mess-table, on account of the alarms, had already been taken and adapted for our prospective wounded, so we had to finish our meal as best we could. For a while there was no further disturbance, and we rested. At 12:50 the Admiral ordered the *Zhemtshug* to fall into line with the *Orel*. At 1:20 P.M. the alarm for battle was sounded, and my man rushed to his quarters. When I got to the forecastle, by our forward gun, our battleships had changed their two-column formation and were now steaming in single column. The transports had taken up a position of shelter under the cover of our cruisers, to starboard of their former course and on the starboard beam of our battleships. Ahead of the *Suvorov* and a little to port of her course, the Japanese battleships were emerging from the fog in one single column; steaming at great speed to meet us. The *Suvorov* was moving very slowly, in order to give time to our sternmost battleships to take up their stations, and our line had become pretty well extended. . . .

What happened subsequently does not admit of systematically detailed description. The booming, roaring, hissing of the big shells, their shrill screaming as they struck the water, causing great splashing clouds of spray, the peculiar noise made by the ricochets, like that of a steamship going at full speed—all these sounds in one inextricable confusion now began. All the shells which struck the water ahead of us and ricochetted, were clearly visible to the naked eye. Spinning round and round, they gave me the impression of the flight of birds overhead. Whenever they struck the water a second time, a high column of water and black smoke was thrown up by the shock. I perfectly appreciated the object of Togo's first manœuvre. He did not bring his fleet along on a cross tack, but when abreast of the leading battleships in our column he put on full steam and went by them. He then described a looped course on their port beam, and, cutting across their bows, went right on until he was on the other side of them, to starboard.

This brilliant manœuvre of the Japanese, which they could not have carried out if their vessels had not been superior in speed, allowed them to concentrate the fire of all their guns on whichever of the leading ships of our column they pleased. And this is exactly what they did. It was at once evident that nearly all their shots were directed at the *Suvorov* and the *Oslabya*. They made targets of them, as it were. . . .

It is difficult to say at what particular time each stage of the fight occurred. It was not as though I could just look at my watch and write down what was happening, for I had my own duties to attend to.

We on board the *Zhemtshug* also kept on firing haphazard on every Japanese vessel that we saw. The uniform grey colour of the Japanese ships made them nearly invisible in the mist on the horizon. Their distance from us at the commencement of the battle was about forty-three cables. Their shells literally fell in showers about us, and how our vessel remained unscathed was simply inexplicable. After a few minutes, as it seemed to me, but in reality after an hour, the *Oslabya* went out of line with a big list to port. By this time the enemy had already crossed to starboard of our column in continuation of their manœuvre; so the *Zhemtshug* had to move away on the port beam of our battleships so as not to be between them and the Japanese, and I lost sight of the *Oslabya* as I was looking after the Admiral's flagship. I was afterwards told that within a few minutes of this she turned turtle. Some torpedo-vessels also succeeded in reaching the spot where the battleship sank. At the same time as the *Zhemtshug* crossed over to the port beam of our ships, fires broke out on board the *Suvorov*. Suddenly a huge column of flame and smoke shot from her after turret and its cover was blown up as high as the tops. These moments were, I think, the decisive ones. The *Borodino* now left the line, and a fire on board the *Alexander III* broke out by her forward funnel. The *Suvorov*, however, shattered and wrecked as she was, mastless, and with both her fore and aft bridges on fire, still maintained her place as leading ship and kept on firing from her undamaged turrets. This was about three o'clock in the afternoon. The Japanese fire was still concentrated on our four leading vessels. Now fires began to break out on our other ships, and the *Borodino*'s forward bridge was ablaze. The nervous qualms to which the flight of the first few shells had given rise had vanished altogether; one could evidently get used even to this. Every minute shells were flying over our heads, and often burst quite close to the side. It was after the destruction of the *Oslabya* and the explosion on board the *Suvorov* that we were hit for the first time. The firing from our own ships and from those of the enemy, and the flight and bursting of the shells, made such a din that the noise the shell made as it crashed into us was indistinguishable from the general uproar. I heard a shout of "stretchers" from the poop. The shell was from a 6″ gun, and must have passed through the entering hatch to the commander's cabin and burst. The hatch was riddled with splinters like a sieve, and Lieutenant Baron Vrangel and three others were killed.

The days of the *Suvorov* were numbered; both her funnels were down, and a thick smoke was trailing over her. I saw her bearing away to port, trying to get beyond the range of fire, whilst the squadron continued the battle away to port.

I recollect why the *Zhemtshug* approached the battleship *Imperator Alexander III*, on board which flames had broken out both from the bows and the stern. There were two destroyers by her, and we thought that Admiral Rozhestvensky, who had been taken off the *Suvorov*, was on board one of them. We had begun even to lower a boat, but at that moment shells began to fall thick and fast about us, and one of them struck us on the stern. Those on board the destroyers signalled us to go back, and the *Zhemtshug* steamed away from the *Alexander III*. We were then struck a second time. The shot came from the port side and from astern, and hit our fore-funnel. When we got so close to the *Alexander III*, we were within 29 cable-lengths of the Japanese battleships. The *Nissin* and *Kassuga* were plainly visible from stem to stern. Judging by the hole made in our fore-funnel, the shot must have come from a 6″ gun. The havoc it made was terrible. The whole right side of the funnel was split open; the plates were torn asunder, pierced with splinters, and bent outwards; the splinters smashed the shot-lockers in the starboard-sponson gun, and set fire to the smokeless powder in the four cases inside the lockers, as well as in some others lying on deck. What followed was indescribable. Running, after the shock, from the forecastle to the gangway ladder, I looked upon a seething mass of fire. The flames reached the cutter, which was hanging in the davits, and filled the whole space from amidships to the side. This was the ignition of the smokeless powder in the cartridge-cases. By the light of the flames I could see our wounded writhing in convulsions of pain. By the time the hoses were turned on this spot the fire was already out, but they succeeded at once in extinguishing the woodwork that had caught fire. The powder was alight for only a few seconds. I went down to the deck. Seven dead bodies lay there in strange postures; they had gaping wounds, and the hands and faces were burnt. Amongst them was the chief of a platoon, Midshipman Tavaststern, who had only just been promoted to officer's rank. One unfortunate man had had the whole of his groin torn away by a splinter, and his left leg was bent backwards in an unnatural position. Another had half his face gone, and an arm and part of his neck wrenched off.

The crew stood panic-stricken at this ghastly spectacle. The bodies had to be removed and the spot cleaned. One must wait for fresh men, and then treat the enemy to the same slaughter and destruction as he had dealt to us. The spot was soon sanded over and the guns freshly manned, but we did not so easily get rid of our impressions. It was useless for us to expose ourselves to the fire of the enemy without being able to do them harm in return. The 120 mm. guns of the *Zhemtshug* could scarcely carry 48 cable-lengths, but the fight was continued nearly all the time at just about this distance. . . .

On the way to the battleship *Alexander III,* when the *Zhemtshug* steamed past, the transports collected together in a cluster. The auxiliary cruiser *Ural* struck against our stern, wrenched a torpedo-tube loose, damaged her stern gear, grazed and bent our starboard screw, and smashed in our starboard side. The shock forced our screw through the side of the *Ural* and stopped her engines suddenly, which were going at full speed. A torpedo lay on deck exposed, and ready to explode at any moment. Had the stem of the *Ural* touched its head, the results would have been disastrous both for her as well as for ourselves. Following in wake of the *Vladimir Monomakh,* in rear of our cruiser column, the *Zhemtshug* and she opened fire together on the enemy's cruisers. They were moving to port on a cross tack, and our cruisers, screening the transports, maintained the battle against them at a distance of thirty to forty cables. Our fire evidently told, for I could clearly see how the enemy altered their course and increased their distance from us. During this time our battleships had drawn ahead and had re-formed, having the Japanese to starboard. I counted the ships in the column, and assured myself that there were ten, and all sailing in perfect order. This spectacle had a pacifying effect on our overwrought nerves. It meant that only the *Kniaz Suvorov* and the *Oslabya* had gone; that all the others had got under the fires which had broken out on board, and, notwithstanding their damage, were continuing the battle. In front were the *Borodino* and *Orel*; behind them came Niebogatov's flagship, *Nicholas I,* three battleships of the *Admiral Ushakov* type, then the *Alexander III, Sissoi Veliky, Navarin,* and *Nakhimov.* The battleships were sailing approximately N. to N.W., and the enemy, holding the same course, and being to starboard of our column, were overtaking it as the battle continued.

It was about six o'clock in the evening. The cruiser *Svietlana* had become separated from the other cruisers and transports, which by this time were crowded together on the port beam of our battleships and out of range of the enemy's fire, and held a course parallel to the battleships.

We followed in her wake. The sun sank lower and lower, and it began to get dark. The flames of the fires on board some of the battleships stood out in clear bright patches.

Suddenly we noticed that the leading ship began to heel over on her starboard side, and in a few seconds the red painted part, normally below the waterline, was visible; the battleship still floated for a few moments on her side, and then disappeared beneath the waves. The end of the *Borodino* was heroic. Never leaving the line, notwithstanding all the damage she had suffered and the fires which had broken out on board, she still struck back at the enemy's vessels. Already heeling over to starboard, she kept on firing, and at the very moment of turning over on her side, she got away a shot from her after-turret. The red disc of the sun had sunk to the verge of the horizon. The atmosphere had now become clearer, and we could plainly see that well away forward to the N.W., and astern of the enemy's battleships, stretched a line of nine Japanese torpedo-boats, approaching to cut across our course. It was at this moment, I remember, that the signal was hoisted,—I do not know on board which ship first, for it was repeated by all—"The Admiral transfers the command to Niebogatov," and "Bear N.E. (to Vladivostok)." The battleships continued the fight. Darkness had fallen. The *Svietlana* then signalled, "I see torpedo-boats across my course," evidently the same that we had noticed earlier, and turned S.W. to avoid them. Complete disorder now reigned amongst our cruisers, transports, and torpedo-boats. The *Svietlana* was evidently disabled, for she was down by the bows, and began to circle round on the same spot. The *Zhemtshug* tried to keep in her wake, but afterwards abandoned the attempt. The transports and torpedo-boats were driven together, passing us at full speed. We noticed the *Oleg* (flying Admiral Enquist's flag), the *Aurora*, and after her the *Dmitri Donskoi*, and the *Monomakh*. . . .

It is very difficult to describe in detail what occurred in the dark. The *Zhemtshug* followed in the wake of the *Oleg* and the *Aurora*, and lost them, owing to the fact that these vessels were steaming in pitch-darkness, without lights. We turned towards the N.W., got within range of our retreating battleships, and finally picked up the *Oleg* and *Aurora* once more. They had been following in each other's tracks all the time. The last ships I was able to make out near us in the darkness were the transport *Irtish*, the cruiser *Vladimir Monomakh*, which had outstripped us, and a few torpedo-boats. All our men, while maintaining outward calm, were fearfully shaken and fatigued, both physically and morally, by the events of the battle and its impressions. The sight of the burning and sinking battleships could not but have its effect on their minds.

28 / ACROSS SIBERIA AND MANCHURIA

In the ethos of our day, imperialism stands condemned. But to dismiss Russian expansion merely as "bad" or to illustrate it exclusively with contemporary warnings, even to document it in terms of territories and peoples added, will not give us an understanding of the motivations, ambitions, self-justifications, in short the general outlook, that propelled the Russians forward. To understand what made Russian imperialism "tick," we must probe into the Russian mind.

In the following selection Dmitrii Abrikossow lays bare his thoughts as he recalls his first voyage across Siberia and Manchuria in 1908 as a young diplomat en route to Peking.

On my way to Peking I had to cross the whole of Siberia, Manchuria, and North China. No one can fail to be impressed by the journey through Siberia, especially the first time. The dimensions of Russia are staggering. You travel a day, you travel a week, you travel ten days, and you are still in Russia. Except for the Ural Mountains and a stretch near Lake Baikal, the country is absolutely flat. After you leave European Russia the population becomes very scarce; you pass hours and hours without seeing any village or habitation. Near the stations there are a few houses. Usually, when the express train arrives at the station, the entire local population comes to stare at the travelers. Especially in the evenings, when the train is brilliantly illuminated by electricity and the elegant figures of some inhabitants of Shanghai or other Far Eastern ports are visible inside, the travelers must appear to the local residents like men from another planet. What envy and dissatisfaction the exotic creatures in furs must provoke in the hearts of those doomed to spend their entire life in some miserable station!

I imagine a young girl who has not yet lost the capacity to dream waiting on the station platform. She hears the express approaching and sees it all illuminated. The train stops for five minutes. The passengers, looking like people from a fairy land, jump on the platform; they laugh and joke. There is a whistle, the train with its passengers disappears, and darkness, emptiness, and dullness reign again.

It is unjust that some should move from place to place in luxury, while others must remain in some forsaken place in misery. Small wonder that this should cause irritation and discontent. I am convinced that the

The Memoirs of Dmitrii Ivanovich Abrikossow, MS, I, 191-194, as edited and translated by G. A. Lensen. Published with permission of the Archive of Russian and East European History and Culture, Columbia University. The entire memoirs have been edited for publication by the University of Washington Press in Seattle.

Siberian express played an important part in the awakening of the population of Siberia and thereby hastened the coming of the revolution.

The sight of unlimited space and the absence of life begins to affect you, and the passengers prefer to pass their time in the diner, drinking endless glasses of tea and playing cards. . . .

Soon we found ourselves entering Manchuria. To my great disappointment, except for the ever-increasing crowds of Chinese, who made an awful noise, as if they were perpetually quarreling with each other, everything remained more or less identical—the same Russian train, the same Russian station with the Russian stationmaster in the red cap, the same three bells at the departure of the train, and, as we entered Harbin, the same Russian provincial town.

My first acquaintance with the Chinese Eastern Railway filled me with great pride. To come to the wild, robber-infested country and create in such short time the enormous enterprise that brought the vast region to life was proof of Russian genius. Once only a small Chinese village, Harbin was now a flourishing Russian town. It attracted many thousand Chinese who grew rich as a result of the Russian activity.

But we Russians had forgotten, when we created all this, that success provokes envy and that to maintain one's success one must be able to defend it. Furthermore, success breeds pride and greed. Unwilling to share our fortune with others, we did not realize that if the Chinese, the real owners of Manchuria, were too weak to do anything alone, they could intrigue and collaborate with envious neighbors. Unwittingly we were confronted with a great danger and were unable to cope with it. As a result the Russo-Japanese War ensued, and we lost half of our great work in Manchuria. But now, three years after the conclusion of peace, following an agreement with Japan, we have resumed our work, limiting our activity to northern Manchuria. Thus even after the lost war, as a Russian entered this part of Manchuria, where the influence of Russia could be seen at every step, he could not but take pride in the tremendous effort that his country had made in bringing this part of the world to life. I realize that the Chinese cannot share this feeling, but if they are incapable of doing the job themselves, surely they can allow others to do it for them, especially since they themselves will be the first beneficiaries. Alas, the word *independence* has such an attraction for human beings that they prefer to live like pigs but feel independent.

29 / MANCHURIA: A SENATOR'S VIEW

Dmitrii Abrikossow's pride in the civilizing rôle of Russia in Manchuria was not baseless. Manchu attempts to keep Chinese settlers out of the land of their forefathers had created a cultural as well as a human vacuum in this region. The eyewitness reflections of Senator Beveridge on the Russian occupation of Manchuria in the wake of the Boxer Rebellion dwell on Russia's greatest asset: the Russian people.

Russia, for all practical purposes, holds every foot of Manchuria in her firm, masterful, intelligent grasp. Russian law, in the sense that all shall have justice regularly administered; Russian order, in the sense that murder and outrage by robber bands and savage clans shall cease; Russian system, in the sense that regularity and method shall succeed continuous social, political, and commercial disturbance—Russian law, order, and system, as thus understood, are there, and, it appears to the observer, are there forever. Chinese law still exists in Manchuria; but it is now promptly and impartially administered. Forever is a long time; but it is not extravagant to use the word with reference to Russia in Manchuria, because it is a fact, to which attention will be hereafter given, that Russia has seldom, if ever, permanently retreated from any spot where her authority has been established, except Alaska, which she believed she was selling to a permanently friendly nation. But whether she remains or departs will be a sheer question of what she wants to do, and not a question of what she must do. Even temporary evacuation will mean little as to her ultimate purposes; for she will leave behind her foundations of permanent occupation, to which at any time she can return. An achievement so vast, so quietly accomplished, so cheaply secured, so easily consummated, so important in itself, and so beyond calculation in its influence upon the rest of the world, compels the admiration of every thinking mind, no matter whether you regret or whether you applaud while you admire.

And you are struck by the fact (nay, if you be Anglo-Saxon, you are startled by it) that all of this mingled motley of humanity get along in perfect harmony. The bronzed Korean, the queued Chinaman, and the blue-eyed, yellow-haired Russian soldier arrange themselves on an open flat-car in a human mosaic of mutual agreeableness. There is no race prejudice here then! Superior to all the world, as the Russian believes himself, he shows no offensive manner towards the other races with

Albert J. Beveridge, *The Russian Advance* (New York: Harper & Row, Publishers, 1903), pp. 9-10, 16-17, 21, 23-26, 29-32.

which he so picturesquely mingles. It is a thing you must have noticed up in Siberia, where the Russian peasant is also coming in contact with semi-Oriental peoples. But, with the blood of racial bigotry coursing through your veins, here this social fusion of races startles you. It is a strange page suddenly opened before you. And it is a page you will read again and again every day as long as you are in Manchuria. And from a reading of it a lesson may be learned, and part of Russia's secret of dominion revealed.

It is more than a hundred miles into Manchuria that you encounter this striking material evidence of the Russianization of the country—a Russian town being built side by side with the decaying, germ-infected collection of hovels which compose the Chinese town. The residences of this Russian town are of wood perhaps, or stone, as taste determines. They are pleasant to look upon, too. Indeed, the homes of merchant or miner or officer, or even of moujik [a Russian peasant] in Siberia are often much handsomer than those ordinarily occupied by the same class in Russia; and it would seem that this comparative superiority is to be repeated in Manchuria. Generous verandas circle the home of a railway official; cool awnings of blue, shifting with the sun, protect these porches from its rays. Young trees are planted along the new-made streets. Occasionally a block is reserved for a miniature park; and, again, there are trees fresh planted, and the color and fragrance of flowers. This, in contrast, is the order, the loveliness, the system, the cleanliness which Russia in Manchuria is building over against Chinese aggregations of corruption, disease, disorder, and all unsightliness. If the Russian is uncivilized, as it has been the fashion to declare, at least in Manchuria he is erecting precisely those very things which, in America, we look upon as the results and proofs of civilization.

Again and yet again you are impressed with this—the Russian soldier in Manchuria is a laboring man first and a military man afterwards. It is an item not to be overlooked—indeed, the Russian soldier must be most carefully considered by those who are estimating the forces influencing the world at present. No toil is too heavy for him; no hardship is to him a hardship at all. He will fell trees, excavate ditches, build houses with the same good-humor with which he will go into action where wounds and death are his sure reward.

In Manchuria there are three classes of the Russian soldier: the Cossack first, then the railway-guard, and then numbers of that host of which the Russian army is composed, the common soldier of the empire. . . .

The Russian women in the interior of Manchuria are wives of those hearty, wholesome-looking, bearded giants, the railway-guards. Even at the dangerous period, when the journey was taken which these chapters chronicle, and at points hundreds of versts in the interior, these women-mates of Russia's workingmen-soldiers were seen at the scarce-erected stations of the railroad which was then being constructed. They were there selling milk or melons or berries or quass (a non-intoxicating Russian drink made out of black bread or berries). So far have Russian and Siberian conditions reproduced themselves in Manchuria that the only difference observed at the railway-stations was the unfinished nature of the road and the increasing number of Koreans and Chinese.

For the Russian peasant is there, as he is in western Siberia, and the Russian peasant's wife is there, as she is in Siberia, and the little, white-haired children, with the pale-blue eye of the Slav, are there, as they are in Siberia; and, as in Siberia and Russia, the little girls from eight to twelve are universally carrying in their arms infant brothers and sisters of as many months or even weeks, for Russian children are being born in Manchuria. And a land where a people's dead are buried, where a people's children are born, becomes to that people sacred soil. Russian homes, not for railway official only, but for the "peasant guard," are springing up throughout Manchuria. Manchurian fields are being languidly cultivated by Russian hands. It is all quite "temporary," of course; you can read it for yourself in the treaty. And, besides, the railway-guard's term of enlistment—or, rather, his contract—is for only five years. But the Slav root strikes quickly into new soil, and having struck, history tells us that, usually, it stays.

30 / MONGOLIA

Mongolia was another region that Russia coveted. During the service of Dmitrii Abrikossow as Second Secretary of the Russian Embassy in Peking, in the years centering about the Chinese Revolution of 1911-12, Russia presented China with a number of claims. Most of these, as Abrikossow recalls, concerned Mongolia. In this excerpt from his memoirs, Abrikossow shares the frustrations as well as the machinations and ill-gotten gains of imperialism.

Most of these claims concerned Mongolia, which until the Chinese Revolution was considered part of China. As this huge but sparsely

The Memoirs of D. I. Abrikossow, MS, I, 225-230, as edited and translated by G. A. Lensen. Published with permission of the Archive of Russian and East European History and Culture, Columbia University.

populated land was situated along the Siberian frontier, far from any other country, the temptation to submit it to Russian influence was very great. After all, the forward movement of Russia into Asia, which had started in 1581, when some 840 Cossacks under the command of Yermak had conquered nearly the whole of Siberia, had never stopped. In subsequent years Russian expeditions had brought order to the newly acquired lands. Different Tartar and Mongol chiefs voluntarily submitted to the White Tsar, as the Asian tribes called the Russian Emperor, and by the twentieth century all Siberia from the Ural Mountains to the Pacific Ocean had become an inalienable part of Russia. Today this would be labeled "aggressive imperialism," but I think it would be more correct to call it the healthy growth of a big state, which cannot tolerate at its frontiers vast, undefined empty lands with nomadic tribes in a very primitive state of civilization wandering about. The Chinese realized this and in the years before the Revolution began to colonize these lands and submit them to Chinese administration. The Mongols did not like it and with their horses and sheep moved to the north, where they fell under Russian influence and easily became tools in anti-Chinese intrigues. This created a great deal of misunderstanding between Russia and China and gave the clever and ambitious Russian representatives in Peking the opportunity to display brilliant diplomatic fireworks.

I remember how one morning, when I was trying to put the archives into order, the Minister entered after his morning ride and said that he was greatly annoyed by the tendency of our Foreign Office to let slip by all opportunities for the adjustment of our relations with the Mongols, and then he asked if I had not found in the archives something exciting with which we could arouse St. Petersburg from its slumber. I replied that only the day before I had found some correspondence about the part of Outer Mongolia known as Uriankhai. According to this correspondence some fifty years ago an officer attached to the governor general of Irkutsk had discovered in the archives that during the reign of Catherine the Great the Khan of Uriankhai had submitted to the Empress by agreeing to pay an annual tribute of several skins of sable. With time the Khan had disappeared, no skins were sent, and the land, with the rest of Mongolia, became Chinese territory. The governor general had sent the officer to Uriankhai, where he had discovered some stone markers, which could be taken as proof that according to the old frontier this land was Russian. The governor general had sent a report to St. Petersburg and the Emperor had written on it that it was inadmissable that part of Russian territory should be included in the Chinese Empire. The report was sent to the Foreign Office which, fearing complications, had given the Emperor some explanation and the whole matter had been forgotten. The Minister asked me to send him the whole correspondence. The next morning I found him beaming. He said that the correspondence was ideal for his purpose and at once sent a report to the Foreign Office and the governor general of Irkutsk, expressing astonishment that nothing had been done to implement the decision of the Emperor. In vain the Foreign Office tried to stop the Minister—the matter came to a head by a representative of the governor general of Irkutsk coming to Peking to aid the Minister. At the same time the governor general of the Priamur region sent a colonel to claim some territory along the Amur, insisting that the river which served as a frontier between Russia and China had changed its course and that the land from which the Cossacks had used to get hay for their cattle found itself on the Chinese side. Each colonel tried to persuade the Minister that his claim was more important than the other's. Each took his affair so much to heart that they quarreled and stopped speaking to each other. In the end the Chinese, whose troubles were increasing daily, agreed to satisfy both claims. Russia got a piece of land bigger than the whole territory of France, and the Cossacks got the fodder for their cattle. The peace was restored between the two colonels, and at the farewell dinner in their honor they got slightly drunk and sang an endless duet about some prisoners in Siberia.

As stated already, Mongolia had proclaimed its independence following the abdication of the Chinese Emperor. Russia, not wanting a change that might provoke international complications, made an agreement with the Chinese in which Russia promised to persuade the Mongolian government to recognize the suzerainty of China in return for Chinese recognition of the autonomy of Mongolia, which implied that no Chinese soldiers or officials were to be sent there. The Mongols proved more difficult to persuade than the Chinese, but our former Minister in Peking who was sent to Urga succeeded and a Russo-Chinese-Mongolian tripartite agreement was concluded. Thus without hostilities, annexation of territory, or international complications, the vast Mongolian region was opened to Russian political and commercial activity. By the time the foreign powers began to take interest in the matter, everything had been finished in such a way that there was no cause for any legal argument against the arrangement. Our legation had a right to be proud of this diplomatic triumph. What we did not know at the time was that the coming revolution in Russia would compromise all the advantages acquired by the old Russian diplomacy.

The problem after the conclusion of the agreement mentioned above was to create in Mongolia a government capable of ruling the autonomous country. There were two authorities in Mongolia: the princes who ruled the separate parts of the territory; and the body of lamas, clergy of a branch of Buddhism in which the innumerable monks who filled the monasteries played the chief rôle, because the general superstition of the people wielded great influence throughout the country. The head of those lamas, the so-called Hutukhtu in Urga, was considered to be a reincarnation of Buddha. These Living Buddhas usually came from Tibet, where they were chosen by the local monasteries, after complicated ceremonies, from among the newborn babies; after strict religious training, at the age of eight or ten, they were sent to Mongolian monasteries, where they were ruled by the lamas, and became objects of great veneration. In order to avoid a civil war, that would inevitably have ensued if one of the princes had been placed at the head of the government, the Russian advisers decided to follow the example of Tibet, and put at the helm of the state the Hutukhtu of Urga and a Council of Ministers chosen from among the princes—the Russian Consul General at Urga playing the rôle of chief adviser to the new government in order to train the princes in the art of ruling. At present such a setup would be called a "puppet government," but if a people is absolutely incapable of ruling itself, such a puppet government is the only alternative to complete subjugation of the country to alien rule. There could be no doubt that the Mongols had not progressed since the time of Genghis Khan, who had led them to world conquest; indeed they had so degenerated that they were incapable of ruling themselves and could not keep their independence, and Russia had all the trouble of creating a semblance of self-government. A Russian officer who served as instructor of the new Mongolian Army related how once, when a Russian general arrived to inspect the Mongolian troops, the Mongolian Minister of War was invited to be present at the review, but could not be awakened after a heavy dinner. When he did come at last, he showed no interest in the proceedings until he espied the general's spurs. Then he came to life, squatted down behind the general, and started to turn the little wheels. With such material it is difficult to build anything other than a "puppet government." As to the Living Buddha, he was perpetually drunk and created a scandal by taking a wife who ruled in his place.

IV / SINCE THE REVOLUTION

INTRODUCTION

Japan's victory over China dispelled Western fears of China's potential power—the hidden dissuader, restraining Western ambitions until that time—and opened the floodgates to imperialistic demands for bases and spheres of influence. At the same time, Japan's leap to modernization upset the applecart of White Supremacy in the Far East. Relations there could no longer be viewed exclusively in terms of Western action and Asian reaction. Asia, in the person of Japan, had begun to do some initiating of its own. No longer were Far Eastern international relations a mere extension of European rivalry to the Orient; increasingly they became an integral part of world affairs.

In the days of the pony express and sailboats, foreign policy was to a large extent the policy of those abroad rather than of statesmen in the capitals. This was true not only of Russia but also of England, the United States, and other countries. As long as Russian forays were directed at sparsely inhabited political no man's lands, individual adventurers could bear the mantle of imperialism. But confrontation with civilized states, capable of organized resistance, changed the picture. By the beginning of the twentieth century, Russian expansion, like that of other powers, had become more directly the handmaiden of the state.

The Communist Revolution of 1917 dramatically altered the international position of Russia. Withdrawing from the war, the Bolsheviks forfeited the empire in the west; refusing to honor the commitments of their predecessors and seeking to ignite the fuse of world revolution, they aroused a wall of hostility that ostracized their country. But there was strength in their weakness. To the people of Asia, especially the Chinese, who had been shortchanged at the Paris Peace Conference when the Allies had handed to Japan the German holdings in China instead of returning them to the latter, Western dislike of Bolshevik Russia was a recommendation, and Communist professions of anticolonialism a welcome serenade.

Denied by China the concessions and extraterritorial privileges extorted by the Tsarist government, the Communists made a virtue out of their weakness and glibly renounced in theory the fruits of imperialism, which they had already lost in fact. As they consolidated their power and were able to flex their muscles, they modified their self-denial with equal agility. By 1929 Russia and China were practically at war over the Chinese Eastern Railway. Here as elsewhere, ideology proved the servant rather than the master of the state—national interests reasserting themselves increasingly in Soviet thinking.

During the period between the two world wars Russia's Far Eastern policy was relatively passive as she licked the wounds of civil war and foreign intervention and groped with internal problems. To be sure, she had her collisions with China and Japan, set up a puppet government in Outer Mongolia, and radiated agents in every direction, but all in all, she was subjected to more pressure than she exerted. It was the destruction of the balance of power in the Far East by Allied elimination of Japan in 1945 and the collapse of Nationalist China by 1949 that created a power vacuum into which Russia was sucked with relatively little exertion on her own part. The revolutions that flared up throughout Asia, ignited as much by internal combustion as by external subversion, burned a path for renewed Russian eastward expansion.

31 / THE SCYTHIANS

The Russian people were the first victims of Communism. Among the freedoms they lost was the freedom to go abroad at will. In time the barrier that separated them from the rest of the world became so formidable as to be labeled the "Iron Curtain." While the civil war was still in progress, however, thousands upon thousands of anti-Communists, ranging from Monarchists to Social Revolutionaries, were able to flee in all directions. Very many made their way across Siberia to Manchuria, China proper, and Japan.

Losing their citizenship as they refused to recognize the Soviet regime, the refugees were neither colonists nor political agents of Russian expansion. But there were many intellectuals among them, and they were disseminators of Russian culture, especially in places where they settled

Sir Cecil Kisch, *Alexander Blok, Prophet of Revolution: A Study of His Life and Work Illustrated by Translations from His Poems and Other Writings* (London: Weidenfeld and Nicolson, 1960), pp. 152-54. Reprinted with permission of George Weidenfeld & Nicolson Ltd.

in "colonies" of countrymen. At the same time the majority had lost their possessions and were forced to live hand-to-mouth in squalor.

Poverty is a great leveler. The appearance of the Caucasian, who heretofore had insisted on his superiority, in a position of equality, indeed of inferiority, made a profound impression on the Chinese and Japanese. It was another nail in the coffin of white domination.

While many Russians were fleeing abroad to escape the new order, the spectre of Allied intervention in the Russian civil war haunted those who remained behind. To keep the foreigners at bay the well-known Russian poet Alexander Blok reminded them of the vital rôle that his country had played in shielding Europe from Asia. Stressing Russia's Asian roots, he extended the hand of friendship, while threatening at the same time that if her friendship should be rebuffed, Russia would step aside and let the yellow hordes overrun the West. Russia gazed upon Europe, he wrote, "with hate and love," and reminded the would-be intruders that "there still dwells on earth a love that can both burn and kill!"

The Scythians

*Panmongolism! Though the name is fierce
Yet it caresses my ear.*

VLADIMIR SOLOVYOV

You're millions, we are hosts—and hosts—and hosts!
    Engage with us and prove our seed!
We're Scythians and Asians too, from coasts
    That breed squint eyes, bespeaking greed!

Yours are the ages—ours is but one hour
    We, slavelike, to obedience steeled,
Have between Europe and the Mongol power,
    Two foemen races, held a shield!

From age to age your ancient forge has pealed
    And drowned the avalanche's din:
What tale of horror was for you revealed
    By ruined Lisbon and Messine!

For aeons towards the East you looked in quest
    Of gems to fuse, of pearls to weigh:
You thought it but a time, with mocking jest,
    The barrels of your guns to lay!

The hour has struck. Winged cares rush on apace:
    Offense each day still ranker grows!
The time shall come when none perhaps shall trace
    Where once your walls of Paestum rose.

Old world, while unto death thou art oppressed,
   While life from sweets of torment sinks!
Stay, greatly wise, like Oedipus, to test
   The ancient riddle of the Sphinx!

Russia's a Sphinx! Triumphant, though in pain,
   She bathes her limbs in blood's dark stream.
Her eyes gaze on you—gaze and gaze again
   With hate and love in single beam!

With love, as our blood learns to love from birth,—
   With such love you long ceased to thrill!
Forgot by you that there still dwells on earth
   A love that can both burn and kill!

All things we love. Cold numbers breathing fires,
   And visions, too, from God consigned.
All things we sense, how Gallic wit inspires,
   How gloom enshrouds the Teuton mind . . .

All things we recollect, the hell-racked street,
   Of Paris, cool Venetian airs
That waft from lemon groves a fragrance sweet,
   Cologne that spreads her smoke-clad squares . . .

And flesh we love, its colour and its taste:
   Flesh with its mortal stifling smell . . .
What blame is ours if your bones crush to waste?
   The clutch of our soft hands is fell!

We're trained to seize the bridle of the horse,
   That with undaunted mettle plays,
To smite his hardy flank of stubborn force,
   To tame the slave-girl's mulish ways . . .

Come you to us! Abandon war and death—
   Come, choose the kiss of peace! Agree
While still 'tis not too late, old swords to sheath . . .
   Comrades, let us true brothers be!

If you renounce, will it for us be worse?
   We know the ways of treachery!
From age to age you'll know the morbid curse
   Of a remote posterity!

Afar through densest woodland we'll retire
   And leave fair Europe in our rear,
And backwards on you we shall so conspire
   To turn our Asiatic leer!

Go, go you all, to Ural's distant land!
We clear an open space for swords
And iron chariots with precision planned—
There meet the savage Mongol hordes!

No more ourselves shall be your shield and foil;
Ourselves no more to fight shall rise!
Spectators we, as war's grim cauldrons boil,
Shall stare with narrow-slitted eyes!

We shall not stir when those wild Huns shall search
The pockets of the slain for spoil,
Burn towns and stable horses in the church
And fat of our white brothers boil!

Old world—once more—awake! Your brothers' plight,
To toil and peace, a feast of fire.
Once more! Come, join your brothers' festal light—
Obey the call of Barbary's lyre!

JANUARY 1918

32 / THE COMMUNIST WORLD VIEW

It is a tenet of Communist doctrine that the prosperity of the capitalist West rests on the exploitation of China and other colonial or semicolonial countries. The strengthening of the position of these nations vis-à-vis the West, be it even through the support of an anti-Communist regime, is regarded as tantamount to pulling the rug out from under the feet of Western capitalism.

It should not be surprising, therefore, that the Communists had barely come to power in Russia when they offered their support to the Chinese revolutionaries, who were struggling to erect a workable republic on the ruins of the Manchu monarchy. Western reluctance to help Sun Yat-sen, the most democratic of the revolutionary contenders, in his desperate struggle with rival cliques of war lords guaranteed the acceptance of Russian offers of aid; and in 1923, a year before the conclusion of the first Sino-Soviet treaty, Chiang Kai-shek was sent to Russia to study Communist military strategy and organization. In 1924 Mikhail Borodin helped Sun rebuild the Chinese Nationalist Party on the Soviet framework and trained Chinese cadres in the techniques of successful revolution. In 1926-27 the forces of Chiang, Sun's brother-in-law and successor, extended their control in the country, thanks to Soviet advice, notably that of General Galen (Vasilii Blücher).

The reunification of China had not been completed when Chiang, fearful lest Soviet guidance mature into Soviet dictation, abruptly turned against the Communists and expelled the Russian advisers. In 1929 China and the U.S.S.R. crossed swords over the Chinese Eastern Railway. Nevertheless, in spite of continued friction and animosity, the Soviet government until the closing days of World War II generally continued to support Chiang more than the Chinese Communists. The idealism of world revolution had been overtaken by the realities of national security and the Soviet Union needed a strong China as a buffer against Japan. Until 1945 Chiang seemed the only man capable of rallying his countrymen in common resistance to Japanese aggression. At the same time Chiang's nationalism fitted into the over-all Communist objective of destroying Western domination in the Far East.

Open support of revolutionary movements in foreign countries was not always politic, and Lenin camouflaged Russian subversion in the Comintern, the Communist International, an association of Communist parties of the world, founded by him in 1919 and dominated by the Russian party. It was the Executive Committee of the Comintern which convened the First Congress of the Toilers of the Far East (January 1922) as a countermove to the "capitalist" Washington Conference. The Manifesto of the Congress, a vivid sample of the ideological diatribe that was to garb Communist pronouncements, shows how Russia sought to undermine the position of the colonial powers from "within." When her own national interests were at stake, however, the Soviet Union did not hesitate to act directly. An article regarding the Sino-Soviet conflict of 1929, translated from the Young Communist, *illustrates the chauvinism, vituperation, and "double-think" of Communist writing.*

Manifesto of the Toilers of the Far East

Toilers of the Far East!

Workers and peasants of China, Korea, Japan, Mongolia, the Pacific Isles, Indochina, and the Dutch Indies!

Enslaved nations of the Far East!

For many years you have been suffering from the robberies and the savage club-law of the European, American, and Japanese vultures. The Japanese oppressors have bespattered Korea with blood from end to end. The Japanese, American, French, and English robbers are plundering and tearing to pieces China, with her four hundred million population, and are building their own welfare on the blood and tears of the Chinese people. They do not look upon the representatives of the oppressed nations as human beings. They want gold that glitters, profits, wealth, and to get them they are ready to sacrifice hundreds of millions of human

From *Soviet Russia and the East 1920-1927: A Documentary Survey* by Xenia Joukoff Eudin and Robert C. North, pp. 230-31. Copyright © 1957 by the Board of Trustees of the Leland Stanford Junior University. Reprinted with the permission of the Stanford University Press.

lives. Chinese and Koreans are not allowed to enter the gardens and other public places in the foreign quarters of Peking, Shanghai, Tientsin, Hong Kong, Seoul, and Chemulpho—on a par with dogs. In these quarters foreign bourgeois, fattened on other men's blood and sweat, ride about in carriages drawn by men-horses, the rickshas, hastening them with kicks and sticks. The most oppressed and browbeaten slave of the rich of the world—the Chinese coolie—works for these parasites to a state of deadly exhaustion. The Chinese peasant toils beyond his strength sixteen and eighteen hours a day at a stretch, only to see his labor enrich the foreign money-lenders and bloodsuckers and their mercenary lackeys. The Korean pauper has no land to work on for his daily bread. The land is in the hands of the Japanese planter, the landowner, and the capitalist, who with their [minions'] guns and bayonets force the refractory to do the work. Every word of protest, every cry of desperation, is smothered by the rattle of mass shootings in the Philippines, on the island of Formosa, in Indochina and the islands of the Dutch Indies, as well as in near-by British India, which has long been a terrible prison for a people of three hundred millions. Millions of people who are toiling on rice, coffee, cotton, and other plantations, are most cruelly exploited. Only recently has Mongolia been able to free herself from Japanese and White Guard clutches. In Japan, where the ruling classes gained the nickname of "hangmen of the Far East," the factory workers and the peasant-laborers—partly daily laborers on rented land—lead an existence fit only for lower animals. The heavy groans of enslaved hundreds of millions are heard everywhere. The oppressors will hear nothing of freedom and independence for the oppressed nations, nor of their human rights. They have met lately in the halls of the American Exchange in Washington, in order to come to an understanding on how to plunder anew the countries of the Far East. There they have signed their alliance of the four bloodsuckers. Korea, the Russian Far East, and Manchuria have been given over to be robbed and pillaged by Japan. The principle of equal rights of robbery in China has been set up, leaving the leading role in this base affair to American capital. The consortium of 1918, invented by America, was to make all the Chinese peasants into tributaries of American capital: they were to pay a considerable tax to the American bankers. Chinese industry was to become subordinate entirely to American. Nothing came of this enterprise in 1918 owing to differences among the oppressors and the unanimous protest by the masses of the Chinese people. Now the vultures desire to create a new consortium—an international firm for the military, financial, and industrial robbery of China. Japan, America, England and France have, for the time being, put off a war, which was ready to break out, for domination over the Pacific. They have postponed it (but not given it up entirely) in order to be able to continue to rob in unison a little while longer.

The World War of 1914 has undermined their strength. The workers' revolution has taken them by the throat in Europe on the very spot of their bloody crime. They have struggled for four years against the Soviet republic, the promised land of all the oppressed and exploited, and they now must openly recognize its strength and their own inability to defeat the Soviets. They hope to re-establish their undermined power in the Far East at our expense and at the price of our lives, our blood, and our toil. They bring new chains, new horrors, and a still more terrible enslavement to the patient and resigned peoples of the Far East.

This must not, this shall not be! We desire to become the masters of our own fate and to stop being the playthings of the imperialists' cupidity and greedy appetites.

The Communist International has sent out a great appeal: World proletarians and all oppressed nations of the world, unite!

We will carry this appeal to our destroyed villages, to the slave plantations, to the factories, schools, and barracks.

We have met in the Red capitals of the Soviet republic—Moscow and Petrograd—in order to raise our voices from this world tribune against the world executioners and against the Washington union of the four bloodsuckers. . . .

The Little Napoleons of Nanking

The old Chinese dynasties trained a particular type of diplomat—the Mandarins. These diplomats had to be extraordinarily shifty and impudent, able to distort and garble [facts], to lie straight into one's eyes, in short, to swindle right and left. The new Chinese diplomats (new, incidentally, only in Kuomintang "form," but not in feudal-bourgeois essence) have fully mastered the science of diplomatic deceit left to them as a legacy by Imperial China.

With such a diplomatic "apparatus" the Nanking leaders have embarked on a dangerous voyage on the Chinese Eastern Railway. It is well-known already that the conflict which had arisen "unexpectedly" had been thoroughly considered by the Nanking leaders together with the Manchurian robber-generals.

The conflict was a test of strength for the loving concord of the

Dmitrii Lebedev, "Nankinskie napoleonchiki" (The little Napoleons of Nanking) *Iunyi Kommunist*, 1929, No. 19, pp. 10-12, 15. Translated by G. A. Lensen. Nanking was the capital of China at that time.

Nanking-Mukden military. The Chiang Kai-shek clique, after disposing of the Kwangsiites and temporarily crowding out Fêng Yü-hsiang, had proud dreams of a grand entry in the diplomatic arena of the world. Many had already tried to find a Napoleonic cocked hat on the Soviet borders. Kolchak, Denikin, Yudenich, Chaikovski, Skoropadski, Pilsudski —which of these did not many times, in the innermost circle of his attending lickspittles, try on this cocked hat?

On our Manchurian and Mongolian frontiers the marshal baton had already smiled at Kolchak, Semenov, Ungern, Chang Tso-lin. "These no longer exist, the others are far away." Chang Hsüeh-liang, the pitiful offspring of his bloodthirsty pop, thought more about drawing-room pleasures with high-ranking prostitutes and about a good portion of cocaine than about testing strength with the Soviet giant. But that which is not lawful for an ox is quite lawful for Jupiter. The young god [Chiang Kai-shek] of the Chinese bourgeoisie convinced Chang Hsüeh-liang that a conflict with the Soviet Union can give them both marshal batons and international glory as champions of civilization.

The trick was simple, and so was the calculation:

> We shall insult the U.S.S.R. The U.S.S.R. will declare war. Before she realizes what happens, we shall cross the frontier. America, England, Japan come to our aid. And then—an effective raid through the spaces of Siberia and glory to the deliverer of world civilization from the sore of bolshevism.

The calculation failed. The U.S.S.R. would not be provoked. With firmness and determination, the U.S.S.R. demanded the resumption of the interrupted normal work of the road and took measures to defend its borders. Further provocation was attempted. As a precaution Chang Hsüeh-liang left on an extended vacation in order to shift the blame onto local officials—the "switchmen" on the wide road of Chinese diplomatic deceit. Once again the provocation did not succeed. Instead the position of the U.S.S.R. hardened further. The border proved closed. The leading workers of the road departed for the U.S.S.R. The majority of the others refused to work. The road stopped.

Then the most dangerous provocation was begun: White [Russian] Guard sorties along the border. The very first scouts laid down their heads in inglorious clashes with our border units. At Pogranichnaia, Chalainor, and other border points, the Mukden forces chanced provoking the Red units into a clash. The provocation had a sad ending: the Soviet bayonet endured the trial with honor, and the lovers of frontier adventures had their paws chopped off.

The failure of the "positive" policy, i.e., of the policy of direct action, forced the Nanking leaders to embark on the tried road of diplomatic deceit. That is when the experience of the old Mandarins came in handy! To be sure, dishonest experiments had been undertaken already in the first stage of the conflict. After the attack on Soviet organizations in Harbin, the Nanking diplomats had asserted in broadcasted interviews that they had not been privy to it, that the Mukden authorities had staged this "local pogrom" on their own.

When the arrest of Soviet citizens and the deportation of leading workers of the Chinese Eastern Railway began, it became already very difficult to demonstrate the nonparticipation of Nanking, and the Nanking diplomats thereupon feverishly advanced the argument of propaganda. It was a cheap, trite trick, long ago exploited by all kinds of Curzons, Briands, and similar Chamberlains. Chinese diplomacy proved to be by no means the first student of Downing Street.

For a while the inventiveness of the Nanking Chamberlains was confined to this. But, as the conflict unfolded, they began to show their existence with extraordinarily fertile "information," which like a torrent of dirty lava suddenly gushed down the broad river bed of the imperialistic press.

There was not a day in the history of the Sino-Soviet conflict that the countless Chinese telegraph agencies—all kinds of Kuo-wen, Kuo-min, Ta-chun, and the like—did not clutter up the telegraph and the radio with their abundant fabrications. In China every self-respecting governor general has his own agency to make mankind happy with his political revelations. It is easy to understand that under the circumstances the creativity of the political leaders of Nanking has no bounds.

The first thing that could be determined under such guidance of public opinion was that the U.S.S.R. persistently sought the receiving of its diplomats by Nanking, which, however, maintained a firm and uncompromising position. Alas, there exists in China in addition to the Chinese press also a foreign press, English, American, Japanese, and the like. It discovered instead, that at the very moment that these militant pronouncements were being made, the plenipotentiary of the Mukden rulers, Tsai, bombarded the Soviet authorities of the Far East with his proposals.

These proposals paved the way for the peaceful settlement of the conflict. Tsai, in essence, accepted the proposal of the Soviet Union. This peace-loving policy was dictated to him by the Mukden rulers, who had experienced on their own skin all the unpleasant aspects of the conflict: bankruptcy, chaos in transportation, the shattering of all border adventures, the lording of White Guardsmen in Harbin and along the Chinese

Eastern Railway, with the resulting disorganization of the economy of the region.

But the Nanking Napoleon managed to put an end to this peaceful conspiracy in time. Chiang Kai-shek was not at all disposed to give up this easily his hope for a marshal's baton. Furthermore, the first clash with the Red Army would fall with all its weight onto the shoulders of Chang Hsüeh-liang. The destruction of the Manchurian dictator was fully in the interest of Chiang Kai-shek, as it would remove from his path one of his strongest rivals. As to further consequences, Chiang Kai-shek does not consider them: sweet dreams becloud his reason.

The attempt of the Mukdenites fell through. In reply to the clearly expressed readiness of the Soviet government to expedite the peaceful settlement of the conflict, the Nanking diplomacy played a deceitful trick: Chang Tso-lin came forth with "peace" proposals, which in actuality nullified everything that Tsai had proposed.

This was but a "pen probe" of the Nanking swindlers. Events soon showed that there were experts in this business in Nanking. Soon the international press learned that the U.S.S.R. still strove to negotiate and that, in general, the matter of China was in the bag, that all that China had to do was to wish. . . . China, of course, was eager for peace and was ready at this very moment to come to terms, but the U.S.S.R. was being difficult. The U.S.S.R. insisted on its proposals. The U.S.S.R. was attacking. Help! China, and with it the whole of world civilization, was in danger.

From the very beginning and throughout the entire development of the conflict the wretched Nanking diplomats resorted to deceitful profiteering methods, attempting thereby to justify their provocotive actions. It was a characteristic measure of this policy to falsify the last Soviet proposals in the matter of the appointment of a director of the Chinese Eastern Railway. The Soviet government proposed to appoint a director immediately. In reply the Nanking diplomats agreed with innocent faces that the Soviet Union immediately "recommend" such a director. After thus twisting the Soviet note unsuccessfully, the Nanking bandits in diplomatic clothing rejected all the proposals, which had been made by the Soviet government from the very beginning of the conflict, as the only condition of solving it peacefully.

The new Nanking proposal, transmitted thereafter through the German Embassy, proved a usual, no-less-unscrupulous attempt of the Nanking good-for-nothing diplomats to catch the Soviet government by means of a very simple trick. Substituting for the question of the appointment of the director the question of the appointment of his assistant, the Nanking government tried to legalize those infractions of the Peking and Mukden agreements which had precipitated the break.

At the same time there continues the torrent of fabrications about the continuing negotiations with the U.S.S.R.: these fabrications are to persuade the toiling masses of China of the "love of peace" of the Nanking bandits. But simultaneously armed raids against our border continue. Entangled in insoluble internal contradictions, which threaten to erupt in renewed general fighting, the Nanking diplomats continue to count on the support of the League of Nations or the American capital. All their unsuccessful tricks are only hopeless attempts to escape from these contradictions. These wretched diplomatic dodges are the best proof that the necessary solution of the conflict can be guaranteed only by a firm position on the part of the Soviet government. . . .

A firm position on the part of the Soviet government is the only guarantee of peace. All that the Nanking military has to oppose this position are the deceitful methods of its diplomacy and the shaky internal condition of China, where the first general fighting is already imminent and where the wave of revolutionary movement is rising steadily.

The Sino-Soviet conflict is not yet over, but its outcome is already taking shape to the disadvantage of the Nanking government. Once again Soviet diplomacy and the Red Army have shown to the whole world the might of the Soviet Union, whose stronghold has shattered ingloriously the proud dreams of the unsuccessful Chinese Napoleons.

33 / THE NON-RUSSIAN RUSSIANS

Russian activity beyond her own frontiers did not signify a bursting at the seams. Far from being overpopulated, Siberia was still underdeveloped in men and machines. But the balance was gradually changing. Russia's eastward expansion, within her own borders, was a continuing process.

In the United States we constantly speak of "Russia." But in the Soviet Union "Russia" is little used. The many nationalities of which the Russian Empire is composed receive greater play in the term "Union of Soviet Socialist Republics." The Soviets lose no opportunity to lambaste segregation in the United States; yet actually the "separate but equal" approach is more in line with their own thinking than is integration, which, in their view, would deprive the minorities of the opportunity to develop their own cultures. While Americans of Chinese and Japanese ancestry want to be regarded as Americans and look at any identification by race as

Walter Kolarz, *Russia and Her Colonies* (New York: Frederick A. Praeger, Inc., 1952), pp. 303-304, 307-13. Reprinted with permission of Frederick A. Praeger, Inc.

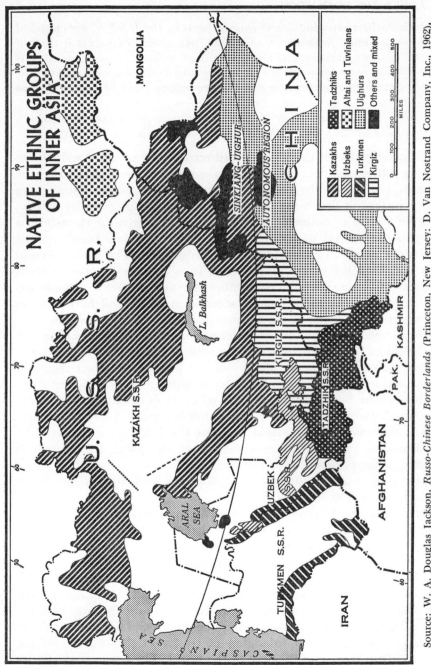

Source: W. A. Douglas Jackson, *Russo-Chinese Borderlands* (Princeton, New Jersey: D. Van Nostrand Company, Inc., 1962), p. 8. Reprinted with permission of the publisher.

potentially discriminatory, their counterparts in the U.S.S.R. are classified as "Chinese" and "Japanese" rather than "Russian." The same is true, of course, of Jews, Armenians, Georgians, and other nationalities. But if Russification is no longer policy, it yet remains an inescapable fact of life, for the heartbeat of expansion and the generating force of modernization are Russian.

In the following selection Walter Kolarz compares the nationalities policy of the Communists with the Russification policy of the tsars.

An investigation of the Soviet record territory by territory and nationality by nationality does not bear out the claim of the Kremlin that the U.S.S.R. has solved the problem of nationalities. Soviet nationalities policy, instead of destroying Russian imperialism, has in reality tried to preserve and to consolidate it. This has led to a crisis in the relations between the central authorities of the Soviet Russian State and the dependent peoples fighting for national liberation. The Second World War laid bare the extent of the crisis in a number of areas (North Caucasus, Crimea, Ukraine, etc.). Since the war the Soviet régime has tried to solve it by tightening up security measures and by increasing the might of the centre at the expense of the non-Russian peoples.

The blame for the failures of Soviet nationalities policy cannot be put on the Soviet Government and the Communist Party alone. A number of factors obstruct a genuine solution of the problem on lines suggested in the Bolshevik programme. They have nothing to do with the shortcomings of the Soviet régime, but are inherent in conditions within the Russian Empire, independent of any political régime. These factors are:
1. The numerical disproportion between the Russian people and the non-Russians, particularly the non-Slavs of the Soviet Union, which naturally ensures Russian domination.
2. The geographical distribution of Russians and Ukrainians almost throughout the territory of the U.S.S.R.
3. The numerical weakness of many Soviet nationalities which prevents their independent cultural and political development.

Other more weighty reasons for the failure of Soviet nationalities policy are connected with the political philosophy and strategy of what is called "Stalinism" with its totalitarian atmosphere of compulsion rendering impossible the cultural and political unfolding of all the nationalities of the U.S.S.R. From the point of view of the communist ideology itself the Soviet nationalities policy was a failure because it did not and could not succeed in establishing a federation of equals in the territory of the U.S.S.R., thus setting an example to the world. The Soviet nationalities policy did not fail in an absolute sense, however, since it greatly increased the efficiency of the Russian "melting-pot," under the neutral term of "Union of Socialist Soviet Republics."

The U.S.S.R. as a melting-pot of races is in many ways similar to that other big melting-pot, the United States of America. The melting-pot process, while disposing in the long run of the problems of nationalities in a given territory, provides no model for a global solution. Neither the American nor the Russian pattern can be schematically applied to Africa, Eastern Europe or South-East Asia.

There are, of course, notable differences between the American and Russian melting-pots. The Europeans who are being Americanized as citizens of the United States enter the melting-pot of their own free will; from the outset they want to become English-speaking Americans and they want their children to absorb English-American culture. The Soviet melting-pot is of a strongly compulsory character and produces some modified specimens of Russians linked together by the doctrine of Leninism-Stalinism. On the other hand, the color problem which prevents the full integration of an American nation is absent in the Soviet Union. Because there are no Negroes in the territory of the U.S.S.R. it is impossible to assess with certainty whether color prejudice is non-existent or whether it is nonexistent in the higher sense of complete racial equality. It is a fair assumption, however, that were a large colored population included in the framework of the Soviet Union it would not suffer from any special racial discrimination but only from the same repressive measures which the Soviet Government imposes on all peoples, their national cultures and traditions, within the boundaries of the Russian Empire. The Soviet Government would undoubtedly try to break the Negroes spiritually just as it has tried to break other nationalities and races. As long as the communist dictatorship lasts, racial equality in Russia will mean nothing but equality of subjection.

As far as absence of color prejudice in Russia is a fact, it goes to the credit of the Russian people and not of the Soviet régime. The Russian attitude to racial problems is by no means unique but is characteristic of all peoples who, in the course of their history, have been exposed to a process of drastic racial intermixture. In view of this intermixture which educates towards racial tolerance and broadmindedness, the Russians, irrespective of the régime under which they live, would never insist on a policy of segregation, even to one slightly approaching that prevailing in the Southern States of the U.S.A., or in the Union of South Africa.

34 / RUSSIAN IMPERIALISM OR COMMUNIST AGGRESSION?

The Russo-Japanese War and World War I plus the Revolutions of 1905 and 1917 took the wind out of the sails of Russian expansion. Initiative on the Asian continent passed into Japanese hands. In 1915 the shadow of Japanese domination hung over China, in the early 1920's over Siberia itself. Western opposition induced Japan to pull back, but throughout the 1930's she continued to test the Soviet frontier. Communist Russia's involvement in the Nationalist Revolution in China ended disastrously and, though she crossed swords with China and Japan in the interwar years, she needed above all else peace for internal reconstruction.

The exhaustion of Nationalist China at the hands of Japan and of Japan at the hands of the Western Allies in World War II benefited the Soviet Union, which entered the conflict, under the wire, at Allied request. Unfortunate as American solicitation of Russian aid may have been in retrospect, one must remember that in February of 1945 no one could count upon the effective use of the atomic bomb in the war against Japan, and that American planners estimated that eighteen months of fighting after the not yet attained German surrender and at least 500,000 American casualties—perhaps one million—would be required to subdue Japan, even with Soviet help.

At the Yalta Conference, in February of 1945, the bargain guaranteeing Russian entry into the Pacific war was sealed. Russia was promised southern Sakhalin, which had been ceded to Japan in 1905, as well as the entire Kuril Archipelago. The preservation of the status quo in Outer Mongolia (the Mongolian People's Republic), the internationalization of Dairen, the lease of Port Arthur, and the Russo-Chinese operation of the Chinese Eastern and South Manchurian Railways were guaranteed also.

The growth of the Soviet Empire in the aftermath of World War II brings to mind the warnings of old, uttered by statesmen from London to Tokyo. Was not the Monroe Doctrine rooted in Russian encroachment?

There is no denying that in the history of Russia, as in the history of many other countries, including the United States, there is a streak of expansionism, be it branded as "imperialism" or sugarcoated as "manifest destiny." But does the persistence of geographical factors equate Tsarist and Communist needs and ambitions? Is the Soviet Union the menace that was Tsarist Russia? Was Tsarist Russia the menace that is the Soviet Union? Is there a difference merely in degree or also in kind? Are Monarchists and Communists right when they insist, though for opposite

N. S. Timasheff, "Russian Imperialism or Communist Aggression?" in *Soviet Imperialism: Its Origins and Tactics*, ed. Waldemar Gurian (Notre Dame, Indiana: University of Notre Dame Press, 1953), pp. 19-25, 27-30, 32-34. Reprinted with permission of the University of Notre Dame Press.

reasons, that tsarism and communism are different in nature or is it true that the more things change, the more they remain the same? With questions such as these in mind, N. S. Timasheff, a Russian-American, holds Tsarist imperialism against the yardstick of world history and finds it not abnormal. He then measures it against Soviet imperialism and determines some distinct differences. "There is a good deal of irony in the fact that, today, to prove that Russia always was a particular villain, one cites Marx and Engels," Timasheff observes; "it was only after having imbibed the teaching of these prophets that Russia assumed that role."

In the course of a millennium, from the 9th to the 19th centuries, the state later on known as Russia expanded from a moderately large area consisting of the basins of the Dnieper, the Dvina and the Volkhov, into a vast Empire reaching from the Easternmost spearheads of the Atlantic to the Westernmost spearheads of the Pacific. Russia has tremendously expanded; *ergo,* she was expansionist; but was this peculiar to Russia?

It was not. The process may be analyzed into four components, each of which has counterparts in the history of other great nations.

There has been, first, occupation of empty space adjacent to the habitat of a vigorous and rapidly multiplying nation. This process took place in waves. During the 10th and 12th centuries the Russians expanded from their original home to the basin of the upper Volga and beyond it, particularly towards the Northeast; in the 12th century a town was founded in the newly occupied area which received the name of Moscow. From the 16th century on, the Russians expanded in the vast area between the Volga and the Urals and, having crossed those mountains, occupied the almost empty spaces of Siberia. By 1650, they reached the Pacific Ocean, 5,000 miles East of Moscow. Simultaneously, step by step, they occupied the Northern part of the fertile plain which separated them from the Black Sea and which, prior to that, had been the home for nomads. Somewhat later, they expanded into the Northern Caucasus. What was the moving spring behind this process? Exactly the same as the one behind the movement of the Americans to the Pacific Ocean: the attraction of free land where new and better homes could be built.

Second, there was the process of unification. While originally appearing in the form of a body politic with Kiev as its center, the land of the Russians, both the original homeland and the area added to it in the way just described, was divided into a number of small and almost independent principalities. Moreover, a large part of the original homeland was conquered by the Lithuanians and Poles, who seized the opportunity created by the conquest of the major part of Russia by the Tartars. Later on, the trend reversed. Step by step, the particular principalities and the area conquered by the Lithuanians and the Poles were reunited around the Duchy of Moscow. This was the exact counterpart of the unification of France around the domain of the Kings in the *Ile de France*, of Spain around Castile and Aragon, of Italy around Piedmont, of Germany around Brandenburg-Prussia. The integration of the Russian principalities was accomplished in the 15th century, while the reconquest of the lost provinces (except Eastern Galicia around Lvov) went on until the end of the 18th century. In one major case, namely the recovery of Northeastern Ukraine, the process was peculiar. The people revolted against their Polish masters, and succeeded in gaining independence, but found out that they could not preserve it by their own strength; so they declared their will to come under the scepter of "The Russian Tsar." What was the moving spring behind this process? Exactly the same tendency of dynastically divided nations to integrate around an energetic center which also created the national states of France, Spain, Italy and Germany.

Third, there was the process of building up a colonial Empire by drawing a number of retarded nations and tribes into the political and economic orbit of Russia. This happened in the Caucasus, Central Asia and the Far East. Again, a particular case deserves special attention. In 1801, the Christian kingdom of Georgia, situated beyond the crest of the Caucasian mountains, feeling unable to survive the incessant attacks of the Turks and Persians, both Moslem nations, voluntarily surrendered its sovereignty in favor of the Russian Empire.

The process, as a whole, was the exact counterpart of the formation of the colonial empires by Spain, Portugal, the Netherlands, England and France, with this difference: while the empires just mentioned consisted of overseas possessions, the colonial Empire of Russia has been constituted by lands adjacent to the area of expansion. Today, colonialism is frowned upon, especially in this country and, naturally, in large parts of the colonial empires themselves. But fifty years ago colonial conquest was by no means peculiar to the Russians. The wars which the Russians had to wage in the Caucasus and Central Asia throughout the major part of the 19th century were very similar to those waged by France in North Africa and by Great Britain on the periphery of her empire.

In Russian expansion there was, however, a fourth component, a struggle for access to the sea understandable on the part of a land-locked nation. It seems on first thought to be an exception. But one must take into consideration that the original homeland of the Russians had access both to the Baltic and the Black Seas. Trade between Novgorod and the German *Hansa* cities was active until the Swedes cut the communications by occupying the mouth of the Neva. Still more important was the trade with Byzantium, across the Black Sea. In this trade, H. Pirenne sees the key to the marvelous cultural progress of Russia during the first centuries of her existence. Later on, it was cut off by nomads of Turkish origin. To restore a direct outlet to Europe, Russia, under Peter the Great, waged a long war and conquered, along the Eastern shore of the Baltic, the lands which later on became known as Estonia and Latvia, plus a slice of present day Finland. At that time, these lands were provinces of Sweden. The inhabitants did not lose independence; they only changed masters. Similarly, wars with Turkey were necessary to acquire access to the Black Sea, since, in the period of her greatest expansion, Turkey had acquired its Northern shore. With the exception of the Crimea, which was a vassal state of Turkey, the conquest by the Russians meant only the change of masters. Of course, this was aggrandizement; but aggrandizement was considered, in those days, a legitimate goal of national policies and often took place for much less valid reasons than Russia's advance toward the seas.

It took centuries to consolidate into one body politic the vast area which, in 1914, found itself under the scepter of the Tsars. In other words, Russia's expansion has been rather slow, except in cases when she acquired almost uninhabited areas. It was continuous, though time and again interrupted by setbacks. When these occurred, the Russian nation never despaired, but resumed her advance when opportunity presented itself. This advance was carried out in a remarkably cautious way. With a few exceptions, of which the Russo-Japanese War (1904-5) was the most spectacular, expansion was undertaken only when the chance of success was overwhelming.

About the end of the 19th century, Russia's historical tendency to expand seemed to have come to an end. Russia's Western boundary did not materially change from 1815 to 1914. In 1860, the boundary with China was stabilized. After 1870, only minor adjustments took place in the Caucasus (1878) and in Central Asia (1885).

But early in the 20th century the expansionist tendency of Russia reasserted itself. She waged a war against Japan, the aim of which was to get undisputed overlordship in Manchuria and perhaps Korea. Soon after the beginning of the First World War, she announced a peace plan including the acquisition of Eastern Galicia, as well as of the straits and of a large slice of Asiatic Turkey.

Of course, these phenomena were tantamount to the resurgence of expansionism, but this was not anything peculiar to Russia. Around 1900, China was considered to be a "sick man," and spheres of influence were carved out for Russia, England, Germany, France and Japan; Italy wanted to follow suit but was rebuked, since she was not strong enough to conduct a truly imperialist policy. During the first year of the First World War, a treaty was signed in London assigning large portions of Turkey to Russia, England, France and Italy; once again, the latter did not get her share (neither did Russia), but England and France inherited the German colonies and, temporarily, a large part of Asiatic Turkey (Syria, Lebanon, Iraq, Transjordan, Palestine).

. . . Yes, Russia advanced 700 miles toward Berlin; but, from the day the United States gained independence to the end of the Mexican war, in other words, in 65 years, the United States advanced toward the Pacific by 1,500 miles. Yes, Russia acquired a large area between 1853 and 1914. But, between the same years, Great Britain, France, Germany, Italy and Belgium partitioned among themselves the continent of Africa which, in 1853, belonged to the Europeans only in its periphery. Only a few would know that the Belgian share of Africa, the so-called Belgian Congo, is approximately as large as the totality of the Russian acquisitions between 1853 and 1914 which have so frightened Secretary of State Byrnes, and that the share of France, 3.5 million sq. mi., was approximately four times larger.

These facts put Russia's alleged super-expansionism into the right historical perspective: the 18th and 19th centuries were, in general, a period of the formation of national states and colonial empires. This might not be a valid justification of the conquests made by Russia and other powers, but disposes of the idea that Russia was always the particular villain.

In 1917, Russia's expansionism seemed to have come to an abrupt end. In November of that year, the Russian nation inflicted on herself a crushing defeat. This it did in allowing the Communists to gain power. Had Russia preserved the Provisional government and continued as a member of the grand coalition, perhaps a passive member only, then, at the peace conference, any unfavorable change of boundaries would have been out of the question, except in regard to those around Poland proper which had been granted independence by the Provisional government.

But the Russian nation allowed the Communists to become their masters. This is not the place to inquire why that happened. Only this fact is important: the Communists gained power after a defeatist propaganda and had to take the consequences. Under the Communists Russia experienced the rather exceptional fate of becoming a defeated member of a victorious coalition. According to the rules of the game between the states, defeat is penalized by loss of territory. So the Russian dominated part of the Eurasian continent substantially shrank. The nadir was reached on the day when the Brest Litovsk peace treaty was signed (March, 1918). The Russian Empire was dismembered. The Baltic States, the Ukraine, the Transcaucasian States became independent, not to speak of Finland and Poland. In fact, Russia's Central Asiatic possessions were also gone.

This defeat was only temporary. In three steps, an Empire was built much larger than the Russian had been. The first (1918-22) was the reunification of the old Empire minus the Western borderlands. The second (1939-40 and again 1944-5) was the reannexation of the provinces lost after the First World War and not yet recompensed, with some substitutions. The third (1945-9) was the formation of a girdle of satellite states along the Western boundary and the conquest of China.

Let us now consider these three steps from the point of view of Russia's historical expansionism which, as has been shown, did not differ much from that of other powers. As for the first and the second steps, these would probably have been made even by a non-Communist government of Russia. The reasons for such an assumption are as follows:

When one compares the Western boundary of the Soviet Union as of September 1, 1939, and today, one perceives advance along the whole line. In other words, aggrandizement is apparent. But when one compares the present day boundary with that of 1914, there is no aggrandizement at all. In 1914, Russia possessed the whole of Finland and the rump of Poland, around Warsaw; these lands have not been reabsorbed. Of course, in 1914 East Prussia, Eastern Galicia, Carpathorussia and Northern Bukovina did not belong to the Empire of the Tsars. But these acquisitions hardly compensate Russia for the loss of the lands mentioned above.

The same pattern of reannexation is apparent in the Far East. The Soviets have occupied or *de facto* annexed the two areas lost to Japan in the course of previous events, both Southern Sakhalin and the Kuriles, the former exchanged for the latter in 1875 and then lost in 1905, as the consequence of defeat in the course of the Russo-Japanese war. The Sino-Soviet treaty of 1945 restored to Russia the positions lost in 1905 and 1937: the Chinese Eastern railway, both the trunk line and the Kwantung branch, and dominance in Port Arthur and Dairen. Another zone of influence, the Northwestern part of Iran, has however not been recovered.

As the result of these events, by 1945 the body politic formerly known as Russia and now called the Soviet Union, had acquired approximately the same extension as in 1914. This signifies the recovery of territory and the regaining of strength by a great nation after suffering temporary eclipse.

Such recoveries are frequent in history. . . .

One may assert that even if Russia were not in Communist garb, her government, either Imperial or democratic, would have used victory to trace the boundaries approximately where they were traced after the two V-days. There would, however, have been this substantial difference: While the men in the Kremlin proceeded by unilateral action and gave to Russia's recovery the unpleasant flavor of aggression, another government would have resorted to negotiations and most probably would have obtained what they demanded.

The Soviets, however, preferred unilateral action, a modality of aggression as an instrument of recovering that (or approximately that) which had been Russian before the losses of 1918-21. The situation was indeed peculiar. In general, up to recently, the striving for national goals, especially for the recovery of lost provinces, by means of aggression, was considered as being in accordance with international law. Therefore, Soviet expansion, within the limits just stated, was in conformity with a model of action which was held valid in the 19th century but which is now obsolescent. It is obsolescent because the most advanced nations of the world no longer believe the model justified. They frown upon aggression even if it is tantamount to the reconquest of formerly lost lands, except when in accordance with the clear and unequivocal will of the people concerned.

Communist expansion is, moreover, not limited to that which has actually been acquired. The third step could be followed by a fourth, fifth and so on, whenever the opportunity should present itself. Virtually, its limit is the totality of the globe which, most definitely, was not the case of historical Russia. It is obvious that behind the present day aggressiveness of the body politic which is now the Soviet Union and formerly was known as Russia, there is a new force. This force cannot but be Communism.

35 / THE SHIFT OF RUSSIA'S ECONOMIC BASIS EAST

Russia's eastward expansion entailed a shift in the center of gravity of the state. The census taken in 1959 reveals that while the population of European Russia increased by only about two million people in the period since 1939 (from about 144,000,000 to about 146,000,000), the population of Soviet Asia rose by about sixteen million (a jump from about 47,000,-

000 to 63,000,000). In other words, there was a definite flow of population eastward. Hand in hand with this shift in population, indeed one of its causes, was the industrialization of Siberia. The preponderance of energy resources in Soviet Asia made this economic development possible; the German invasion and postwar strategic considerations made it necessary.

The development and growth of four Siberian cities are realistically described by an American newspaperman. A more exuberant Soviet account of a fifth city follows. Marxism is more than an interpretation of history. It is a projection of the past into the future, drawn with imagination and faith rather than scientific accuracy. But the future is a guidepost for the present, and the radiant vision of Vladivostok as a rival of San Francisco in beauty and greatness, voiced by the chairman of the Vladivostok City Council, must not be dismissed as mere civic pride. It is a tonic that sustains Russian efforts.

Urban Development in Siberia

When a Soviet city wants to blow its horn these days, it outlaws horn blowing on its streets.

That is what they are doing in Irkutsk and Khabarovsk, thinking of doing in Chita and dreaming of doing in Yakutsk. Everyone talks about the new law (old in Moscow). It implies deafening traffic noises and is far better testimony to the new urbanity in remote Siberia than anything you might see on the inevitable Lenin or Karl Marx Street.

Irkutsk, Chita, Khabarovsk, Yakutsk. The names sound strange in New York, exactly half way around the world from Irkutsk.

But thousands toil there in summer heat and winter cold to overtake the United States some day in industrial output and standard of life. The American learning about the Soviet Union can no longer look only to Moscow, unfamiliar enough as are its ways.

What lies beyond, far beyond?

Optimism despite hardship. Opportunity despite nature's limitations. A pattern of growth imposed from afar, through seven-year plans and by officials and scientists come to serve higher ambitions than those of the parochial local Siberian.

Yet throughout Siberia there is pride and hope. Soviet plans for Siberia are grandiloquent, and many Russians seem willing to work and wait for the new world of communism.

These are some notes on four cities far from Moscow yet large on the Soviet map of the future.

Dispatch by Max Frankel, "Four Siberian Centers Typify Soviet Effort to Overtake U.S.," *The New York Times*, April 28, 1959. Copyright © 1959 by *The New York Times*. Reprinted with permission of *The New York Times*.

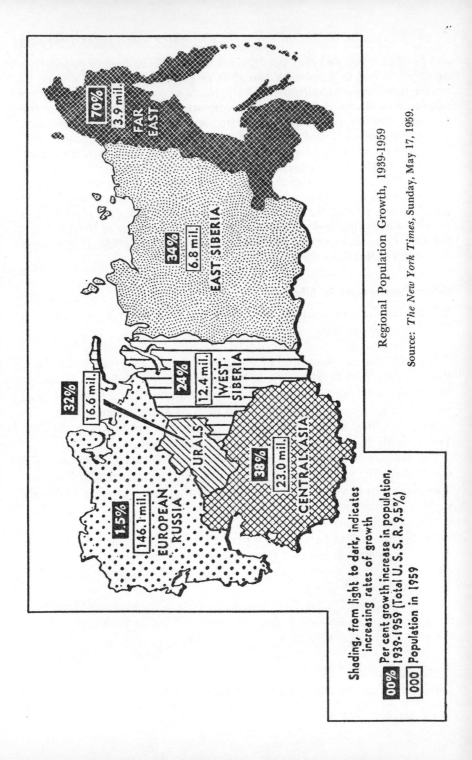

70% **3.9 mil.** FAR EAST

34% **6.8 mil.** EAST SIBERIA

24% **12.4 mil.** WEST-SIBERIA

32% **16.6 mil.** URALS

38% **23.0 mil.** CENTRAL ASIA

1.5% **146.1 mil.** EUROPEAN RUSSIA

Shading, from light to dark, indicates increasing rates of growth

00% Per cent growth increase in population, 1939-1959 (Total U.S.S.R. 9.5%)

000 Population in 1959

Regional Population Growth, 1939-1959

Source: *The New York Times*, Sunday, May 17, 1959.

Irkutsk

Irkutsk is 2,600 miles from Moscow, but only half way to the Pacific from the border of Europe and Asia in the Ural Mountains. It is as far north as the northern tip of Newfoundland yet in the southernmost part of Siberia crossed by the Trans-Siberian Railway to the sea.

For weeks police cars have been chasing the many lumber-bearing trucks and the few passenger cars to enforce the no-honking statute.

Thus there are a few decibels less din in the sprawling, bleak city. All the clearer, therefore, the deep-throated moans and shrill howls of the trains chugging through railroad yards. The air is still but clouded by smoke that pours from chimneys of factories where gold dredges and agricultural machinery are produced.

About 340,000 persons live in Irkutsk. That puts it in the class of Rochester, N.Y., the visitor notes before he disciplines himself to forget about comparisons. Beside the chimneys in the skyline are the remains of twelve large churches that once served the fortress city. Some churches are now meeting halls, others are abandoned. One twin-domed church is a planetarium.

Czarist Irkutsk had a few dozen other large stone buildings. But most residents today as before the Bolshevik revolution live in the snug, small wooden Siberian homes, with slant-eye windows surrounded by intricate carved-wood lace. The homes snuggle against each other at rakish angles along little hills on both banks of the powerful Angara River.

But stone is coming. And the sight of red brick and tall cranes lugging it skyward to the men and women on the scaffolding arouses the warmest feelings all over Siberia.

The strategy of growth is remarkably alike in this huge land. The stately old buildings that survived revolution and civil war have been turned to social uses. The turreted headquarters of the former Russian-America Company is a hospital facing a gesticulating statue of Lenin on Lenin Square.

Other old Czarist buildings house science and education, the twin pillars on which Siberia expects to build. Irkutsk is to be the center of learning and research in Eastern Siberia, and the two disciplines also get the choicest new structures.

Around another large square are other imposing façades, including one for the local railroad authorities. Communist party and Government offices are also settled well.

Needed scientists and educators, party officials and factory managers must be housed, too, and new apartment buildings blossom all over town.

It will be a long time before all of Irkutsk can live in such houses. But people take heart from what they see and work on, for their children if not for themselves.

At the new Angara dam near Irkutsk, a smooth-cheeked, agile, alert young engineer named Makhorin, in his late twenties, two years out of engineering school, runs perfunctorily through power statistics, then speaks romantically of the beauty of Lake Baikal, which feeds the river. . . .

At a collective farm near Irkutsk, old-time Siberians live on the main street, near the club and school, in fenced-in little yards with woodshed, cowshed and small overheated house, stuffed with furniture, draped in lace and festooned with greenery. The new settlers are up on the hill, piling fresh planks upon planks with the help of neighbors.

The farm population of 1,800 struggles with 22,000 cold acres for rye and wheat and with 3,700 acres for potatoes and vegetables for the builders in town. There are 800 cows, soon to be supplied with self-feeders, two greenhouses, thirty-six tractors, nineteen combines. Twelve hundred more workers are needed and solicited through modest advertising.

Of 930 families, eighty-seven have arrived since 1950. The average family earned 3,600 rubles, 3,000 pounds of grain, some honey and vegetables last year. Nine farmers got vacation passes to the Caucasus. Most of the peasants venture into town, 15 miles away, only during vacations.

At Listvyanka, forty-five miles from Irkutsk, 2,000 settlers live on the magnificent shore of Lake Baikal, larger than Lake Erie, deeper (more than a mile in spots) than any lake in the world.

Boys play ice hockey on the lake, but trucks did not long trust the ice during the warm winter. Soon hunters will inch out on treacherously thin ice to await the Baikal seals as they break through toward the spring sun and the boys will switch from study and play to work in the local boatyard.

Even here one large new brick building rises among the wooden homes. It is for the hundred scientists come to Listvyanka to serve Siberia.

Chita

Move 400 miles east from Irkutsk, two hours by plane, twenty-two by train. You are now in Chita, capital of a Siberian province larger than California.

In a way the history is the same: from railroad stop to village to city to provincial capital, big stone façades and block upon block of log homes.

But this is home to a different 175,000 persons. They are in a picturesque valley surrounded by wooded hills, their air so pure and dry that at night you stare at a planetarium sky, wonderful for watching satellites, you are told.

It is easier to take 40 degrees below Fahrenheit here than 20 below in Moscow, Chita residents insist. The visitor takes a stroll at 20 above without overcoat to prove them right. But spring may not be here yet. At the barbershop they still talk about the six men who froze to death back in 1939 when their car broke down sixty miles from town—on an April 26!

The pattern of progress in Chita is the same as in Irkutsk, though on a smaller scale. New buildings are set far back from the roadway in anticipation of a boulevard that is to be built some day, after the last wooden home is gone, when the lamp-posts are installed, when the side streets are paved.

Traffic is even less of a bother than in Irkutsk, but at the movie a short graphically depicts the plight of the careless pedestrian.

No fruit in town at the moment, but pleasant waitresses serve tasty Ukrainian dishes to parties of army officers. Russians and Ukrainians predominate among the residents all along the Trans-Siberian Railway.

The local railroad administration has a huge new building, the industrial management regional offices have moved to where the railroad was and a polyclinic has inherited the local headquarters of the gold-mining industry. Thirty-two physicians and dentists—all women—tend to 700 or 800 outpatients until 3 P.M. at the clinic and then start their home calls.

Doctors and teachers are needed in this and other Siberian regions. Chita has begun to train its own. Yuri D. Ryzhkov, a biochemist, is director of the six-year medical school, with 1,200 students and a staff of 140. The first class of 200, chosen from 800 applicants, will graduate this year. By design, half are men.

The medical school is housed in two old army staff buildings, dark, narrow and small. The students have set up their own models, charts and museum, they have good microscopes and basic equipment, a vigorous, young faculty of physicians from Leningrad and Kiev.

Across the street, the first building of a new campus is going up. The director inspects it every day. Summers and in spare time, the students help cart bricks. . . .

The students, 18 to 35 years old, live in a four-story dormitory, four or five to the room. Cleanliness is policed by the school's Young Communist League. Students do their own cleaning and repairs, paint the walls when necessary. They seem ambitious, courteous and proud.

Chita's main factory, built up by women and children to make agricultural machinery during the war, was converted last year to the production of fifty compressors a month and 350 medium-size refrigeration units a year. Most of its 900 workers today are young men and women who came from school for on-the-job training.

With twice as many workers the factory hopes by 1965 to triple the output of compressors and to turn out six times as many refrigeration units. A new main building is going up and the workers, in free time, help build "because they know working conditions will be better in the new plant," the director says.

Water for showers is still trucked to the machine factory, but pipes are on order. Across the street, the fourth of several planned twenty-unit apartment buildings is going up and the half-dozen officials who met the visitor are especially proud of the new food store. . . .

Up on the hill, in the new sports compound among the evergreens, are a new wooden stadium for 15,000, courts and rinks, a gym and a busy modest swimming pool. The cement is already poured for a new Olympic-size pool, with grandstand and all.

Khabarovsk

Almost at the end of the Trans-Siberian line, nine days' train ride and nine hours' jet flight from Moscow, is Khabarovsk.

Still the pattern holds. The imprint is Moscow's, not that of Manchuria, forty miles away, and not that of the Pacific, 200 miles away.

Khabarovsk is the turntable of the Soviet Far East, wheeling and dealing out all manner of goods along the two railroad lines to the ocean and along the Ussuri and the mighty Amur Rivers.

The city developed hastily after the Bolshevik Revolution of 1917. Its population today is about 300,000, but it seems greater. The city is a producer as well as trader, with scores of plants for heavy and light industry.

Khabarovsk gives the impression of a city working hard to get itself out of the slum-and-mud state, to atone for years of hasty growth. At the center are the older buildings, again the party headquarters and party school, the waterway and railroad administrations, the large officers' club and the telegraph office, the government agencies running large parts of the Far East, all housed well.

And again, all around, the neighborhoods of wooden homes that cannot be uprooted while there is a shortage of housing. Then come some marshy gaps, where the Amur spills over in summer, and on the outskirts, new little communities of brick, rising up to only five stories to save the cost of elevator installation.

New buildings often go up at strange angles to the old, betraying plans for future street patterns. Near a flour mill are a new hospital and school. The Park of Culture and Rest is being leveled, the river beach widened and improved for the hot summer. Railroad engineers are being trained in a large colonnaded new school.

Khabarovsk is not an attractive city, but it seems ambitious and important. Much work is still to be done by the builders, and also by new citizens' groups being organized all over the country to fight drunkenness and other public misbehavior.

The visitor, sitting at the railroad station, happy to be leaving, is reminded that, ugly or not, Khabarovsk represents a home and a future to people. . . .

Yakutsk

Technology and geography will probably conspire to bring plumbing and jet plane service to Yakutsk at about the same time.

It now takes a twin-engine passenger plane, with crates of fruit aboard, seven hours to reach Yakutsk from Irkutsk. The 300-year-old frontier post and former fortress is about 3,000 miles from Moscow.

Yakutsk is the capital of Yakutia, an area twice the size of Alaska and only somewhat more densely settled with a population of 450,000. The Yakuts, a people of Turkic origin, dominate the rural population and are in the majority even among the nearly 100,000 in the capital.

Until recently, gold and guts seem to have kept the place going. Vodka probably helped.

Now have come discoveries of diamonds and the promise of natural gas. Soviet planners have begun to talk of a rail line. Scientists are encamped in a large gleaming white building. Past the building trudge the long-haired Siberian horses lugging water and sewage to and from the neat and sturdy wooden Yakutsk homes.

The visitor keeps his coat on in the Yakutian spring. Residents reminisce about a December and January of constant 50 to 75 degrees below, and await the brief summer, usually in the eighties.

Yakutsk, too, is building for a future. A new theatre opened last year, its imposing front and glittering chandeliers probably short-changed by a mere 500 seats. Going up are a hotel, a post office, and the first brick apartment houses, with plumbing, in which the editor of a local paper, for one, finds he can live "as well as in Moscow."

Work on a . . . university campus will begin this year. But the training of teachers, doctors, physicists, geologists, linguists, engineers, veterinarians and botanists in the newest and most northern Soviet university is not deferred. For three years, the 1,428 students, including 829 Yakuts, and a faculty of 156, have been meeting wherever there is available space.

The projected classroom building, for 2,500 students, will be the largest in Yakutsk. Graduates will be expected to stay in the region.

The Yakuts are the most numerous of the original Siberian peoples. They not only are talented in the regional arts of hunting, fishing, reindeer breeding, but have raised many of their sons in learned professions. The university president is a Yakut. The city of Yakutsk is truly bilingual, with a radio station, newspaper and theatre vaunting communism and Shakespeare alike in the Yakut language.

Small plants in the city serve local needs. Bread and beer are made from grains raised on the shores of the Lena, still another great Siberian river, ten miles wide at Yakutsk. It is navigable from the end of May to early October.

Hundreds pass through Yakutsk daily and camp in the small wooden air terminal to await the scheduling of flights to gold fields, hunting camps and other remote outposts.

A traveler coming from the south finds the city surprisingly characterless and primitive. But a few minutes' watch shows what the city means to local transients: new boots for the Yakut farmer, Volume V of a world history series for the teacher from the Aldan gold area.

There is as fine a collection of materials in the main store as in most places in Siberia. Tea at the restaurant comes with lemon and the transients suck the lemon dry and talk about vitamins.

Films are shown in the Yakutsk Central Theatre at about the time they play in Moscow. But life for most is not at all like life in Moscow. In Yakutsk, you wash in ingenious tin basins, the water running from a shoulder-high can to a pail below. If you live in Yakutsk, you bed your family among reserves of potatoes and cabbage to tide you over the unavoidable periods of shortage, as they are described.

As recently as five years ago Yakutsk and other parts of Siberia were found by a Western correspondent to be dispirited and overspirited, bawdy and ill-disciplined. Today the visitor does not argue with the Moscow actor's judgment that this and other icy outposts will some day outgrow the frontier phase. And it is on the Yakutsk run that the shawled woman shouts to her passenger-comrades: "Let's go, we must be first, hurry!"

The Vladivostok of Tomorrow

It was only after the Revolution that our city really began to grow. Take the population—during the Soviet period its rate of increase has been six times higher than in czarist times. This, in a way, reflects the very rapid development of the whole Maritime Territory.

Our land is very rich in natural resources. We have coal, iron ore, tin, lead, graphite, gold and tungsten. All these treasures, buried and unused in the old days, are being tapped now, and Vladivostok is playing a pioneering role in the economic expansion of this frontier region.

Our leading industries are ship repairing, fish processing, woodworking, coal mining and production of building materials. The city's life is in many ways connected with the ocean. Vladivostok is home port for our Pacific merchant and fishing fleets. Fishermen, crabbers, whalers, seal hunters leave here for far-off fishing grounds and return for unloading and repairs. Radiating from Vladivostok and its young neighbor, the port of Nakhodka, are sea lanes to Chukotka, Kamchatka, the Kuril Islands, the Okhotsk coast, Sakhalin and many countries of Asia and America. Cargoes of coal, oil, timber, cotton and machinery are loaded here for other cities in the Soviet Union and abroad.

Besides being an industrial and shipping city, Vladivostok is an important cultural center. Back in 1914 there was only one college in our city with 200 students. Now we have almost 16 thousand students enrolled in six institutions of higher education and nine specialized secondary schools. Most popular among young people are Far Eastern University, Far Eastern Polytechnic Institute, Far Eastern Medical College and the Higher Merchant Marine School.

The Siberian Branch of the USSR Academy of Sciences has its Far Eastern Department in Vladivostok. There are also several research centers, like the Institute of Ichthyology and Oceanography, the Hydrometeorological Institute and the Geological Institute. The main direction in their work is the study of the region's natural wealth and the investigation of possibilities for its use.

Much has been done to rebuild Vladivostok from a town of wooden houses into the modern city it is today. We are proud of our beautiful city with its wide streets and hillsides terraced right to the harbor. All along the beaches of golden sand are health and vacation resorts and clubs for water sports.

Boris Averkin, "Vladivostok," *USSR*, XLIX, No. 10 (October 1960), 20-21. Reprinted with permission of *USSR*.

In the near future our city will become even more beautiful. These next six years we expect to build more new housing than in the entire hundred years since Vladivostok was founded. We are building dozens of schools, kindergartens and nurseries. In addition to the three theaters we now have, we will build a drama theater and a circus.

A group of new factories is being built in Vladivostok to provide all the materials needed for this large construction program. All over the city old houses are now being torn down and new ones put up. We are also in the middle of a big face-lifting job for our waterfront and beaches. The fishing and freight wharves are being modernized, and the port buildings are being remodeled.

When our construction program is completed, our city will look more like a resort than an industrial and port town, with parks and greenery and flowers everywhere. Most beautiful will be Primorsky (Maritime) Boulevard that will run through the city along the shore of Amur Bay and merge with the resort area in the suburbs.

San Francisco, our neighbor across the ocean, is acknowledged to be one of the beautiful cities on the Pacific coast. We hope, in a future not too distant, to be competing with San Francisco for the title of *most* beautiful.

36 / THE NEW FRONTIERSMEN

The vastness of the old Russian Empire, no smaller for its Soviet garb, contains within itself the space for continued eastward expansion. The German invasion of World War II contributed to this movement by pushing Russian industry to the security of the interior. The apparition of a rejuvenated China, which may well look upon Siberia as a logical outlet for its teeming population, has made the settling of Russia's eastern regions with Slavs a matter of urgent necessity.

But the Soviet regime is not as omnipotent as often imagined. It does not develop its Far Eastern territories simply by decree. Not that it has any compunctions about administrative fiat, but even a totalitarian state must reckon with the human factor. As the sole employer, the government can and does force-feed the Siberian labor market by manipulating job openings. A graduating class of prospective teachers, for example, may be given a choice of placements in a long list of communities, all of them in Siberia. But a disgruntled worker is an unproductive worker, and the government makes every effort through propaganda and fringe benefits to garland necessity with the flowers of enthusiasm.

Broadly speaking, the parallel of American and Russian expansion persists. In January of 1963 "CBS Reports" presented a dramatic television documentary on the continued migration of Americans westward, especially to California, and of the living meaning of the frontier in

American society. Like California, Siberia remains a land of opportunity, but more like the California of the nineteenth century than of the twentieth.

In the following brief selections the Australian writer Wilfred G. Burchett conveys the rosy view of the government come-on; the American journalist Theodore Shabad, the hard facts of colonization. An Associated Press dispatch shows how the conservative moral fiber of the Russian peasant women rebels at the continuing tendency of the government to exile shady characters and nonconformists to Siberia for rehabilitation.

Come East, Young Man!

At the small town of Ossipovichi, about sixty miles southeast of the Byelorussian capital of Minsk, a significant and moving ceremony took place in the early summer of 1960. Soldiers of the Fifth Red Banner Heavy Tank Division paraded for the last time in a sunny, grass-covered barracks square. Their commander, Colonel of the Guards Ivan Velichko, made a short speech reminding them of the fine record of the Division. From its birthplace in Tadjikistan the Division helped expel the Nazi invaders from the North Caucasus, chased them out of the Ukraine and Moldavia back across Eastern Europe—through Rumania, Hungary, Yugoslavia and on to Austria. Now the Division was to be disbanded—one of dozens of complete units being dissolved following a January 1960 decision to reduce the Soviet armed forces by another 1,200,000 men. Colonel Velichko recalled Khrushchov's words: "We need strong hands and warm hearts all over our country—in Kazakhstan, Siberia and the Altai Territory. . . ."

The divisional banner which they had borne half-way across Europe was carried down in front of the tribune. Officers, non-coms and privates, representing their different units, stepped forward and knelt to kiss the flag. An order was given that it be consigned to the Soviet Army Museum in Moscow. Following a final march past their commander, the troops were dismissed. A Soviet tank division ceased to exist.

All the soldiers, all the non-coms and most of the officers were now demobilised. And forty per cent of them had volunteered for the virgin lands.

I spoke with one trio of lance-corporals: Ivan Kokoshkin, Mikhail Zhukov and Mahmet Tulokov—stocky carefree youngsters of twenty-two. They had served two years, and were being demobbed a year ahead of time. They had volunteered to go together to the Altai regions, just across Kazakhstan's northeast border with Siberia.

What to do? I asked.

Wilfred G. Burchett, *Come East, Young Man!* (Berlin: Seven Seas Publishers, 1962), pp. 55-57. Reprinted with permission of Seven Seas Publishers.

"We'll learn to drive combines," said Kokoshkin, and Tulokov added with a laugh: "Driving a combine or a tank's not much different—except for the results."

They would go first to an Altai school for tractor- and combine-drivers and then be allotted to a sovkhoz.

"We're determined to stick together," Zhukov said. "Others have already formed bigger teams of drivers and mechanics. They've elected their own leaders from specialists and we hope to work together as a unit."

An hour or two later, another ceremony took place at the railway station. Thousands of people had turned out to see the ex-soldiers off. There were some moving speeches from the local population. The words of one young woman stuck in my memory for a long time:

"Your leaving us shows again that our leaders are for peace. Peace! Peace is our good morning; our joyous day; our peaceful night. Success and happiness for all of you in your new life."

As they embarked aboard the waiting train, people surged forward smothering them with flowers and embraces—and good advice about raising bumper crops in the virgin lands. There were plenty of wet eyes among those departing and among farewellers as the train glided slowly away—carrying these young people to join the hundreds of thousands who, since 1954, have responded to the call "Come East, Young Man!"

Reluctant Pioneers

Ambitious Soviet plans for the development of Siberia are being handicapped by an excessive turnover of labor, according to a Soviet labor economist, who blames poor living conditions there.

Citing previously unpublished spot surveys, the economist reported that about half of those who move to Siberian cities leave them within three years. He lists inadequate wages, bad working conditions and housing as some of the factors causing their departure.

Noting that recent settlers have been attracted to Siberia mainly by financial inducements, he said that this additional capital could have been invested more effectively in housing and consumer services.

The findings of the surveys were published by V. I. Perevedentsev in the current issue of the economic journal Voprosy Ekonomiki (Problems of Economics).

Mr. Perevedentsev is on the staff of the Institute of Economics and Organization of Productions of the Siberian Division of the Academy of

Theodore Shabad, "Workers' Exodus Hampers Siberia," special dispatch, dated Moscow, June 24, 1962, The New York Times, July 1, 1962. Copyright by The New York Times. Reprinted with permission of The New York Times.

Sciences. The institute, situated in Novosibirsk, has been engaged in a long-range study of the Siberian manpower problem.

One of the Soviet Union's richest resource regions, Siberia covers about 60 per cent of the nation's total area. Its population of 25,000,000, only 11 per cent of the Soviet total, is concentrated in a narrow economically developed belt along the Trans-Siberian Railroad.

Mr. Perevedentsev wrote that the manpower shortage had caused the rate of growth of Siberian industry in the Nineteen Fifties to remain roughly the same as that of the Russian republic as a whole despite Soviet plans for a more rapid expansion in Siberia.

He said the situation was particularly acute in rural areas, where labor resources are inadequate to handle the most essential farm work. As a result, industrial workers and students have had to work on farms in the summertime. For the 1956-1960 period, the economist found that 700,000 persons moved to Siberia under various forms of government incentive and even migrated on their own initiative. Yet the total outflow from Siberia during this period exceeded the number of arrivals.

The institute's spot survey of sixty industrial plants of Krasnoyarsk, a city of 470,000, disclosed that 4,700 workers left in the second quarter of 1960.

According to the survey 17.5 per cent expressed a desire to rejoin their families as a reason for leaving and nearly all left. About 11 per cent mentioned poor housing and more than half left Krasnoyarsk.

Mr. Perevedentsev noted that of those who quit because of low wages or poor working conditions a quarter left the city.

Pointing out that the financial incentive was evidently inadequate to assure the settlement of Siberia, the economist suggested that living conditions be raised to the level of European parts of the country.

"Experience shows that wage increases that are not accompanied by opportunities to spend such wages do not promote the creation of a stable labor force," he wrote.

Playgirls Not Wanted

Irate Siberian housewives protested yesterday against exiling big city playgirls to their villages.

Speaking for the aroused village women, Mrs. V. Marina of Irkutsk, voiced the protest in the Moscow newspaper Literaturnaya Gazeta.

Mrs. Marina said she was incensed by reports from Leningrad that a young woman of easy virtue named Tosca was slated for exile to Siberia to mend her ways.

St. Petersburg Times, Friday, March 15, 1963, p. 3A.

"This is simply offensive and insulting for us Siberians," she wrote. "Won't this piece of goods from the capital find admirers even in a new place? She probably will.

"I know that the wives of a few Bodaibo miners, for example, turned to the authorities with a request to quit sending the likes of Tosca to Bodaibo."

Mrs. Marina's attack on the flashy homewreckers from the big cities was the latest in a series of complaints from the provinces about the flood of hooligans, idlers and undesirables who have been exiled to villages.

The exiles are supposed to be re-educated through manual labor on the farms. But reports indicate they are mostly drinking, brawling, thieving and loafing.

So the peasants are mad at the city people for dumping their problems on them.

"This desire to push their unfinished goods onto others is wrong," Mrs. Marina wrote.

37 / THE ACADEMIC CITY OF NOVOSIBIRSK

U.S. senators, even former senators, have a way of getting around. While ordinary mortals from the West cannot explore Siberia beyond Irkutsk and Lake Baikal, their title seems to unlock the gates of closed areas like a magic wand. Thus former Senator William Benton, publisher of the Encyclopaedia Britannica, *visited Novosibirsk and its nearby Academic City of science.*

A mere village at the turn of the century, Novosibirsk, at the juncture of the Ob River and the Trans-Siberian Railroad, had grown into a small city at the time of the Revolution. Its industrial development had been accelerated in the 1930's with the construction of a factory for agricultural machinery. But its real boom was promoted by the German attack on Russia and by the consequent shift of industrial machinery and skilled labor to Siberia. Today Novosibirsk boasts a population of almost one million, heavy industry, and an "Academic City," which is to serve as model for similar scientific centers in Irkutsk, Kemerovo, and elsewhere.

The following personal observations, dictated by Senator Benton on this spot in the summer of 1962, are excerpted from a mimeographed transcript graciously made available for use in this book.

Now the great Institutes are nearing completion. They are to be finished and in full operation by fall—fifteen Institutes with brand new laboratories supplied with the latest scientific equipment. A new University is springing from the recently cleared forest land. We inspected

Senator William Benton, "The 'Closed' Academic City of Novosibirsk," mimeographed impressions, dictated in Novosibirsk, transcribed in New York, July 4 and July 5, 1962, pp. 1-2, 26-29. Reprinted with permission of Senator Benton.

its first building—for physics and chemistry, and again replete with the most modern laboratories.

Plans for this "Academic City," the latest example of Soviet dedication to scientific research, were submitted to Premier Khrushchev five years ago. The President of the USSR Academy of Science opposed the scheme. He said, "You won't be able to persuade the top scientists to move to Novosibirsk." Khrushchev said, "Go ahead; you can get the brilliant young ones and you can train them; they will learn to do the best research."

First the buildings were erected to house the construction workers. 12,500 are now in residence. Then came the Institutes and the University—the shiny new apartment houses for the workers—and comfortable modern cottages for the top scientists and research directors—cottages and houses which certainly rival those within the financial means of the professors at our leading American universities. About 12,500 staff members are now in residence for a total of 25,000. As the construction workers finish up and move out, they will be replaced by more staff workers. The research group is to be built up to 50,000 in 2 or 3 years.

However, it is not anticipated that the construction workers will leave in the immediate future. There is no end to the expanding building plans for the Institutes. But as they leave—and *if* they leave—their quarters will be taken over by the workers in the Institutes.

This "Academic City" has been carved out of the forest—about a half hour's drive on a modern highway from the Square in the center of Novosibirsk. It is a mile or two from the Sea of Ob. This is a great lake, 200 kilometers long at the most, and 40 kilometers at the widest. (It's a tribute to the Soviet propagandists that this artificially created lake is called a "sea.") It was created by the dam put up across the River Ob five years ago when the "Academic City" was planned—to provide hydro electric power for the city of Novosibirsk and the "Academic City." All heat and hot water for the "Academic City" are furnished centrally through this dam. And there won't be any smoke in the "Academic City"!

Let me describe the new University of Novosibirsk as seen through the eyes of its Rector, Academician Ilya Vekhua, a distinguished mathematician who resigned his chair of mathematics at the University of Moscow to respond to the challenge of the new frontier in Central Siberia. Mr. Vekhua is a Georgian who entered the University of Velizh in 1925. He later served for many years as Pro Rector of the University of Velizh, and for one year as Rector. . . .

Academician Vekhua now has 1,000 students in his new university which was created in 1958 coincident with the creation of the "Academic City." Only 100 of these students are in the humanities. And these in only three fields. He does not intend to enlarge this number even when he reaches his anticipated enrollment of 4,000 students.

I asked him to explain to me how the University of Novosibirsk is different from other Soviet universities. He said,

> We are very lucky to be here in this great new Academic City. We are affiliated with 15 great Research Institutes. We shall seize this chance to improve the training of students. Of course during the first two years, the students will devote themselves wholly to their academic studies at the University. But in the second term of the third year, they will begin to work with the Institute in their field of specialization. They will spend about two days a week with the Institute throughout their third and fourth years. In the fifth year, they will spend five out of every six days at the Institute. They will work on team projects—or be given individual assignments. This affiliation with the Institute brings them step by step into research. We shall thus be able easily to spot the gifted students. We shall keep them in the Institutes. This will be their sure way into science. Of course it is better for a child to learn how to swim step by step—but there is also a second way of teaching a child how to swim: throw him right into the water. This second way cuts down on the period which was formerly obligatory before a man could launch on pure research.

Academician Vekhua manifestly took this assignment to head this new university because of its pioneering opportunity. . . .

The Academician explained that all the key people in the Academic City had previously had big jobs—mostly in Moscow. Yet they came here even though the salaries are the same. Yes, they came here to get the better laboratories. But there were other reasons, too. The institutions in Moscow are old. They have many men who are getting along in years who are entrenched in their jobs. There is a better chance for initiative here. Novosibirsk opens up new vistas. "There is a chance to create a new team." Men can go ahead faster here. "There is no rigidity here." Then Academician Vekhua gave Academician Sobolev, Director of the Institute of Mathematics, as an example. Academician Sobolev was the head of the Mathematics Department of the University of Moscow. But here he has his own Institute. He is the head man instead of merely the head of a department. He has 500 young men under him and within two years will have 1,000. (This will show the size and scope of these Institutes!) He can do a better job in building his staff. In Moscow, when he thought he was about to get the people he wanted for his department, he couldn't get apartments for them. Here he can give them the apartments. Further, the apartments are bigger and better. . . .

In addition to all these practical advantages, there is "the excitement." There is the thrill of adventure in the great pioneering of this new Academic City.

CONCLUSION

In the Soviet Union, as in the United States, technological progress has lifted the face of expansion. Modern trains and sleek jets have replaced dogsleds and prairie schooners. But the frontier remains, and the transcontinental trek continues. In the old days, fur and plunder, free land, and refuge from the law beckoned the pioneers. Today jobs and professional opportunities are beacons of migration to the Pacific shores.

Separated from the cultural centers of old, the uprooted make their own traditions. There is no comparison, in terms of standard of living, of the Russian East and the American West today, but the faces and attitudes of the inhabitants of Irkutsk and Vladivostok are as refreshingly different from those of fellow-citizens in Moscow and Leningrad as are the faces and attitudes of the people in Denver and Seattle from those of fellow-citizens in New York and Chicago. A similar shift in the center of gravity, cultural as well as industrial, is occurring—though at a slower pace—in the Soviet Union than in the United States. Impressed by the growth of Novosibirsk, which in World War II received entire industrial plants, removed from war-torn Europe, Senator Benton could not help observing: "But no one is speculating on the boom which could be Novosibirsk's were it an American city located in the midst of a vast and undeveloped continent replete with fertile and undeveloped farm lands; great unexplored forests; and untold mineral wealth."

In theory, a planned economy provides the U.S.S.R. with unparalleled means and efficiency of operation; in practice, the all-pervading bureaucracy chokes the life out of individual aspirations and initiative and often does more to brake than to accelerate economic development. The changing character of the Russian leader is brilliantly lampooned in the Soviet take-off on V. M. Vasnetsov's famous painting of the Valiant Knights ("Bogatyri"), depicted in the frontispiece to this volume.

Expansion is the natural growth of a state and is relatively healthy (or at least was so regarded in the nineteenth century) when it is the vehicle of civilization in sparsely populated, largely nomadic, regions. Such was the "manifest destiny" of Russia and the United States in their national development, unfortunate as this was at the time for the natives of Asia and America. The early pioneers were forerunners rather than bearers of civilization, and the exploitation of Asian tribesmen by Cossack marauders was on the same ethical plane as the actions of those in America who felt that the only good Indian was a dead Indian. As maturity caught up with growth and as law and order settled over the land, some of the advantages and disadvantages of civilization were extended to natives as well as to settlers.

In spite of Indian Reservations, Chinatowns, and segregation, the United States is a melting pot, compared with the Soviet Union, whose nationalities, inhabiting separate republics, keep alive their linguistic and cultural heritage. While second- and third-generation offspring of Chinatown residents are as American as popcorn and often do not know or use Chinese, the people of the Georgian Soviet Socialist Republic, not to mention the people of Uzbekistan, converse in their own tongue and reserve Russian for Russians. Thus an American who in Moscow or Leningrad will be regarded as a "foreigner" will find himself in Bukhara or Samarkand as a "guest"—on the same level, more or less, as the Russian.

All this has interesting implications in the ideological conflict between the United States and the Soviet Union and the increasing rivalry between the latter and China, for the Soviet Empire has a soft belly, like the old Austro-Hungarian Empire. The Soviet call to colonial peoples to rise against their Caucasian masters could well be turned against themselves. This is not to say that the fragmentation of the Russian Empire into its component nationalities in Asia would be in the interest of the United States or of the nationalities themselves, since they would merely find themselves in the magnetic field of Communist China. But the incomplete assimilation and regional compartmentalization of minorities in Russia leave the Soviet Union with the appearance and characteristics of empire and colonialism, a matter of increasing embarrassment to the Russians. Thus in response to the rhetorical question of the British U.N. Representative Sir Patrick Dean in New York in December of 1962 about what target date the Soviet Union had set for the independence of Azerbaidzhan, Kazakhstan, Turkestan, Turkmenia, and other imperialistic acquisitions, the official Soviet Labor newspaper *Trud* deemed it necessary to publish a series of "letters to the editor" denying that the Soviet Union was a colonial power.

The swift emergence of the People's Republic of China, rising like a demon from the corpse of the Nationalist government, was as much of a surprise to the Russians as to the Americans. A younger brother, not a son, of Moscow, the Peking regime soon displayed more signs of sibling rivalry than of filial piety. The border regions were like toys, now shared, now fought over.

In Manchuria and in Sinkiang, China re-emerged dominant, the Yalta concessions notwithstanding. In the Mongolian People's Republic or in Outer Mongolia, on the other hand, the Russians have been more successful in preserving their influence.

The eastward expansion of Russia, like the westward expansion of the United States, was less permanent overseas than on the continent. Relatively nearby possessions—Sakhalin and Hawaii—were retained, but more distant ones—Russian America and the Philippines—were cut loose. At the same time the power struggle and juggling for positions between the United States and the Soviet Union in the years after World War II have given a new twist to American and Russian expansion through their political, economic, and military involvement in distant regions.

The American and Russian parallel must not be overdrawn. There are profound differences in the historical development of the two countries. But the impetus of expansion and the influence of the frontier are a common denominator, which have made for greater similarities in American and Russian outlooks on life than the present ideological controversy allows. Indeed, one may wonder whether the Messianic character of the Russo-American conflict, so startling to many Europeans and Asians, is due to the fact that Americans and Russians are so different or so much alike.

FURTHER READINGS

The clash of American, Russian, and Chinese interests in the Far East since World War II has focused public attention on Russia's eastward expansion, but the outpour of books has been confined largely to the Soviet period. Space does not permit mention of all the recent publications, nor indeed of the many scholarly works in Russian, German, and other languages. The titles suggested below have been selected with the general reader in mind.

The Russian drive across the continent is traced vividly in Vladimir, *Russia on the Pacific and the Siberian Railway* (London: Sampson Low, Marston and Company, 1899) and F. A. Golder, *Russian Expansion on the Pacific, 1641-1850* (Cleveland: Arthur H. Clark Co., 1914, recently reprinted by Peter Smith, Publisher, Gloucester, Mass.). Its motivating force and characteristics are analyzed in Robert J. Kerner, *The Urge to the Sea: The Course of Russian History* (Berkeley: University of California Press, 1942), Raymond H. Fisher, *The Russian Fur Trade 1550-1700* (Berkeley: University of California Press, 1943), and Donald W. Treadgold, *The Great Siberian Migration* (Princeton, N.J.: Princeton University Press, 1957). A readable sketch of the geography and climate of Siberia is found in Emil Lengyel, *Siberia* (New York: Random House, 1943). E. G. Ravenstein, *The Russians on the Amur* (London: Trübner and Co., 1861) gives a detailed account of the Amur region, including the personal observations of Russian travellers; Albert J. Beveridge, *The Russian Advance* (New York: Harper and Row, Publishers, 1903) is an absorbing American eyewitness view of Russia's eastward expansion. George Frederick Wright, *Asiatic Russia* (New York: McClure, Phillips and Co., 1902, 2 vols.) offers a remarkably comprehensive survey of Siberia, including its history.

The relations of Russia with Asia in general (the Near East, Central Asia, and the Far East) are examined in Prince A. Lobanov-Rostovsky, *Russia and Asia* (New York: The Macmillan Company, 1933, reprinted in 1951 by G. Wahr Publication Co., Ann Arbor). A less scholarly, highly biased yet fascinating account, penned at the turn of the century, is Alexis Krausse, *Russia in Asia. A Record and a Study 1558-1899* (New York: Holt, Rinehart & Winston, 1901). An important survey of Russian penetration of Manchuria and Korea is Andrew Malozemoff, *Russian Far Eastern Policy 1881-1904* (Berkeley: University of

182

California Press, 1958). Continued Russian interest in Manchuria and Mongolia is related in detail by Peter S. H. Tang in *Russian and Soviet Policy in Manchuria and Outer Mongolia 1911-1931* (Durham, N.C.: Duke University Press, 1959). The influence of the Revolution of 1905 on the peoples of Asia is told in Ivar Spector, *The First Russian Revolution: Its Impact on Asia* (Englewood Cliffs, N.J.: Prentice-Hall, Inc., 1962, A Spectrum Book, S-27). Books on the Soviet period include Xenia Joukoff Eudin and Robert C. North, *Soviet Russia and the East 1920-1927* (Stanford: Stanford University Press, 1957), a documentary survey, and Max Beloff, *The Foreign Policy of Soviet Russia, 1929-1941* (London: Oxford University Press, 1947 and 1949, 2 vols.), and *Soviet Policy in the Far East 1944-1951* (London: Oxford University Press, 1953). Difficulties within the Soviet empire are aired in Geoffrey Wheeler, *Racial Problems in Soviet Muslim Asia* (London: Oxford University Press, 1960).

Early Russian voyages in the Pacific are recorded in William Coxe, *Account of the Russian Discoveries between Asia and America* (London: T. Cadell, 1780); a lively account of subsequent exploration is Harold McCracken, *Hunters of the Stormy Sea* (Garden City, N.Y.: Doubleday and Company, Inc., 1957). S. B. Okun, *The Russian-American Company* (edited by B. D. Grekov, translated by Carl Ginsburg; Cambridge, Mass.: Harvard University Press, 1951) traces the history of Russian activities in America up to the sale of Alaska. Hector Chevigny dramatizes it by focusing on two key figures: *Lost Empire. The Life and Adventures of Nikolai Petrovich Rezanov* (New York: The Macmillan Company, 1937) and *Lord of Alaska. The Story of Baranov and the Russian Adventure* (New York: The Viking Press, 1943). A fascinating interpretation of Russo-American relations up to 1917, well written and beautifully illustrated, is Alexandre Tarsaïdzé, *Czars and Presidents. The Story of a Forgotten Friendship* (New York: Ivan Obolensky, Inc., 1958). Russo-American rivalry in Asia is covered in Edward H. Zabriskie, *American-Russian Rivalry in the Far East* (Philadelphia: University of Pennsylvania Press, 1946), Pauline Tompkins, *American-Russian Relations in the Far East* (New York: The Macmillan Company, 1946), and John L. Snell (ed.), *The Meaning of Yalta. Big Three Diplomacy and the New Balance of Power* (Baton Rouge: Louisiana State University Press, 1956).

Surveys of Russo-Chinese relations from ancient times to the present include A. K. Wu, *China and the Soviet Union* (New York: The John Day Company, Inc. 1950) and J. V. Davidson-Houston, *Russia and China From the Huns to Mao Tse-tung* (London: Robert Hale, 1960). The most detailed account of Russo-Chinese relations prior to the eighteenth century is John Baddeley, *Russia, Mongolia, China* (London: Macmillan and Co., Ltd., 1919, 2 vols.). More concise but informative accounts reaching into the eighteenth century are Gaston Cahen, *Some Early Russo-Chinese Relations* (translated and edited by W. Sheldon Ridge; Shanghai: The National Review Office, 1914, reprinted in Peking, 1940) and Joseph Sebes, *The Jesuits and the Sino-Russian Treaty of Nerchinsk (1689)* (Rome: Institutum Historicum S. I., 1961). Modern relations are stressed in Ken Shen Weigh, *Russo-Chinese Diplomacy* (Shanghai: The Commercial Press, Ltd., 1928). Studies of the Soviet period include Robert C. North, *Moscow and the Chinese Communists* (Stanford: Stanford University Press, 1963, 2nd ed.), Allen S. Whiting, *Soviet Policies in China, 1917-1924* (New York: Columbia University Press, 1953), Conrad Brandt, *Stalin's Failure in*

China, 1924-1927 (Cambridge, Mass: Harvard University Press, 1958), Martin Wilbur and Julie Lien-ying How, *Documents on Communism, Nationalism and Soviet Advisers in China, 1918-1927* (New York: Columbia University Press, 1958), Charles B. McClane, *Soviet Policy and the Chinese Communists 1931-1946* (New York: Columbia University Press, 1958), and Donald S. Zagoria, *The Sino-Soviet Conflict 1956-1961* (Princeton, N.J.; Princeton University Press, 1962).

Early Russian relations with Japan are narrated in John A. Harrison, *Japan's Northern Frontier* (Gainesville: University of Florida Press, 1953) and George Alexander Lensen, *The Russian Push Toward Japan; Russo-Japanese Relations, 1697-1875* (Princeton: Princeton University Press, 1959). G. A. Lensen's *Report From Hokkaido: The Remains of Russian Culture in Northern Japan* (Hakodate: Municipal Library, 1954) may be of interest for its illustrations; his *Russia's Japan Expedition of 1852 to 1855* (Gainesville: University of Florida Press, 1955) is the story of the Russian expedition which competed with Commodore Perry in the opening of Japan. Russo-Japanese relations since 1875 are examined in Ernest Batson Price, *The Russo-Japanese Treaties of 1907-1916 Concerning Manchuria and Mongolia* (Baltimore: The Johns Hopkins Press, 1933), John A. White, *The Siberian Intervention* (Princeton: Princeton University Press, 1950), James Morley, *The Japanese Thrust into Siberia* (New York: Columbia University Press, 1957), G. A. Lensen, "Japan and Tsarist Russia—the Changing Relationships, 1875-1917" (in *Jahrbücher für Geschichte Osteuropas*, New Series, Vol. X, No. 3 [October 1962], pp. 337-48), in the books of Max Beloff, mentioned above, and in Rodger Swearingen, *Red Flag in Japan* (Cambridge: Harvard University Press, 1952).

Date Due